Microsoft® CRM For Dummies®

C000003692

Reading Your Personal E-Mail

1. At the bottom of the navigation pane, click the Workplace button.

2. At the top of the pane, select Activities.

3. In the Type field, click the arrow to open the drop-down list, and select E-mail.

4. In the View field, click the arrow to open the drop-down list and make your selection.

Linking an E-Mail to a Record

1. On the menu bar (at the top of the screen), choose New➪New Activity➪E-mail.

2. Fill in the appropriate fields (To, Subject, and the like).

3. To the right of the Regarding field, click the magnifying glass icon.

4. Click the drop-down arrow to the right of the Look For field, and select one of the twelve record types in the list.

5. Double-click the appropriate record.

Viewing Your Calendar

1. Click the Workplace button at the bottom of the navigation pane.

2. At the top of the pane, under My Work, click Calendar.

Creating a New Account or Contact

1. Within Sales, Marketing, Service, or My Workplace, select Accounts or Contacts in the navigation pane.

2. In the window's toolbar, click the New button.

3. Fill in the General, Details, Administration, and Notes tabs as necessary.

4. Click Save and Close.

Creating an E-Mail

1. In the menu bar (at the top of the screen), choose New➪New Activity➪E-mail, or click the Create New E-mail icon below the menu bar.

2. Select a recipient of your e-mail as follows:

   a. Click the magnifying glass icon to the right of the To field.

   b. Highlight the record you want.

   c. Click the >> button to move the recipient(s) to the Selected Records pane.

   d. Click OK to close the window and return to your e-mail.

3. Enter a subject.

4. In the open text box below the Subject field, type your message.

5. Documentation of e-mail can be essential. To associate, or link, the message to a record, do the following:

   a. Click the magnifying glass icon to the right of the Regarding field.

   b. Search for and highlight your contact.

   c. Click OK to return to the e-mail window.

6. Add other options as desired.

7. To send your message, click the Send button (next to Save and Close).

Completing an Activity

1. At the bottom of the navigation pane, click the Workplace button.

2. At the top of the pane, under My Work, click Activities.

3. Select an activity that you want to mark as completed.

4. Click the Notes tab and create a note that will be attached to the record.

5. Click the Save as Completed button.

For Dummies: Bestselling Book Series for Beginners

Microsoft® CRM 3 For Dummies®

Cheat Sheet

Creating a Quote

1. At the bottom of the navigation pane, click the Sales button.
2. At the top of the pane, select Quotes.
3. In the Quotes window's toolbar, click the New button.
4. In the Name field, enter some text that describes the quote.
5. In the Potential Customer field, select an account or a contact to associate with the quote.
6. In the Price List field, use the magnifying glass or the Form Assistant to select a price list.
7. Click Save (the disk icon).
8. In the Totals section of the General tab, enter the Quote Discount and Freight Amount.
9. Click the Shipping tab and fill in the following:
   a. Enter information into the Effective From and To, Requested Delivery Date, and Due By fields.
   b. Enter the Shipping Method, Payment Terms, and Freight Terms.
10. Click the Addresses tab enter the Bill To and Ship To information.
11. If you want to associate your quote with an opportunity, do the following:
    a. Click the Administration tab.
    b. Use the magnifying glass in the Opportunity field to find and select that opportunity.
    c. Click OK.
12. Click the Save and Close button to save your quote.

Searching the Knowledge Base

1. At the bottom of the navigation pane, click the Workplace button.
2. In the upper part of the navigation pane, select Service and then select Knowledge Base.
3. On the left side of the Knowledge Base window, click the Search tab.
4. Fill in the following fields to define your search criteria: Unlabeled field, Search for, In subject, and Options.
5. Click the Search button.

Creating a Service Activity

1. At the bottom of the navigation pane, click the Service button.
2. At the top of the pane, select Service Calendar.
3. In the Type field (next to the Look For field), select Service Activity from the drop-down list.
4. Choose a day for the service.
5. In the window's toolbar, click the New button and make your selection.
6. In the Subject field, enter a name for this service activity.
7. In the Service field, select the service you want to schedule.
8. Choose your start and end times as well as the duration.
9. Add any notes.
10. Click the Details tab and fill it in as required.
11. Click the Save and Close button to schedule the activity.

Viewing Announcements

1. At the bottom of the navigation pane, click the Workplace button.
2. At the top of the pane, choose Announcements under My Work.
3. Read the announcements.

Checking the Service Calendar

1. At the bottom of the navigation pane, click the Service button.
2. At the top of the pane, select Service Calendar.
3. Click any resource, and you will see the schedule for that resource in the calendar area.

For Dummies: Bestselling Book Series for Beginners

Microsoft® CRM 3 FOR DUMMIES®

by Joel Scott and David Lee

WILEY

Wiley Publishing, Inc.

Microsoft® CRM 3 For Dummies®

Published by
Wiley Publishing, Inc.
111 River Street
Hoboken, NJ 07030-5774

www.wiley.com

Copyright © 2006 by Wiley Publishing, Inc., Indianapolis, Indiana

Published by Wiley Publishing, Inc., Indianapolis, Indiana

Published simultaneously in Canada

For general information on our other products and services, please contact our Customer Care Department within the U.S. at 800-762-2974, outside the U.S. at 317-572-3993, or fax 317-572-4002.

For technical support, please visit www.wiley.com/techsupport.

Wiley also publishes its books in a variety of electronic formats. Some content that appears in print may not be available in electronic books.

Library of Congress Control Number: 2006920630

ISBN-13: 978-0-471-79945-0

ISBN-10: 0-471-79945-9

Manufactured in the United States of America

10 9 8 7 6 5 4 3 2 1

1B/QV/QV/QW/IN

WILEY

About the Authors

Joel Scott is president of the Computer Control Corporation, headquartered in Connecticut. Since 1991, Computer Control Corporation has been focused on designing and installing high-quality CRM systems. Well known in the industry, Computer Control has garnered numerous industry awards for sales, training, and CRM best practices.

Mr. Scott has authored several editions of *GoldMine For Dummies* and numerous articles and white papers on client retention systems. Mr. Scott can be reached by e-mail at `joels@ccc24k.com`.

David Lee founded Vertical Marketing Inc. in 1983. He has more than thirty years of business experience in CRM and information systems industries.

This is his first Dummies book, although he has written several white papers on CRM and the industry. He can be reached at `dlee@vermar.com`.

Authors' Acknowledgments

Joel Scott: No one writes a book alone. Perhaps it's possible for a work of fiction. But even then, a collection of editors and technicians all have some say in the appearance of the work. It seems unlikely that one or two people can bring a book from the starting line to the finish line by themselves.

First and foremost, I need to thank my co-author, Dave Lee. Our early brainstorming sessions about this book and continuing communications made this writing easier.

I also want to thank everyone in my office and at home for taking up the slack while I was so often sitting in my room moaning and groaning over words I had written and rewritten so many times.

David Lee: Of all the books and articles that I have ever written, this one took the most teamwork. I could never have completed this book and still run Vertical Marketing without a huge amount of help from my secretary, Jennifer Slusher. She reviewed all my work, did all the screen captures (a much tougher job than you might imagine), and updated text based on feedback from the editor and the technical editor. She now knows Microsoft CRM so well that I will probably have to make her a trainer or a designer.

I also need to thank my friend, partner, competitor, and co-author, Joel. He was willing to risk a more than ten-year friendship by asking me to co-author this book. Despite the late nights and deadlines, I still like the guy.

Our technical editor, Ben Vollmer, is also a personal friend. As a Microsoft employee, he has a different perspective on the system. His advice and support have been invaluable.

Susan Pink, our editor, must have the patience of Methuselah. Wiley Press has some pretty specific editorial rules. Working with both Joel and me in that framework has to be harder than herding cats. She somehow managed to keep us on track and pretty much on schedule.

I would also like to thank my staff. With the new release of Microsoft 3.0, we have been extremely busy. They have taken up the slack whenever they were asked so that I could have the time I needed to write.

Finally, I would like to thank you for your interest in Microsoft CRM. CRM is my passion (I am a pretty dull guy), and it is people like you who allow me to do the work that I love.

Publisher's Acknowledgments

We're proud of this book; please send us your comments through our online registration form located at `www.dummies.com/register/`.

Some of the people who helped bring this book to market include the following:

Acquisitions, Editorial, and Media Development

Project Editor: Susan Pink

Acquisitions Editor: Bob Woerner

Technical Editor: Ben Vollmer

Editorial Manager: Jodi Jensen

Media Development Manager: Laura VanWinkle

Editorial Assistant: Amanda Foxworth

Cartoons: Rich Tennant (`www.the5thwave.com`)

Composition Services

Project Coordinator: Tera Knapp

Layout and Graphics: Andrea Dahl, Mary J. Gillot, Stephanie D. Jumper, Barbara Moore, Heather Ryan, Ron Terry

Proofreaders: John Greenough, Leeann Harney, Joe Niesen, Techbooks

Indexer: Techbooks

Publishing and Editorial for Technology Dummies

Richard Swadley, Vice President and Executive Group Publisher

Andy Cummings, Vice President and Publisher

Mary Bednarek, Executive Acquisitions Director

Mary C. Corder, Editorial Director

Publishing for Consumer Dummies

Diane Graves Steele, Vice President and Publisher

Joyce Pepple, Acquisitions Director

Composition Services

Gerry Fahey, Vice President of Production Services

Debbie Stailey, Director of Composition Services

Contents at a Glance

Table of Contents

Introduction

*T*his book is about Microsoft Dynamics CRM Version 3.0, which we refer to as simply Microsoft CRM or just CRM. We assume that Microsoft CRM just showed up on your desktop computer or notebook. Chances are, you already have some experience with one or more of the popular predecessors to CRM — ACT, GoldMine, SalesLogix, or an earlier release of Microsoft CRM. Or maybe you've never had any kind of CRM system — and never wanted one either. In any event, now you have to get yourself up and running with this new software. If you relate to any of this, *Microsoft CRM 3 For Dummies* is for you.

If you're a technical type looking for help with installation, integration, or serious customization, you'll need more than just this book. You'll need some technical references, an experienced dealer, and some time.

If nothing else, Microsoft CRM is an organizational tool. Whether you're in sales, marketing, customer service, or management, this software will provide a significant return on your investment — whether that investment is money or time. Beyond that, if you've fallen in love with Microsoft Outlook and refuse to relinquish it, relax. Not only can you still use Outlook, it's one of the primary means by which you'll communicate with Microsoft CRM.

How CRM Fits in the Market

Microsoft has come to the CRM market seemingly a little late but with a system built on a platform called .NET. With CRM, you work in networked mode or in offline mode. Networked mode does not require a direct connection to your office file server. In fact, with .NET technology, *networked* actually means connected to the server through the Internet. *Offline* mode also takes great advantage of the Internet but enables you to work while disconnected by using a tool that Outlook users will find familiar.

The software itself is aimed at small businesses with a basic infrastructure, medium-sized companies, or departments of large enterprises. Typically, if you have more than ten users, and like the look and feel of Outlook, you're a prime candidate for success with CRM. If you have fewer than ten users, you may want to look at Microsoft Business Contact Manager, which is a free add-on to Outlook 2003 for small businesses.

If you have an IT department comfortable with the care and feeding of servers and have Internet connectivity with good firewalls and security, you should consider installing and using CRM. Otherwise, you can have CRM hosted. The hosting company maintains the equipment and software in return for a monthly check. For more information, see Chapter 28.

How to Use This Book

Microsoft CRM is divided into five major sections: Workplace, Sales, Marketing, Service, and Settings. This book loosely follows these themes. We describe navigating the workplace and CRM in general in Chapter 2. In Part II, you find out all about setting up the system. Then we jump into sales topics, a little marketing, and some customer service.

You should be able to comfortably read the book from start to finish, but for those of you so caffeinated you can't sit still that long (don't laugh, you know who you are), each chapter can stand on its own as reference material. Either way, you have a comprehensive guide to Microsoft CRM.

You'll get the most benefit from this book by sitting in front of your computer with CRM on the screen. It's easy to convince yourself that you've got it by just reading, but there's no substitute for trying the steps yourself. Experimenting with sample data is sometimes just the ticket to an epiphany.

Foolish Assumptions

We assume you have some basic computer and Windows skills. If you aren't comfortable with Windows, you need to get yourself up to speed in this area. Find a local class or seminar, or get one of the *For Dummies* books on Windows. Regarding CRM, however, we assume you just returned from a long mission to Mars and need to start using CRM tomorrow.

We also assume you have a basic understanding of database concepts. If you're comfortable with fields, records, files, folders, and how they relate to each other, you'll be fine. If you're familiar with attributes, entities, instances, and objects, even better. If this is already sounding bad, you can seek help at most community colleges or local computer training facilities.

If you're going to be your own CRM administrator (backing up files and assigning usernames, passwords, and access rights), you need to understand records, files, folders, security, operating systems, and networks. If you just want to be a good day-to-day user of CRM, make sure that you understand what a file is and how to locate one using Explorer.

How This Book Is Organized

Some people just have a knack for organization. Our office manager is highly organized, although her desk looks like a tornado swept through it. However, she assures us that she knows exactly where everything *should* be (and we take no responsibility for her actions if you touch anything). Anyway, we digress. Organization — without it, this book would be a jumbled mess. To cure that, we've organized the book into six parts, each with at least two chapters. Again, the book can be read from cover to cover (who has that kind of time?) or you can refer to it section by section. Each part (and chapter) can definitely stand on its own, but we recommend that you at least skim through the basics and the table of contents before getting started.

Part 1: Microsoft CRM Basics

Just the facts! Part I gives you an overview of what Microsoft CRM is all about and provides a tour of the main windows. We also show you how to use Microsoft CRM offline.

Part 11: Setting the Settings

In Part II, we begin with a discussion of how to personalize your workplace and the software. The workplace is command central in Microsoft CRM. From the workplace, you can access the day-to-day stuff, such as your calendar, assigned activities, and service scheduling. You can also set up business units, security, sales processes, and business rules. Workflow, just so you know, is managed not directly from CRM but from a separate program. Getting to that program and using it is discussed in Chapter 8. The knowledge base, discussed in Chapter 9, collects information for everyone in your organization needing to support staff or clients.

Part III: Managing Sales

In Part III, we explain how to create accounts and contacts in your database and how to locate existing records with Version 3's rebuilt-from-the-ground-up search features. We also show you how to create and manage activities as well as leads, opportunities, and territories. You find how-to information on notes, attachments, and all things e-mail. Then we get into the nitty-gritty and discuss some of the408 more complex functions of Microsoft CRM, such as the product catalog, quotes, orders, and invoices (some of which require integration with an accounting system). In addition, we talk about sales literature and how to track competitors.

Part IV: Making the Most of Marketing

Microsoft CRM Version 3 explodes with all kinds of capability in the marketing arena. Combining the new Advanced Find function with Quick Campaigns and a sophisticated Campaign Management system, Microsoft CRM enables you to do more than just send out e-mails and letters. You'll be able to follow the progress of the campaign, create and delegate tasks, keep track of actual costs compared to the campaign budget, and easily catalog and maintain the responses.

Part V: Taking Care of Your Customers

Customer service is a big issue, no matter how big your company. In this part, we show you how to track and manage customer service issues using cases and the special Service Calendar. We talk about workflow and your business processes and how Microsoft CRM can easily handle incoming service calls and e-mail and their responses using queues. We discuss contracts and tiered levels of customer service and how to organize this division to handle service issues efficiently and quickly.

Part VI: The Part of Tens

As new as Microsoft CRM is, third-party developers have brought many complementary products to the market. We discuss the best and most useful we've found. And, just in case you still need assistance, we also discuss ten ways to get help.

Icons Used in This Book

 You don't want to skip the helpful reminders noted by this icon.

 This icon lets you know that some particularly geeky, technical information is coming up. You can look past this if you want.

 This icon points you to a trick that will save you time and effort.

 Look to this icon to find out what to avoid if you don't want your database to blow up or cause you other types of anguish.

Where to Go from Here

If you're a first-time user, we suggest you begin with Chapters 1 – 3 to get a solid introduction to the basics of living with Microsoft CRM. Then check out Part III, IV, or V, depending on whether you're in sales, marketing, or customer service, respectively. If you're charged with setting up CRM for your company, you would do well to read Part I and then Part II. If you have questions or comments and want to contact us directly, please send us an e-mail at dummy@crmworldclass.com.

Part I
Microsoft CRM
Basics

The 5th Wave   By Rich Tennant

"The new technology has really helped me become organized. I keep my project reports under the PC, budgets under my laptop, and memos under my pager."

In this part . . .

Microsoft Dynamics CRM 3.0 is technically an update to Version 1.0 (and 1.2), but it's really a quantum leap beyond what first came out almost three years ago. Microsoft CRM integrates with Outlook and the web and is now much easier to use. If you're one of the 92 million Outlook users, Microsoft CRM is the comfortable, organizational upgrade you're looking for.

In this first part, you find a general discussion of the features and benefits of Microsoft CRM and how best to navigate through the screens. In addition, we discuss the online versus offline use of Microsoft CRM.

Chapter 1

Taking a First Look at Microsoft CRM 3

*P*ersonal Information Managers (PIM) and Contact Management Systems (CMS) were introduced in the mid-1980s. Both PIM and CMS systems enabled you to organize the names, addresses, and phone numbers for all your business contacts. PIMs were superseded by Sales Force Automation (SFA) systems in the late 1980s. Products such as ACT and GoldMine initially combined scheduling functions with contact management. By the mid-1990s, these systems evolved into simple Customer Relationship Management (CRM) systems, attempting to involve not just salespeople but also customer service and management.

Microsoft Dynamics CRM 3.0 (that's the official name) is the next generation of CRM systems. Microsoft CRM is based on .NET (pronounced *dot-net*) technology, pioneered by Microsoft. Not only does Microsoft CRM have functionality for sales, customer service, and now marketing, it takes great advantage of the Internet, or more specifically, web services. This web service focus is what defines the .NET strategy. In a nutshell, web services enable applications to be easily integrated, rapidly configured to meet your business needs, and extended to both internal and external users.

Tracking Your Contacts

Microsoft CRM has a record type or entity called a *contact*. A contact, in this sense, is a person. It is a concept taken from Microsoft Outlook. In fact, contact records from Outlook are directly transferable into contact records in Microsoft CRM.

Microsoft CRM calls company records *accounts*. Companies (accounts) and the people who work at each of them (contacts) can be related to one another within the system.

A contact is a person and an account is a company. A customer is either a person or a company.

We often hear company executives say that their most important corporate asset is their database of prospects and clients. We couldn't agree more. Neglecting, for the moment, all the powerful tools within CRM, the most basic thing is what pays off the quickest. And *that* quick payoff results from having one central, organized, accessible repository for all the information relating to your customers and prospects. Even if you never create any workflow rules, never connect the system to a web site, or never automate your quotation system, you will be miles ahead just by organizing your data into one coherent database.

You want to store other kinds of information in Microsoft CRM, too. The system is going to be your universal reference tool — your Rolodex, your personnel directory, and your Yellow Pages all in one place. You also want to have records for vendors, employees, and competitors.

In addition, Microsoft CRM holds important information that will help you manage and make better-informed decisions about your business. That information includes opportunities to track your sales cycles, cases to track customer service issues, and campaigns to track the results of your marketing campaigns.

Communicating with the Outside World

Far and away, the primary reason that companies lose accounts is that the customer thinks no one is paying attention. Microsoft CRM gives you the tools to counteract this perception, which, with regard to your firm, is certainly a wrong one. Right?

A handful of ways exist to communicate with customers, and CRM handles most of them:

✔ **Scheduling calls and appointments:** Of course, you will be scheduling all your calls and all your appointments using CRM through Outlook.

✔ **Faxing:** This is built into Microsoft CRM Small Business Edition.

✔ **E-mailing:** Outlook is the champion of all e-mail systems. It is practically the de facto standard. Whether you are operating in online or offline mode, you have the ability to integrate your e-mail with the CRM system. This includes the ability to create e-mail templates and e-mail merge documents to rapidly communicate with your customers.

✔ **Printing:** You can merge and print letters as long as you have Microsoft Word (which, as part of the Microsoft family of products, is well-integrated with CRM).

Integrating with Accounting

In the early years of CRM systems, many companies were reluctant to allow their salespeople access to accounting information. Fortunately, the pendulum has swung back, with the best thinkers realizing that it's helpful for salespeople to have more knowledge, not less. Microsoft has developed links to a line of applications it owns called Dynamics (of which Microsoft Dynamics CRM is a part). These links include the ability to share customer information, product information, and invoice and billing information.

Links to other accounting packages, such as those from Intuit and Sage SAP, are provided by third-party developers.

Why integrate?

Surely, no sales manager wants his or her people spending their time trying to close another deal with an existing customer when that customer has not paid for the previous six orders stretching over the last eight months. Nor would a discerning sales manager want a salesperson quoting a deal that would put customers over their existing credit limit without taking the credit situation into account. By integrating Microsoft CRM with your accounting system, your users and sales managers have the information they need to avoid these situations.

Conversely, before a credit manager calls an existing client in an effort to collect a past-due payment, it may be important for the manager to understand that the sales department is on the verge of closing a megadeal with that very same client. Although the credit department would certainly want to collect that money, understanding the current sales situation may affect how the credit manager's conversation is conducted.

Other accounting systems

Most competitors claim to have integration with one or more accounting packages. Most of the time, a third party does this integration, and that situation has some major disadvantages. If you are relying on three separate companies — your CRM vendor, your accounting vendor, and a third-party developer — to keep your front-office and back-office operation coordinated, you could be in trouble.

One of the ongoing problems occurs when your CRM vendor or your accounting vendor upgrades. That upgrade immediately requires an upgrade to at least one of the other packages. Microsoft has gone a long way toward solving this dilemma because it controls both ends and the middle. Look for integration that is much better coordinated than what has been available in the past.

Setting Up Business Processes

One of the most powerful features in Microsoft CRM is workflow rules. These rules provide a way to automate many routine functions in your organization, such as following up with standard letters after an appointment or alerting members of your team to account-related deadlines.

If you prefer to have Microsoft CRM work for you, rather than you work for it, you should consider implementing workflow rules after you get past the initial effort of organizing all your data.

Every business has processes. Sometimes, they aren't well documented, so they aren't obvious. An example of a process is how your company handles leads from prospective customers.

While designing and customizing your soon-to-be CRM system, you should also analyze (and improve) all your processes.

Good process development has several basic principles:

- ✔ **Assigning tasks:** The first principle is properly assigning responsibility. Each task that needs to be accomplished should have one primary person assigned to it, not a team of people.

- ✔ **Feedback:** Every step of every task should be confirmed. Amazon.com has this procedure down pat. If you're not sure about proper feedback, order a book from Amazon. Almost any *For Dummies* book will do.

When you place the order, you get an order confirmation. When the book is shipped, you get a shipping confirmation. And you may very well get some after-the-fact follow-up (all in an effort, of course, to sell you more books). Their process is well done, and you may want to pattern your processes after theirs.

✔ **Escalation:** Just because a phone call has been assigned, don't assume that it will be completed. Plan your processes under the assumption that, even with the best of intentions, things fall through the cracks. Give each team member a reasonable amount of time to accomplish a task. If the task isn't completed, make sure that the next person on your organization chart is notified. Continue escalating and notifying until something is done about the situation.

✔ **Reporting and measuring:** It isn't a real process unless you can measure it and then improve it. Design into each process an appropriate report that allows the necessary analysis that leads to continual improvement. A good way to begin designing a process is to mock up the reports first. These reports help determine what data is necessary for proper tracking.

With workflow rules, you can program the business processes you design. Workflow rules can access any of the data files in Microsoft CRM and create activities for your users or send out correspondence through fax or e-mail. These rules can notify you of overdue activities and can escalate important issues.

Some of the best new stuff in Version 3

Chapter 29 details the ten best new features in this Version of Microsoft CRM. Microsoft made a quantum leap with Version 3 — so much so that they decided to forego calling this latest release Version 2. (Versions 1.0 and 1.2 are the immediate predecessors of this version.)

Microsoft has worked to improve usability and has increased functionality. Both were major issues before, and both issues should now be laid to rest.

In addition, there aren't nearly as many separate windows to click through. It's harder to get lost inside the system. More information is displayed in each window. All good things.

Marketing has been added. The Advanced Find feature now let's you locate records much more easily and across more than just one entity. After you've created a good search query, you can save it for future use. CRM integrates nicely with both Word and Excel, and you will probably make extensive use of this connection when writing quotes and reports.

The very best thing is that Version 3 is a pleasure to use.

Implementing business processes within the scope of workflow rules is the heart and mind of a good CRM system and is also probably the most under-utilized area of CRM. Too often, companies relax after their data is properly imported and their users have received a little training. Properly implemented workflow rules will pay you back for your investment many times over. Do not neglect this powerful feature!

Coordinating Microsoft CRM with Your Success Plan

A disappointing number of CRM projects don't live up to their expectations. The first issue to consider is the one of expectations. The second issue involves planning.

If all your expectations are built on what you heard from your salesperson or what you read in the promotional materials, you may be in for an unpleasant surprise. And, of course, the old axiom applies: If you fail to plan, you plan to fail. Microsoft has released a comprehensive CRM planning guide. It's available on their web site or at www.ccc24k.com.

Defining your goals

You may be tempted to wing it. Maybe someone promised the sales staff that a system would be in place before the next annual sales meeting. That was 11 months ago. If you're thinking you have a month to buy the software and get it implemented, forget about it. Your project should be done in bite-sized chunks with measurable goals at each step.

The first step in a project with the complexity of a Microsoft CRM implementation is to do a needs analysis. Most of the more sophisticated dealers will do this for you, although you should expect to pay for it. Some dealers offer a free needs analysis. Remember, you always get what you pay for.

A true needs analysis involves interviewing representatives from each department that will be using the system. It involves collecting a considerable amount of information on what is being done at your company today and how you want that to change. It involves determining what software may meet your requirements and does not presume that it is necessarily Microsoft CRM or any other system. A needs analysis includes detailed pricing, schedules, and the assignment of responsibilities.

Making Microsoft CRM part of your client-retention program

Out of the box, Microsoft CRM comes prepared to assist you with closing business with new customers. It has records for leads that are expected to grow into opportunities. It has fields in the account and contact records that are meant to assist you in organizing your efforts to make a deal.

With a little forethought and customizing, you can use Microsoft CRM to ensure that you keep the customers you already have. CRM vendors have put little emphasis on customer retention, but it is relatively simple and will provide that return on your investment that everyone looks forward to generating.

We think a good needs analysis (or at least a detailed, written plan) is an essential ingredient to a successful implementation.

Microsoft provides some documents if you decide to go it alone. Look in the *Implementation Guide* for basic planning documents to make sure you get the most out of your system,

Implementing a pilot program

Everyone is conservative by nature when thinking about spending money. So a pilot program is often a useful way to make sure the project will be successful. Typically, a pilot program involves a select group of users, not the entire company. If you're going to go this route, make it a representative sample, not just the brightest or most enthusiastic people and not just people in one small department.

Most projects never get beyond the pilot stage because a hundred or a thousand steps are needed to implement any project like this successfully. Invariably, as the pilot project struggles to the finish line, you find two or three nagging items that have not been conquered. And these unresolved items are what everyone is suddenly focused on. In some people's minds, these unfinished items remain a good reason to declare failure or to refuse to move on to the full rollout.

Before beginning a pilot, you must define what determines success. These conditions must be written down and known to all. If they are met, full rollout should be triggered automatically.

Deciding Whether Microsoft CRM Fits Your Needs

Microsoft CRM is not for everyone, but it's inevitable that an enormous wave of companies will adopt it. It will probably achieve a critical mass, much like other Microsoft applications, and may eventually become the de facto standard for CRM.

Microsoft has targeted Outlook users. If you're comfortably using Outlook to maintain your list of contacts and to handle your e-mail, you should become a satisfied user of Microsoft CRM. The look and feel of Outlook has been transferred into the Outlook version of Microsoft CRM. And Microsoft has provided an import facility for transferring your Outlook data into Microsoft CRM.

If you are coming from one of the enterprise-level CRM systems, such as Siebel or Oracle, you will be impressed with the relative ease and user-friendliness of Microsoft CRM — as well as the ability for Microsoft CRM to adapt to the way you do business as opposed to the other way around.

If you are a salesperson who operates more on your own than as a member of a team, you will be right at home. The security built into the system will provide you with a sense of well-being, and you'll have just enough ability to coordinate activities with other members of your team when you are compelled to do so.

On the other hand, if your experience is with another CRM package (such as ACT or GoldMine) that was built for small to medium-sized businesses, you are about to enter a new world. Your first issue will be getting your existing data into Microsoft CRM, which is no easy task. See Chapter 28 for a discussion of third-party add-ons that address this problem.

Some of the basic calendar and literature management functionality that you are accustomed to are just plain missing. If you are used to looking up other people's schedules, you will need to learn a new way of handling this.

If you have five or fewer people using the system, you'll probably find that setting up CRM is too expensive and technology-intensive. Enter Business Contact Manager, which Microsoft makes available for free for up to five users of Outlook 2003. Microsoft CRM will automatically import all data into Microsoft CRM when you grow into it.

Using Microsoft CRM Successfully

The difference between a successful implementation and a flop is often the investment of a little more time, thought, money, and commitment. Microsoft CRM won't let you down as long as you do the following:

- **Have a needs analysis completed by a competent dealer.** Spend the money. It's well worth it.

- **Make sure that every user finds an advantage to using the system.** Otherwise, you won't get good acceptance or consistent use, which will inevitably lead to the collapse of the system. You have to sell your team on it. Solicit ideas from team members. Have each of them invest in the effort.

- **Plan your technology infrastructure.** Microsoft CRM demands a series of servers (or at least a Small Business server) and good network connectivity. You may need to update your operating systems and install SQL and Exchange Servers.

- **Organize your existing data.** You probably have your data in more places and formats than you realize. Take a survey of all your users so you know the location of all the data. Plan to eliminate unnecessary records and collect as much missing information as possible.

- **Install your Microsoft CRM software and customize it with regard to any additional fields and reports you need.**

- **Set up your organizational structure with business units, roles, and teams.**

- **Import all the data and train your users almost simultaneously.** As soon as training is complete, you want your users to have immediate access to their own data so they can start using it before they forget what they learned in class.

- **Don't take your eyes off your data.** As soon as you turn your back on the data, it will turn into garbage. Put someone in charge of data integrity.

- **Plan to continually improve the system.** The system will never be finished and will never be perfect. It's a process that evolves and changes as your organization changes. Don't lose sight of where you came from.

Chapter 2

Navigating the Microsoft CRM System

*R*emember the home page in CRM Versions 1 and 1.2? Well, the home page is gone, and its functions have been blended into what Microsoft calls the *workplace.* In this chapter, we explain the main features of the workplace screen and the other common screens and provide you with the skills to get from one screen to another without getting lost.

Whirlwind Tour of the Screen

The workplace is the first thing you see when you start Microsoft CRM, so that's where we'll begin our discussion of what's what on the screen. Figure 2-1 shows a typical workplace screen.

Many elements in CRM are context sensitive, which means that what they contain differs depending on what part of the program you're viewing, what access rights you have, or both. In addition, you can change your personal settings (as described in Chapter 4). Those personal settings may further influence what you see on each screen. And, one more caveat: Microsoft CRM is highly customizable. If someone in your organization or your CRM dealer has already customized your system, your screens may not be exactly the same as those that came out of the box. (For this book, we used all out-of-the-box screens.)

If you've used Microsoft products before, you'll find that some of these elements are familiar. Let's start from the top.

Menu bar

The *menu bar,* which appears below the title bar, is context sensitive, which means that the choices you have depend on the screen you are logged on to (such as Accounts or Activities) and the access rights you have. On the far right of the menu bar is the name of the currently logged-in user. Typically, that will be you.

Toolbar

Menu bar

Window

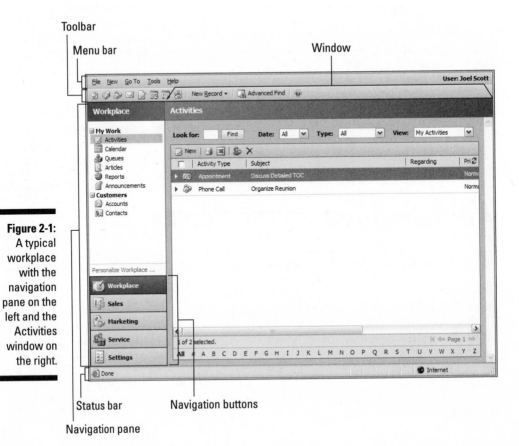

Figure 2-1:
A typical
workplace
with the
navigation
pane on the
left and the
Activities
window on
the right.

Status bar

Navigation buttons

Navigation pane

Toolbar

Next up after the menu bar is the *toolbar.* This area contains buttons for common tasks. For example, in the Activities window (refer to Figure 2-1), the first few toolbar buttons (from left to right) are used to create a task, fax, phone call, e-mail, and letter. The New Record button on the toolbar leads to a screen where you can create each of the different types of records. Use the Advanced Find button to quickly search for a set of records based on one or more fields that the program has defined as searchable. The results of the Advanced Find operation are shown in the listing in the middle of the window.

Navigation pane

The navigation pane is the column on the left side of the screen. As mentioned, many screen elements are context sensitive, but no area is more so than the navigation pane. The navigation pane is split into two major areas. What button you click at the bottom — Workplace, Sales, Marketing, Service, or Settings — determines what you see at the top. Click Sales, for example, and you might see a screen like the one in Figure 2-2.

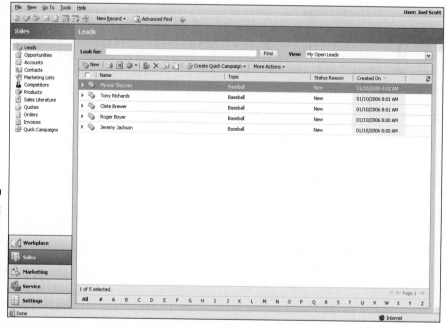

Figure 2-2:
Clicking the Sales button displays a list of your current leads.

When you are using one of the modules, the navigation pane is always available, and you can use it to get back to the workplace at any time. For those people just getting started with a CRM application or those coming from a simpler system, it's easy to get lost in what may seem to be a myriad of similar screens. The Workplace button in the navigation pane is always there for you, like a trail of bread crumbs leading you home.

If you're suddenly lost while entering information, remember that Microsoft CRM does not automatically save data for you. So click the Save button (the disk icon) on the toolbar before returning to the workplace.

Status bar

At the very bottom of the screen is the status bar with several indicators. The *Done* indicator tells you that CRM has finished retrieving the information you requested. If CRM has not finished, you see an indication of what it is currently loading. If you see a pop-up icon in the status bar, hover your mouse over it and it will tell you whether pop-ups are blocked. The final indicator shows your current Internet security properties. The possibilities are Internet, Local Intranet, Trusted Sites, and Restricted Sites.

Window

The largest part of the screen is what we simply call the *window* (labeled in Figure 2-1). What you see here depends first on what navigation button you've clicked (Workplace, Sales, Marketing, Service, or Settings) and second on what you've clicked in the upper part of the navigation pane. For example, in Figure 2-3, we've clicked Workplace and then Accounts (under Customers).

At the top of the window is the name of the area you're currently working in. Directly below the title of the window you see the Look For field and its Find button as well as the View menu. You use these elements to filter records. We talk more about filtering records later in this chapter.

Next up is a row of toolbar buttons, such as the New button and a printer icon. The toolbar in Figure 2-3 also shows two buttons with drop-down menus, Create Quick Campaign and More Actions. Click the down-pointing arrow, and a list of options appears.

Records are displayed in the main display area of the window. You can view any record that appears here by simply clicking it. To preview additional details about a record displayed in the window, click the arrow to the left of the record name. A small window, called the *preview,* appears in the lower part of the screen with more fields than can be seen in the listing in the main window. However, you can't edit a record in the preview window.

At the top of the record listing are the column headers. Click a column header to sort the records into ascending or descending order. To change the sort order, click the column header again.

To select one or more records for some type of action, such as sending an e-mail, highlight the record. You can select all the records on a page by clicking the top check box (the one that is a column header).

Selecting all the records in the manner just described selects only those records displayed in that particular window, one screen at a time.

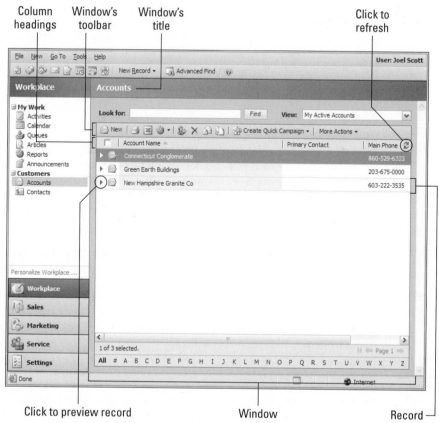

Figure 2-3:
The
Accounts
window.

Column headings   Window's toolbar   Window's title   Click to refresh

Click to preview record   Window   Record

any windows, particularly those with a list view such as the Accounts window, have a refresh button just to the right of the column headers (labeled in Figure 2-3). If you've modified a record but there's no evidence of that change in the window, click the refresh button.

Several elements appear at the bottom of the window. The first is the scroll bar. Next, you see a row indicating how may records appear in the window. The current page is on the far right. When a listing has more than one page, the arrows surrounding the page number are no longer dimmed and you can use them to move from one page to another.

The final element in the window is the CRM alphabet bar. Click a letter in the alphabet bar, and you see only records beginning with that letter. This is a quick way to sort and find records.

First Things First — Signing On

Now that we've described some of the basic screen terminology, it's time to talk about navigating through the CRM system. But before you can navigate to and through Microsoft CRM, you have to sign on. Although that sounds like a simple thing, you might encounter a gotcha or two.

Microsoft CRM does not require a separate login for the program like other CRM systems you may have used. It is integrated with Microsoft Active Directory, which means that it gets your login information from your computer. However, before you can access CRM, your administrator must set you up in the system with at least one security role. Your role in the organization and your access rights will determine, to a large part, what sections of the system you can get to and what you can do when you're there. For more on roles and access rights, see Chapter 5.

Microsoft CRM is normally an intranet-based application, so you access the application from your web browser. Therefore, the application is hosted on your servers, generally with none of the information accessible from the Internet — unless you set it up that way. To use the system from your computer through the Internet — the higher the speed, the better. A dial-up line might work, but you won't be a happy camper over the long run. DSL, cable, or a T1 line are all better options.

If your browser has a pop-up blocker enabled, this may prevent you from even getting into Microsoft CRM. From the Internet Explorer main toolbar, go to Tools⇨Pop-up Blocker⇨Turn off Pop-up Blocker. However, this may not be enough if you have other pop-up blockers enabled. For example, if you use Yahoo!, it has its own pop-up blocker (on its main toolbar) that must also be disabled.

The Workplace Is Your Starting Point

When you have conquered the mysteries of Internet connectivity and pop-up blockers, you will land on the sign-on screen. After you enter your username and password and click OK, CRM automatically brings you to your workplace.

The workplace is not only the first place you see after signing on, it's the place you should always go back to if you find yourself adrift in a sea of screens.

The CRM program contains five modules: workplace, sales, marketing, service, and settings. The three application modules — sales, marketing, and service — can contain many individual records, such as an account or a contact or a case. In this section, we discuss how to get to the application modules and, from there, how to get to individual records.

Navigating at the application level

You can navigate to the three application modules from the workplace in two ways: the navigation pane or the Go To menu (on the menu bar). Our choice is to use the navigation pane, which contains buttons for all five modules (including the workplace itself). If you instead choose the Go To menu, you are presented with a drop-down list of the same five choices available in the navigation pane.

The settings module is one you will visit infrequently, when you want to change a personal setting on your system. That leaves the three application modules: sales, marketing, and service. Depending on your role in your organization, you'll probably be spending most of your day in just one of these modules.

At the application level, the windows you see are similar to those of the workplace, but they do have a few differences. Figure 2-4 shows a sample window with a listing of contacts.

Navigating at the record level

From the application level, you can drill down to the record level, where the meat of your data actually lives. Figure 2-5 shows a typical contact record. The record level shows detailed information about each subarea (Contacts, Leads, Opportunities, Accounts, and the like). To access the record level, you simply double-click a record in the particular window's listing.

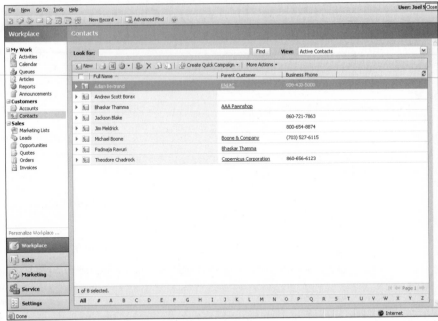

Figure 2-4:
Everyone I
should be in
touch with
all the time.

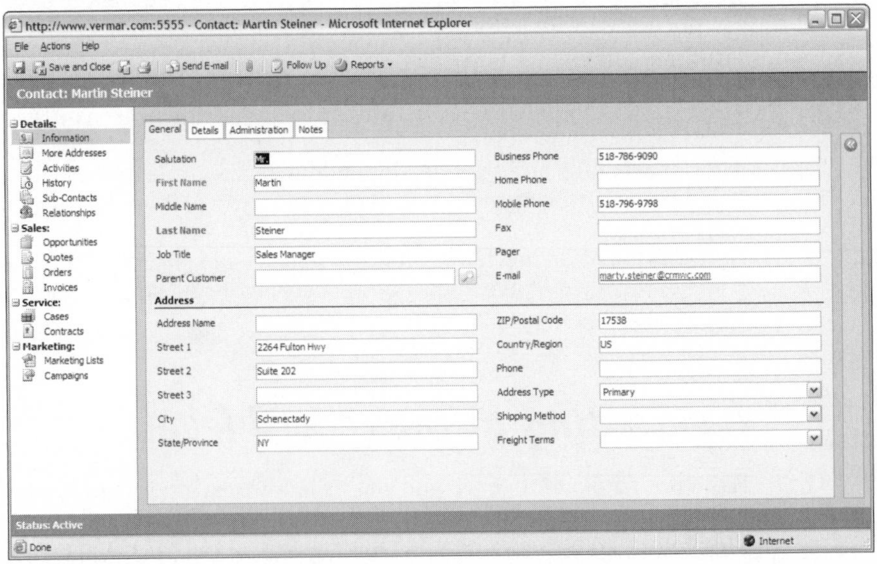

Figure 2-5:
A typical
contact
record.

Your first navigation lessons

Navigating through the Activities window is typical of more general navigation through CRM. You will almost always need to create and edit appointments (which are a type of activity), so we'll use appointments as an example. You can create (also called *schedule*) an activity in many ways, but the fastest and easiest way is to use the workplace:

1. **At the bottom of the navigation pane, click the Workplace button.**

2. **At the top of the navigation pane, click Activities.**

   The Activities window appears.

3. **In the Activities window's toolbar, click the New button.**

   The New Activity dialog box appears.

4. **Double-click the icon for the activity you want to create.**

   You're creating an appointment, so you would double-click Appointment. A window appears for entering the relevant information, as shown in Figure 2-6.

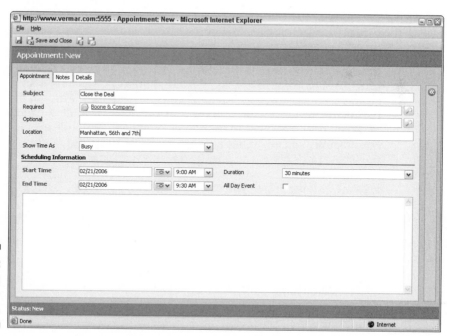

Figure 2-6:
Scheduling
an appoint-
ment.

5. **Enter text in all the necessary fields.**

   For an appointment, you'd enter the subject (why you're making the appointment), the account or contact with whom you're scheduling the appointment, and all scheduling information.

6. **CRM doesn't save anything until you tell it to, so click the Save and Close button (below the menu bar).**

   You return to the workplace.

Now that you've created an appointment, you can practice changing one. This should be even easier. We'll start from the Activities window:

1. **In the Activities window, find and then click the activity you want to edit.**

   The activity opens, enabling you to review and change it. If you were changing an appointment, you'd see a screen similar to Figure 2-6.

2. **To change a field, highlight it and make your edits.**

   For example, you might want to change the scheduled time for an appointment.

3. **Before leaving the window, make sure you click the Save and Close button.**

   You return to the workplace.

Now that you've worked on creating, viewing, and editing an appointment, let's take a moment to check out another area of CRM: announcements. From the workplace, click Announcements (under My Work) in the upper part of the navigation pane. In the Announcements window, members of your team can post messages to everyone about company-wide events or issues. For example, you might use an announcement to send reminders about an upcoming price change or a revised holiday schedule.

Figure 2-7 shows some typical announcement postings. Clicking the link in the Announcements window brings you directly to that posting. The posting will include a link to a web site containing additional information, if that link was created when the announcement was created.

If an announcement is too long, or if several active announcements are displayed, a scroll bar appears at the right side of the window so you can review all the posted material.

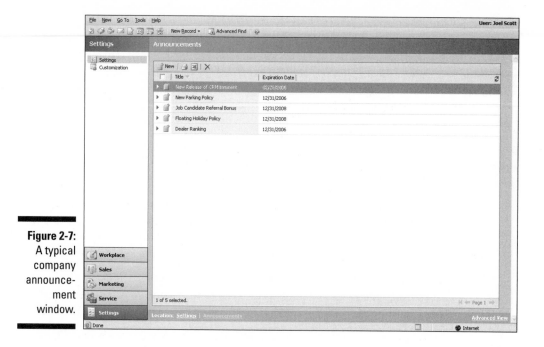

Figure 2-7:
A typical
company
announce-
ment
window.

Filtering and Searching for Records

Since the dawn of mankind, humans have organized things. Of course, if you organize things, you have to filter and search through them at some point. It could be argued that you have to filter and search before you can organize, but that's sort of like trying to determine which came first, the chicken or the egg. Well, Microsoft CRM doesn't answer that question, but the program does offer you an advanced, user-intuitive filter and search capability.

Filtering records

Now how is filtering different from searching? Basically, a filter is a type of search, in that you give the program search criteria and the filter function hunts down all the records that meet your search definition. You can apply this filtering to a list of contacts or leads, to documents in the knowledge base, to service activities, and more. You can use the function to find one record or a thousand records.

In almost every workspace in Microsoft CRM, you'll see a Look For field and a View field, as shown in Figure 2-8.

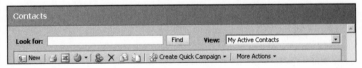

You use the Look For field to enter information free form. If you're looking for an article on brakes, for example, you could type *brakes.* If you're looking for the guy who just called you at the help desk (and got cut off) but all you remember is his first name, Rico, you could type that first name.

Right next to the Look For field is the View field. Basically, this tells the program where to search for and what to search while hunting for the text you entered in the Look For field.

Here's where the filter function shows its teeth. The options you find in the View field drop-down box depend on what section of Microsoft CRM you're working in. For example, if you're in Workplace, under Contacts, the options are geared towards contacts, such as Active Contacts, My Active Contacts, and Inactive Contacts. If you're in Marketing, in the Campaigns workspace, you get options such as My Campaigns and Launched Campaigns.

Searching with the magnifying glass icon

Throughout Microsoft CRM, you'll find a magnifying-glass icon to the right of many fields. Whenever you see the magnifying glass, there's a Look Up Records dialog box waiting for you. Using this look-up feature, you can search almost anything.

Just click the magnifying glass. Like the filter function, the options you see in the Look Up dialog box depend on the field the icon is next to. Figure 2-9 is the one you'll see most often because it lends itself to most searches performed in Microsoft CRM. The drop-down box offered in the Look For field can have two options to search in (say, Accounts and Contacts) or as many as eleven, depending on the type of record you're looking for.

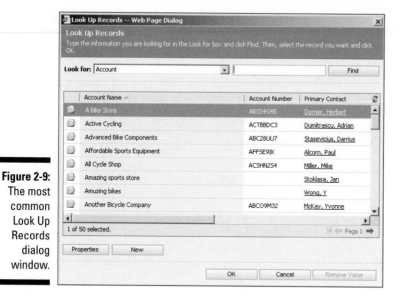

Figure 2-9:
The most
common
Look Up
Records
dialog
window.

Figure 2-10 is fairly simple as well. Just type in your search text and click Find. This particular window is found on some of the price list lookups.

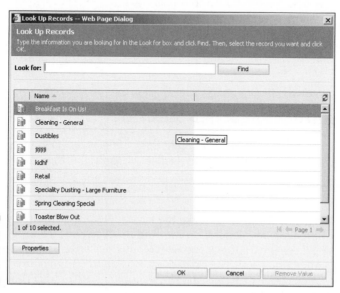

Figure 2-10:
Another
style.

When you're offered to choose more than one option, the window in Figure 2-11 lets you choose which options you want. After you find them in the left pane, just click the double right-arrow to move them over to the Selected Records pane.

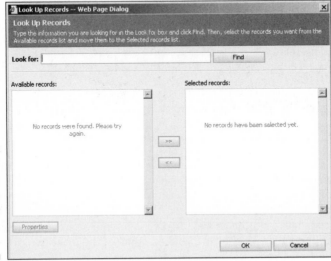

Figure 2-11: This one allows you to select records from a group.

Figure 2-12 is the Look Up window you see when you click the magnifying glass next to a Subject field.

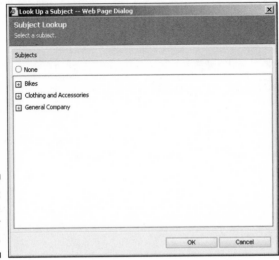

Figure 2-12: Here we're looking for a subject.

Searching with the Form Assistant

The Form Assistant is basically the lookup records feature put right there on the same window you're working in. Every field with a magnifying glass can be accessed and completed using the Form Assistant. See Figure 2-13.

Figure 2-13:
Your friendly neighbor-hood Form Assistant.

Keep in mind that what the Form Assistant shows depends on the field you want to complete.

Searching with the Advanced Find Feature

Almost all CRM software programs have some sort of advanced search fea-ture, but they rarely measure up to the workhorse built into Microsoft CRM. You can search for almost *anything,* from addresses to queues to roles to views. The other cool thing is that Advanced Find is accessible throughout the program (in the main menu bar).

In this section, we look at using the Advanced Find feature. (You can find even more ways to use Advanced Find in Chapter 16.) Follow these steps:

1. **Click the Advanced Find button in the main toolbar, or choose Tools➪Advanced Find in the menu bar.**

   Your location in the program doesn't matter. You can access Advanced Find from Marketing, Sales, Service — even Settings. The Advanced Find dialog box appears, as shown in Figure 2-14, so you can define the values of your search.

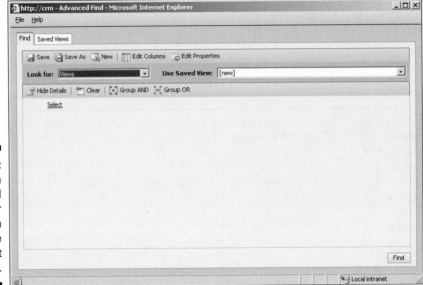

Figure 2-14: With Advanced Find, your search options are almost limitless.

2. **Click the drop-down arrow to the right of the Look For field to select the area or item you want to search.**

   The list has 49 items (or more if you have customized field views). Browse through them to see the available options. The options in the Use Saved View field depend on the category you select in the Look For field. Experiment by selecting various options in the Look For field and then seeing your options in the Use Saved View field.

3. **Choose your search criteria.**

   a. **Move your cursor to the word *Select* below the window's toolbar in the Advanced Find window.**

   A field appears with a drop-down menu.

  b. **Click the field to open the drop-down box.**

  c. **Select a field from the drop-down menu.**

   This tells Microsoft CRM that the search you're about to conduct will look first in the State/Province field.

 Note that after you make the State/Province selection, the word *Equals* appears next to it. To the right of *Equals* is the phrase *Enter Value.* The options in this third lookup file depend on the choices made earlier.

4. **Choose the modifier.**

  a. **Hover your cursor over the word *Equals* to display the field.**

   This should default to Equals, but always check before continuing. We want Equals in this case, but you also have Does Not Equal, Contains, Does Not Contain, and so on.

  b. **Click in the field to open the drop-down box and select the option you need.**

5. **Enter the value for your search to look for.**

  a. **Move your cursor over the words *Enter Value,* and click in the field that appears.**

   Again, these options depend on choices made in the previous steps.

  b. **To follow along with the example, enter NY;NJ in the field.**

   By using the semicolon, you can define multiple possible values for this field.

6. **Click Save.**

 A window pops up, asking for a title of your search.

7. **Enter a name for your search and click OK.**

 This convenient feature saves your search for future use.

 Click the arrow by the Use Saved View field to see all saved searches. Searches in System Views are available to everyone. Those in My Views (including the one you just saved) are available to you.

8. **In the Advanced Find window, click Find (in the lower-right corner) to activate the search.**

 A new window appears showing you a list of all accounts meeting your search criteria, as shown in Figure 2-15.

Didn't see what you wanted? Or worse, your search results returned a gazillion more hits than you thought it would? You can always click Back to Query to return to your search criteria for further definition.

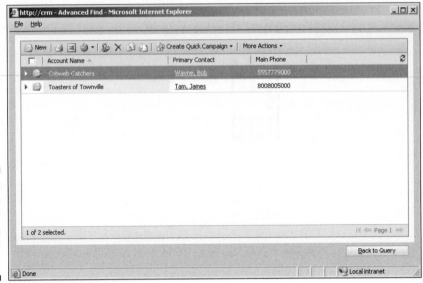

Figure 2-15:
Another
successful
search using
Advanced
Find!

Chapter 3

Using Microsoft CRM
Online and Offline

In This Chapter

▶ Outlining the things the Outlook client can't do

▶ Understanding the Outlook client

▶ Synchronizing

▶ Setting up your workspace in the Outlook client

*Y*ou can use Microsoft CRM in two ways: through the browser (the web client) or through Microsoft Outlook (the Microsoft CRM for Outlook client — which we call the outlook client). The web client is your main access method, the one that everyone in the office will use. The Outlook client is what your traveling folks use as well as the members of your staff who have no life and take their computers home to work from there.

The Microsoft CRM Outlook client has two options for your business: the laptop client, which allows for synchronization, and the desktop client, which is designed not to have a local database. If you are security conscious about data leaving your building or you always work at a desk, the desktop client may be your best option. If you spend most of your life on the road, you may want to use the laptop client because it allows you to make changes while not connected to any networks.

We're basing this chapter on the assumption that you already know Microsoft Outlook, so we don't go over Microsoft Outlook itself in detail. What we do focus on are the two different environments. Despite some functionality issues, how you do Microsoft CRM things in the Outlook client is almost exactly how you would do them in Microsoft CRM's web client.

Functionality

We start with those functionality issues just mentioned. Although you can do tons of stuff from the Outlook client, it can't do a handful of functions from Microsoft CRM. This includes settings as well as administrative and some customer support functions. We've listed them here:

- ✔ Settings
  - Change settings
  - Administer system
  - Configure system
- ✔ Customer service functions
  - Manage knowledge base
  - Manage service activities
  - Manage services
  - View Microsoft CRM service calendar
  - Edit products
  - Edit or manage sales literature

On the flip side, there are a few things you can do from the Outlook client that you can't do from the web client, such as a letter merge.

Last but not least, some things are particular to Outlook and are not incorporated into the Outlook client. For example, attachments might not be accepted in templates. Also, you can't use a drag-and-drop operation to move or copy an Outlook contact into a Microsoft CRM folder. (If you drag a contact to a folder, you create a new e-mail message, but the contact information is not copied.)

When you create an Outlook contact, be sure to click Track in CRM so that the new contact record syncs to your web client.

If you drag an Outlook e-mail message into a Microsoft CRM folder, the message will not appear in the Microsoft CRM folder even though it has been moved or copied to the folder.

The Outlook Client

When you're ready to start working, just launch Outlook. Easy as pie. With Microsoft CRM on your system, the Outlook client is automatically activated in Outlook itself. At this point, you're in the Outlook client, working online. Take a look at Figure 3-1.

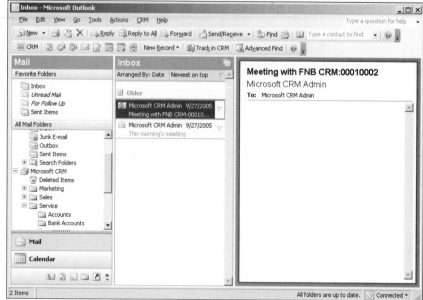

Figure 3-1:
This is how
Microsoft
Outlook
appears
with the
Outlook
client active.

Microsoft Outlook itself offers the ability to work online or offline. You can still use the Outlook client, no matter how you're working in Outlook. Another thing to keep in mind is that when you go offline (or come back online), the Outlook client automatically synchronizes with the main database.

Using Microsoft CRM functions

You can access Microsoft CRM functions in three ways. The first is by using the leftmost navigation pane, which has a Microsoft CRM section. If you open the folders and subfolders in this section, you'll see that most of the options in the web client are also here.

We mentioned that doing Microsoft CRM tasks in the Outlook client is almost the same as doing them in the web client. Let's take a quick peek at sales contacts, so you can see that we weren't kidding!

1. **Under Microsoft CRM in the navigation pane, click the plus sign next to Sales.**

   If a minus sign appears next to Sales instead, there's no need to click, because the Sales folder is already displaying its subfolders.

2. **Select Contacts (under Sales).**

   Now take a look at the right pane, the main workspace (see Figure 3-2). Look familiar? This is almost exactly like the workspace you would see in the Microsoft CRM web client.

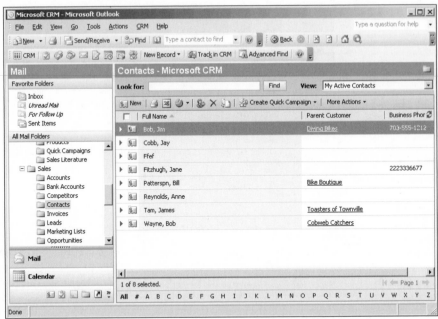

Figure 3-2:
Just like the
real thing.

The other two methods of accessing CRM functions are by choosing the CRM option on the menu bar and clicking the CRM button in the toolbar. The navigation, options, and functionality offered by both choices are identical to the web client. And because we covering those elsewhere in the book, we only mention a few important ones here.

Outlook client mail merge

As any sales rep or marketing guru can tell you, mail merge is one of the best inventions since peanut butter. You can mail merge a document (and envelopes or labels!) to a group of contacts or accounts, so that printing and setting up mailings is a snap. This is one of the few features not found in the web client.

1. **While you're in Outlook with the Outlook client, use the navigation pane to go to and highlight the group to which you want to send the letter.**

   Let's say you're moving the office and need to let your customers know. You would navigate to Sales and then Accounts. In the Sales window, select the view that contains your customers. The workspace on the right looks just like the workspace for Marketing: Accounts in Microsoft CRM (the web client), complete with the same toolbar.

2. **In the Accounts window toolbar, click the arrow on the More Actions button and then choose Mail Merge.**

   The Mail Merge dialog box appears.

3. **Select Template Letter, and then click OK.**

   The browse window appears.

4. **Search for and highlight the document you want to merge to the groups. Then click OK.**

   A list of mail merge recipients appears.

5. **Highlight the recipients you want to send your letter to, and then click OK.**

6. **On the right side of your screen in Word, select Next to preview your document.**

7. **Click Next again to complete the merge.**

8. **Select Print.**

Outlook client e-mail

Only a few differences exist between Outlook client e-mail and web client e-mail, mostly in how you get that e-mail recorded into your Microsoft CRM later. For the most part, sending an e-mail using the Outlook client is just like sending one in Outlook, only better. Read on:

1. **In the Outlook toolbar, choose New↪Mail Message.**

   Your new e-mail window appears (it's untitled, simply because you haven't put anything in the subject line yet). Eyes up: Just under the main menu bar is a new toolbar, as shown in Figure 3-3.

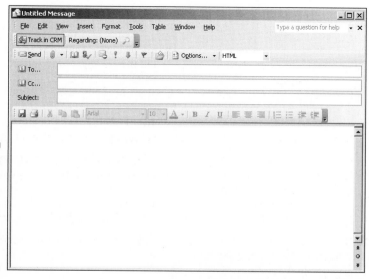

Figure 3-3:
Can you spot the additions to the Outlook client e-mail?

2. In that toolbar, click the Track in CRM button.

Basically, you're telling the Outlook client to attach this e-mail to one of CRM's business objects, such as contacts, accounts, opportunities, or cases.

3. In the same toolbar, click the Regarding button or the magnifying glass.

This is where you can associate the e-mail to the appropriate Microsoft CRM record. Either option opens the Look Up Records dialog box, as shown in Figure 3-4. (You use this dialog box in later chapters too.)

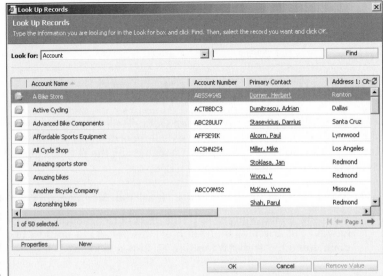

Figure 3-4:
Search for
records
here.

4. Click the arrow in the Look For field and select the type of record you want to associate with this e-mail.

You can search for the record by entering a search term in the empty box next to the Find button and then clicking Find. Because the records are in alphabetical order, you can also page to the entry. The results of your search appear in the Look Up Records window.

5. Highlight the record you want and then click OK.

You return to the new e-mail window. Take a look at the Regarding button. It should now read *Regarding* and whatever client or account you selected.

6. Complete your e-mail message as you normally would in Outlook, and then send it.

The message is now sent and is also tied to the item you selected in the Regarding area. If you were to open that object up and look under History, you would see this e-mail.

If you get stuck and need help with Microsoft CRM while you're in the Outlook client, choose CRM⇨Help on the menu bar in your Outlook window. Outlook's Help files don't contain anything about Microsoft CRM.

Synchronization Settings

No, we're not talking about synchronizing our watches, like a certain spy who has now gone blond. (I still say long live the Scot!) We're talking about getting all the offline work you did at home last night into the office and into Microsoft CRM.

The Outlook client has two types of synchronization: server synchronization and Outlook synchronization. (Microsoft CRM syncs directly to Outlook.) To set up the information available to you in Outlook, you need to tell CRM what data to sync. Here's how:

1. **On the Outlook client's menu bar, choose CRM⇨Options.**

   Your Set Personal Options dialog box appears, with three tabs: General, Synchronization, and Workplace.

2. **Click the Synchronization tab.**

   The screen is divided into two parts: basically, what to synchronize and when to synchronize.

3. **Choose what you want to synchronize.**

   There are three options for the different types of data that will sync: appointments, contacts, and tasks. We recommend that you check them all, just to save you a few steps later.

4. **Choose when to synchronize.**

   Check the box and then fill in the minutes field with however long you want the system to sync. You can also turn off automatic synchronization by unchecking this box. Take note here: the minimum auto sync time that you can set is 15 minutes.

   Your other option is to set up the system so it automatically syncs your Outlook folder when you start your computer.

5. **Click OK to save your settings.**

   The Set Personal Options dialog box closes, and you return to the Outlook client window.

Synchronizing the Outlook client with your server

Outlook client and server synchronization can really be broken down to the idea that you have data flowing in two directions: *From* your server (office) *to* your Outlook client (laptop) and then *from* your Outlook client *to* your server.

The very first step is to set up Microsoft CRM on your laptop with the Outlook client and copy over the data that you'll need when you're working offline. We recommend that you find your IT guys (they're like pens — you can never find one when you need one) and get them to do this part. It could take some time, so be prepared to surrender your laptop to your IT department for this initial setup. Yes, we understand your difficulties in surrendering your laptop, but chin up, little camper. You will survive (plus, for the most part, this is the only time you'll have to give up your laptop to get it ready for sync).

Let's fast-forward a bit. You have your laptop back (and figured out the password that the IT department changed on you as a joke). You took the laptop home and promptly got to work. You worked, played solitaire, chatted with a friend, worked some more, explained to your son that the dog doesn't know how to play ninja warriors, and worked some more . . . until, finally, you're ready to sync. Going offline (and coming back online) is easy. Within your Outlook client, choose File➪Work Offline. When you switch to Work Offline, this option will be checked. Click it again to work online (the check will be removed).

If you have a lot of data, synchronization might take awhile. To check the progress, choose CRM➪Synchronization Progress. The Synchronizing Microsoft CRM Data dialog box appears. You get a comprehensive view of just how your sync is progressing and will be alerted to any errors that occur during the process.

Setting data group (sync) filters

So just how many records (contacts, accounts, and all) do you have in your database? Some companies can have in excess of 40,000. Now let's say that you're the sales rep for Virginia and only 1,000 of those clients are yours. You don't want anyone else's clients; you just want yours. The best thing to do is set a data group filter so that only your contacts come over to your laptop. A *data group filter* tells the system what records to include. It is similar to the Advanced Find function and report filters (see Chapters 2 and 11, respectively, for information on these).

In a data group filter, you can choose from two filter modes: simple and detailed. The simple filter mode lets you change the values to include. The detailed mode lets you add criteria to your rule and gives you access to the Filter toolbar.

We recommend that you write your complex filter expressions on paper first. This way, you can make sure you don't forget some little line or symbol when you enter it in the data group filter.

Here's how you set those data group filters from the Outlook client:

1. **On the menu bar, choose CRM⇨Local Data.**

   The Local Data dialog box appears, as shown in Figure 3-5.

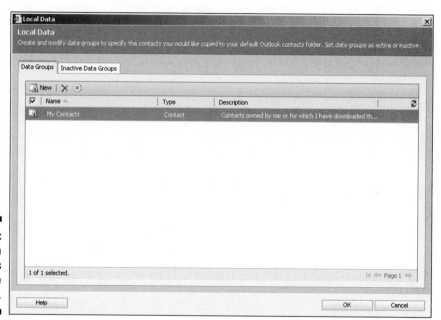

Figure 3-5: All your data group filters can be found here.

2. **Choose the New button to start a new data group filter.**

   The Data Group dialog box appears, as shown in Figure 3-6, so you can set up your criteria. You can also edit your data groups from here, but for now, we show you how to create one. Note the button below the Look For field. If the screen is in Show Details mode — as it is in Figure 3-6 and should be for these steps — the button reads Hide Details. Click it to hide the details and the button changes to Show Details.

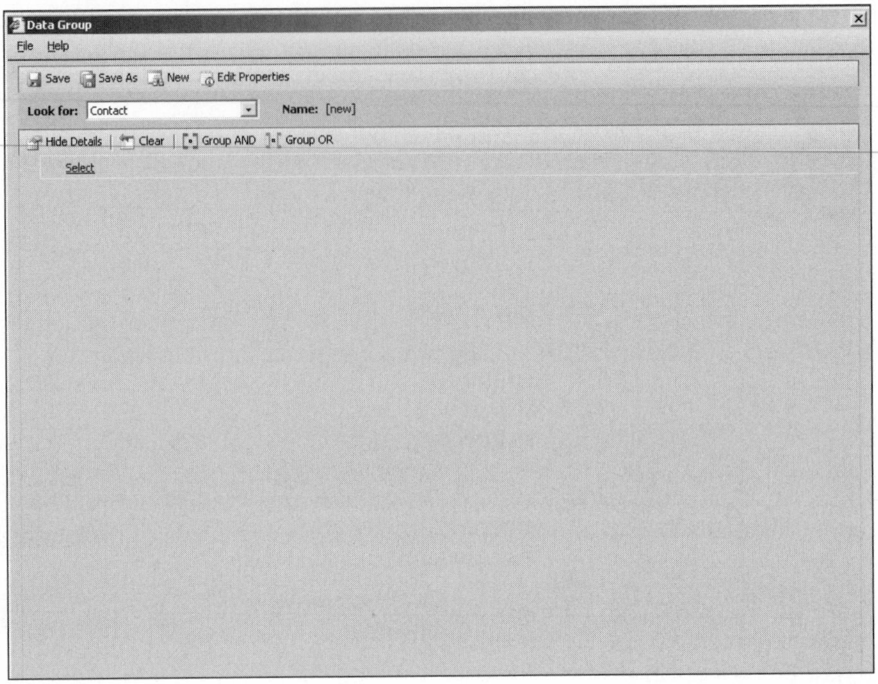

Figure 3-6:
Here are all
the details
for your data
group filter.

3. **Choose the field on which you want to base your filter.**

   Move your cursor to the word *Select* to display the search field. Click it to open the drop-down box. Scroll until you can select the field on which you want to base your filter. For this exercise, we selected Owner.

4. **Choose your qualifier.**

   Move your cursor over the word *Equals* to display the field, and then click it to open the drop-down box. The choices depend on what you chose in Step 3. For our example, we're going to use the default, Equals.

5. **Where the word *Enter* appears, select or enter your search criteria.**

   Depending on what you chose in Steps 3 and 4, this field will be either a free-form field, in which you can manually enter data, or be accompanied by a magnifying glass, which you click to make your choices in the Look Up Records dialog box. After you've entered your data, another Select line appears.

6. **If you want to enter additional search criteria, repeat Steps 3–5 to add additional search criteria.**

7. **In the toolbar, click the Save button.**

   A Data Group Properties dialog box appears.

8. Name this data group, add a description if you want, and then click OK.

You return to the Data Group dialog box. The Name field at the top of the window now contains the group name. You can close this window now if you want. You'll go back to the Local Data dialog box, where your data group appears in the list.

All right, now that you've created a data group, let's go back and edit it. Suppose you want to choose the records owned by Bob, the sales guy, and Stanley, the other sales guy. Basically, you would repeat Steps 3–5 twice: once to choose Bob and once to choose Stanley. Select them both by holding down the Ctrl key and clicking each criteria. Next, choose between Group AND and Group OR.

Group AND tells the filter to search records that contain both or all criteria. If you click Group AND, it will search for records containing both Bob AND Stanley, and because a record can't have two owners, your search results turn up zilch.

Group OR tells the filter to search for records with either Bob OR Stanley as the owner. In this case, this is your best way to go.

Grouping filter criteria works only if you're using criteria of the same type. For instance, the previous example works because you're searching for two owners. However, if you were searching for, say, owner and zip code, you could not group those.

The "last one in" rule

Last one in, close the door, right? According to your mother, maybe, but Microsoft CRM looks at "last one in" a little differently. The last one in rule concerns what happens when two or more people sync changes to the server for the same contact or account.

Let's hop into our time machine to explain a perfect scenario for the "last one in" rule. Last night, you went offline at 5 to meet a client (Ms. Joanne Powers) for dinner at the local greasy spoon. She introduces herself as Joan, not Joanne, so you make a mental note to correct that in your database when you get home. Fast-forward to after dinner, back at your house. Like all of us tech junkies, you go straight to your laptop and change her name and then go on to check your e-mail. But you forget to sync with the office.

Now, this morning, you have to go clear across the state to meet up with another client. You got up late, didn't have time to sync with the office, and ran out the door.

Meanwhile, your trusty sales assistant has come into the office, and she goes to check Ms. Powers's record in Microsoft CRM, using the web client. She thinks Ms. Powers is Jo-Anne (remember, your assistant still sees Joanne) so she changes Joanne to Jo-Anne.

You finally get back to the office around 3 p.m. and power up your laptop and the Outlook client, go online, and sync. Now take a look at Ms. Powers's record: It should say Joanne (and not Joan or Jo-Anne). Even though you made your change last night and your assistant made hers this morning, *your* data was the last (or most recent) data received and therefore is the one the web client listens to.

What if your trusty (and underpaid) sales assistant changed Ms. Powers's last name to Powhers? Both changes would be kept because you're not messing with the same piece of data.

Setting Up the Outlook Client Workplace

Setting up your Outlook client navigation pane and workplace is easy and can be accomplished with just a few clicks. The defaults options are the My Work and Customers options. Here's how you can change these to display the areas you want to work on:

1. **On the Outlook client's menu bar, choose CRM⇨Options.**

   The Set Personal Options dialog box appears.

2. **Click the Workplace tab.**

   The tab has two sides: Preview on the left and Set Workplace Area on the right.

3. **Check the options you want.**

   The Preview pane displays the work available under each option.
   You can check two or even all three.

4. **Click OK to close the dialog box and go back to the Outlook client.**

As you can see, the Outlook client makes it easy to work offline and away from the office. This could save valuable time and expenses and makes things flow just a little smoother, which is the overall goal for Microsoft CRM.

In the following chapters, you find out how to use Microsoft CRM's web client for e-mail, marketing, and service work.

Part II

Setting the
Settings

The 5th Wave   By Rich Tennant

"For 30 years I've put a hat and coat on to make sales calls and I'm not changing now just because I'm doing it on the Web from my living room."

In this part . . .

In Part II, you discover how to make the software fit you and your organization. You read about personalizing the system around your own work habits and schedule. You find out about security and access rights, territories, roles, and business units.

Because workflow is a key component to automating the system around your company's business processes, Chapters 7 and 8 discuss designing and then implementing workflow.

A knowledge base is a collection of articles, materials, and responses to inquiries thats a valuable tool for everyone in your organization. A knowledge base is particularly helpful to new members, who may not know quite as much as you do about the organization and its products, services, and policies. Developing a knowledge base is discussed in Chapter 9. In Chapter 10, you find out how to set up a catalog of products and services you sell.

With Microsoft CRM, you can use built-in reports or create your own. In Chapters 11 and 12, you find out how to run those reports and how to develop template documents and internal announcements.

Chapter 4

Personalizing Your System

• •

In This Chapter

▶ Accessing your personal settings

▶ Understanding your user profile options

• •

*O*ne of the first things you should do is set your personal options to control the way Microsoft CRM displays information. You can use these personal settings to streamline the system so it best suits your function in the organization and your style. For example, you can determine what window appears when you start Microsoft CRM each day. If your role is strictly in customer service, you might want the system to go directly to the listing of your cases.

In this chapter, we discuss what choices you have and how to set them. It's unlikely that you will need to change every option, but it's good to know what's available.

Customization is important, and the process shouldn't take long. A little attention to customization now will enable you to work more efficiently as you become familiar with the system.

Tailoring the System to Suit Your Needs

You can streamline your use of CRM by setting your regular workday hours, how you want your scheduled activities to appear, and the starting point for the system each morning, and many other options. Options like these are called your *personal settings.* Basically, you are telling Microsoft CRM how you like to operate.

To access your personal settings, follow these two steps:

1. **At the bottom of the navigation pane, click the Workplace button.**

   An option to Personalize Workplace appears in blue just above the Workplace button.

2. **Click the Personalize Workplace option.**

The Set Personal Options window appears, with the Workplace tab displayed by default, as shown in Figure 4-1.

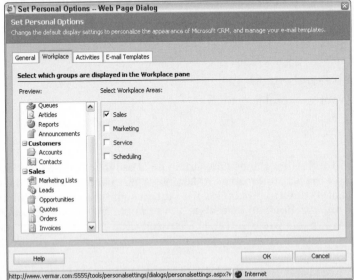

Figure 4-1:
The Set
Personal
Options
window,
showing the
Workplace
tab.

CRM provides you with four tabs, each of which affects various default settings and how information is displayed. None of these settings affect anyone other than *you*, so you should set them to please yourself.

General tab

The General tab (called Miscellaneous in prior versions of Microsoft CRM) contains settings for what you want the system to display upon startup, how many records you want to see at one time, how you want the Find function to work, and what time zone you work in. The General tab is shown in Figure 4-2.

The first group of options on the General tab pertains to your default start page. The Default Pane field has five choices, but you can probably eliminate Settings as a reasonable choice. Selecting Settings means every morning when you sign on, CRM will automatically start up by allowing you to change your Settings. This isn't something you're likely to do regularly. In fact, you'll probably set it and forget it.

If your job function is primarily in sales, marketing, or customer service, it might seem logical to select one of those choices as a starting point for your day. This *might* work for you. However, we prefer to come in each morning and see what's on our agenda. This is best accomplished by setting the Default Pane option to Workplace and the Default Tab option to Activities or to Calendar. (Note that the selections you see in the Default Tab option change depending on your selection in the Default Pane option.)

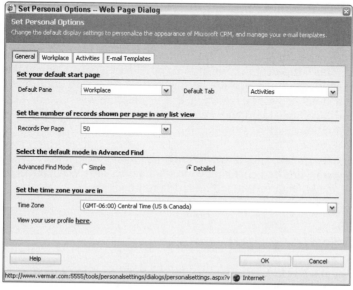

Figure 4-2:
You can tell the system how you want to operate, rather than having it be in charge of you.

To set your default start screen, follow these steps:

1. **Set the Default Pane option as desired.**

   To do so, click the down arrow to the right of the field and then make a selection. The options in the Default Tab option will change, but you won't be able to see that until you position your mouse in that field.

2. **Set the Default Tab option as desired.**

3. **Click the OK button (at the bottom of the window).**

   Your new options are saved, but you will not see the effect of this until the next time you log into CRM.

Now on to the next option on the General tab — the number of records shown on the page. Depending on the size and resolution of the screen you're using, you may want to change the number of records that appear in each list. The smaller your screen or the lower your resolution, the fewer lines you may want displayed at any one time. On the other hand, if you have a large number of records and prefer just scrolling up and down, set the number of records shown to a large number, perhaps 100 or more. The default is 25 records per page; we usually set ours a little higher.

Advanced Find Mode, a new feature in Version 3, allows you to create more complex searches and save search criteria for future use. You can take best advantage of this feature by selecting the Detailed option. If you select the Simple mode instead, you can use predefined searches but cannot create new ones yourself. Even if you have no intention of creating Advanced Find searches right now, don't limit yourself by selecting Simple.

The Time Zone drop-down list contains time zones from all over the world. Choose yours. The goal of setting your time zone is to coordinate your activities with other members of your team who may be dispersed throughout the world. This will assist in coordinating conference calls among team members. For example, suppose you are in New York and set up a conference call with a team member in Sydney, Australia. If you schedule your call for 4 p.m. Monday, the call will show up on your Australian counterpart's activity list for 8 a.m. Tuesday (her time).

In the General tab, and in the other three tabs as well, make sure to click OK when you've finished changing your settings. To see the results of any changes you've made, you have to log out and then back in.

Workplace tab

You use the Workplace tab in the Set Personal Options window (refer to Figure 4-1) to define your role in your organization and to tailor the workplace to show any combination of sales, marketing, service, and scheduling information. When you select the Marketing option, for example, marketing lists, campaigns, and quick campaigns become available to you in the navigation pane. This list of options may also look different depending on how the options were defined by your system administrator or implementation partner.

Simply click to remove the check mark from each of the four options in turn. As you do so, fewer and fewer areas are displayed in the Preview panel on the left. When all four workplace areas are turned off, the minimum areas are available.

We recommend that you select just the one or two roles you usually play in your organization. Selecting more won't damage anything but will clutter the screen with functions you don't need. Our advice? If you're in sales, select Sales or Sales plus Marketing. If you're in customer service, select Service or Service plus Scheduling. If you're in Marketing, don't clutter up your workplace with Service schedules but do select the other three.

Activities tab

Activities is the third tab in the Set Personal Options window. This is where you to specify your default calendar view, as shown in Figure 4-3.

A good choice is the weekly view, which is shown in Figure 4-4. The calendar view, whether daily, weekly, or monthly, displays only appointments and none of the other activities such as scheduled phone calls or tasks . If you want to use any of the calendar views, and you want a realistic picture of what is scheduled for you, make everything an appointment. We think a better option is to use the Activities view, which shows all types of scheduled activities including appointments and phone calls.

The second set of options (Set your default work hours) enables you to specify your typical workday hours. Although a Start Time of 2 PM and an End Time of 3 PM sounds appealing, you should set this more realistically. By default, your workplace calendar displays the hours you've selected as your regular work schedule. If you happen to schedule an appointment outside those normal hours, it will still appear on your calendar.

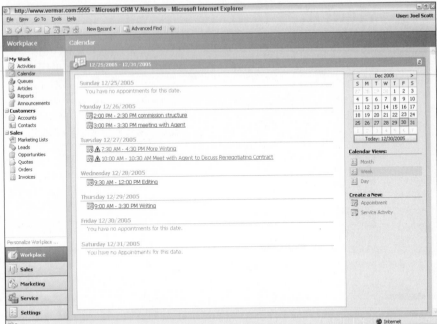

Figure 4-4:
The weekly
calendar
view.

The last area in the Activities tab is meant to allow you to better control the onslaught of incoming e-mail. Microsoft has incorporated a token-based system into CRM 3.0. If you select All e-mail messages, all e-mail that would normally go to your Outlook inbox will go also to Microsoft CRM 3.0. If you select e-mail messages that have a Microsoft CRM token, which means that they were either sent from Microsoft CRM or you click the tracked in CRM button in Outlook, only those messages will be brought into Microsoft CRM automatically.

Each method has its strengths and weaknesses. As a general rule, if you use the Outlook Client for Microsoft CRM, you should have Microsoft CRM automatically capture e-mails with the tokens. If you typically use Internet Explorer to access Microsoft CRM, select All e-mail.

E-mail Templates tab

The E-mail Templates tab enables you to create and customize templates for almost every type of record in the database, assuming your security level allows this. (Security and access rights are described in Chapter 5.) The ones you create in this section are available only to you. To create templates for the entire organization, use the Settings tab of Microsoft CRM.

This important personal setting enables you to create a powerful array of standard documents that you can use, for example, as automatic responses to inquiries about your products or services. This is a great way to expedite your response to sales inquiries. Unlike fine wine, leads never improve with age. From a list of templates you create, you can choose any template and create a *bulk e-mail,* also known as a *direct e-mail* or an *e-mail blast.* Bulk e-mail is a way to send one or more e-mails at one time easily and automatically. Some people associate this with spam. As long as you are legitimately responding to someone's inquiry or have received permission to send electronic communications (also called *opt-in mail*), it is *not* spam and may be an effective way to handle many routine business activities, including newsletters and special announcements.

It is probably to your professional advantage to include a way for your e-mail recipients to opt out of receiving e-mail from you. For more information, read:

```
http://blogs.msdn.com/midatlanticcrm/archive/2006/01/17/
            Managing_Newsletters_and_Blast_Emails_Using_
            Microsoft_CRM.aspx
```

See Figure 4-5 for an example of e-mail template titles. From the E-mail Templates tab, you can highlight and drill down into each of the templates that have been set up for your use. Or you can create new ones by clicking the New button. E-mail templates are discussed in further detail in Chapter 12.

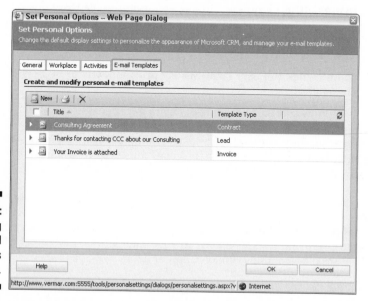

Figure 4-5:
Seasoning your e-mail templates to taste.

Your User Profile

Setting your user profile means telling the system who you are and your role in the organization. Depending on the rights you have to the system, you may need to approach your system administrator to change your user profile.

Even if you don't have the rights to tinker with these settings, you should know what options are available so you can at least provide input to the system administrator.

Your user profile enables you to record information about yourself and your relationship to your company, such as your title, the teams you work on, your roles in the organization, and the times you are generally available. Your user profile settings enable you to participate in one or more team activities and to have a specific role in those activities.

Anyone can view anyone else's user profile, but administrative rights may be required to make changes.

To navigate to the user profile area, follow these steps:

1. **At the bottom of the navigation pane, click the Settings button.**

   A window with 11 choices appears.

2. **In the Settings window, click the first option, Business Unit Settings.**

3. **Select Users.**

   The Users window appears.

4. **Double-click the user (you) whose profile needs to be reviewed or changed.**

   A window similar to the one in Figure 4-6 appears.

Your user profile may be displayed as read-only if your security settings do not allow you to edit it. If this is the case, your system administrator will have to make any necessary changes for you.

Your user profile contains seven categories, each of which is displayed in the upper part of the navigation pane. These seven categories are divided into two groups: Details and Service. The Details group applies to everyone; the Service group applies specifically to customer service personnel. Service groups are discussed in detail in Chapter 22.

Under the Details group are the Information, Teams, Roles, Quotas, and Work Hours categories. You should go through each category sequentially to view how your record is set up and to determine whether any changes are required. Each of these categories defines a different aspect of your role in the organization.

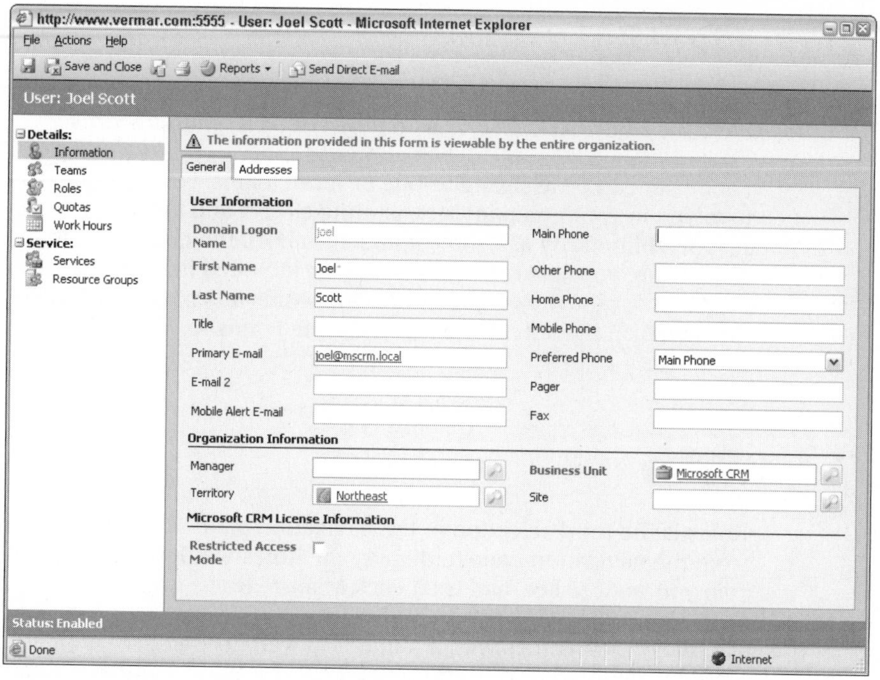

Figure 4-6:
Your user
profile
information.

Information

When you click Information in the navigation pane, you see the User window, with two tabs: General and Addresses (refer to Figure 4-6). The fields labeled in red are required; everything else is optional but recommended. Most of the fields on the General tab are self-explanatory, but several deserve further explanation:

- ✔ **Domain Logon Name:** The server or entire set of resources running your CRM system.

- ✔ **Business Unit:** The organization to which you directly report.

- ✔ **Manager:** Your manager's name. (This field may be important if your system is designed to automatically escalate issues from one level of management to another.)

- ✔ **Territory:** Particularly in sales, efforts are usually divided into regions or territories. Each salesperson is usually associated with one territory.

The Addresses tab allows for two separate addresses. Everyone in your company should use these the same way. We recommend that you use the office address as the Mailing Address and your home address as the Other Address. It could just as well be the other way around, but everyone in your company needs to conform to the same method.

Teams

Teams, the next selection in the navigation pane, is used to group users who have the same basic role or who might need to share records.

Each user can be assigned to one or more teams. For example, you may be involved in your company's consulting efforts and also have some sales responsibilities. By assigning yourself to both the consulting team and the sales team, you assure yourself of being included in correspondence and meetings for those two groups. All the teams in a particular organization are displayed on the left. On the right are the teams to which the user has been assigned.

Roles

Roles is the third selection in the navigation pane. Click the Roles option from the navigation pane to display the Roles window. Highlight the specific role you want to see, and then click Manage Roles from the window's toolbar.

Microsoft CRM comes with a number of well-defined access rights, each associated with different roles that people perform in a company. For example, there's a well-defined set of access rights for an individual salesperson and a different set for the manager of customer service. You should have at least one role and could have several. These assignments are normally part of the initial configuration of the system and are usually the responsibility of your administrator.

Quotas

Quotas is the next category under Details in the navigation pane. For more on quotas, see Chapter 15. Quotas are relevant only for salespeople.

Work hours

The final category under Details is Work Hours. This is where each user's standard schedule is housed. You establish the typical work week and then add specific time off. If your organization runs more than one shift, the Work Hours area is where you indicate what shift each person is working. This area can be used also to indicate, on a day-by-day basis, who is on vacation or otherwise unavailable.

To view or edit a user's work hours, follow these steps:

1. **At the bottom of the navigation pane, click the Settings button.**

2. **In the Settings window, click Business Unit Settings.**

3. **Select Users.**

   The Users window appears.

4. **Select the user whose work hours you want to view by highlighting that user and clicking Work Hours from the navigation pane.**

   The window shown in Figure 4-7 appears.

5. **In the top-left area, click the Set Up button.**

   This button is the key to managing each user's work hours. Three options appear, enabling you to set a new weekly schedule, set a unique schedule for one day at a time, or schedule time off. Each option displays a simple entry screen.

6. **Choose an option, fill in the entry screen, and then click OK.**

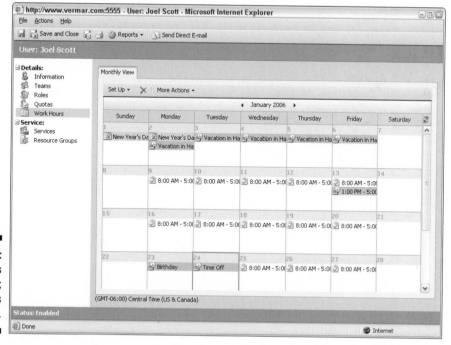

Figure 4-7:
Sometimes at work; sometimes not.

Your user profile coordinates you with your organization, so it's critical that your profile be set up before you and the other users really start using the system. The settings can always be changed as you go along and as your roles change.

Chapter 5

Understanding Security and Access Rights

*I*n this day and age, security is important. As technology advances, so do the hackers, virus writers, and other malevolently minded folks. With Microsoft CRM, you should be concerned with two types of security: physical security and internal security.

Physical security is a defense against everyone you don't know and don't want to meet. These are the people who have nothing better to do than develop and propagate viruses or, worse yet, spend their time hacking into your system to either paralyze you or steal your stuff. This type of security is generally handled by firewalls, routers, and other types of hardware and software. Because the vast majority of CRM installations run only on your intranet, this type of security is beyond the scope of this book. For more information, see the Microsoft *Implementation Guide*.

Information on Microsoft CRM–specific security patches are posted on the Microsoft CRM Community site at

```
http://go.microsoft.com/fwlink/?LinkId=53254
```

Be sure to check the Web site regularly to ensure that you are fully up-to-date on any security issues specifically affecting Microsoft CRM.

The second type of security is aimed at your own usually well-meaning team members. Some organizations, such as brokerage houses, are required to restrict certain records even from members of their own staff. In other organizations, salespeople's opportunities need to be hidden from the other salespeople. In our company, we find it occasionally important to keep e-mails away from prying eyes.

CRM has quite a bit of built-in security. And your system administrator, perhaps with several people from your management team, will probably be charged with setting up security and access rights within Microsoft CRM. In this chapter, you find out about the types of security you should consider and how to regulate your internal security.

Security Overview

Microsoft CRM's security focuses on meeting the needs of most organizations in two ways:

- Role-based security
- Object-based security

Role-based security in Microsoft CRM allows you to create a role, such as Sales Executive, that controls what the user can do and has access to. Your installation can also define its own roles to meet your requirements.

Object-based security in Microsoft CRM focuses on what access the roles have to primary and extended entities (such as leads, opportunities, contacts, accounts, and cases). So you could have the role of Sales Manager and have access to change opportunities (an object) but only read cases (another object).

User Privileges

Privileges are the most basic security option in Microsoft CRM and are generally set up by your administrator. User privileges determine what a user can and can't do, such as creating records or deleting records. (We recommend that only a system administrator be allowed to delete records.) Altogether, a user can do eight basic things: create, read, write (edit or modify), delete, append, append to, assign, and share.

Access Levels

The next step above privileges, *access levels* help determine which records the user privileges should apply to. In other words, your privileges may include the ability to delete account records, but your access level determines exactly which records you are able to delete. Microsoft CRM defines four access levels: user (least authority), business unit, parent/child, and organization (most authority).

Defining Roles

The concept of *roles* marries privileges and access rights. Microsoft CRM comes with 13 predefined roles that are typical of a midsized organization, as shown in Figure 5-1. Making use of these predefined roles saves a lot of time that would otherwise be spent setting up specific access rights for each user.

If you are going to make *any* changes to the default roles, we recommend that you use the functionality Microsoft provides call Role Copy. Refer to the online help on how to use this.

In this section, we show you how to look at the roles that Microsoft CRM ships with. Each of these roles has a complete set of predefined privileges and access rights. The prototypical sales manager is given a default set of privileges and access rights. To see the settings for each of default role, follow these steps:

1. **In the lower part of the navigation pane, click the Settings button.**

   The Settings window appears on the right.

2. **Click Business Unit Settings.**

3. **Select Security Roles.**

   The Security Roles window appears, listing all existing roles (refer to Figure 5-1).

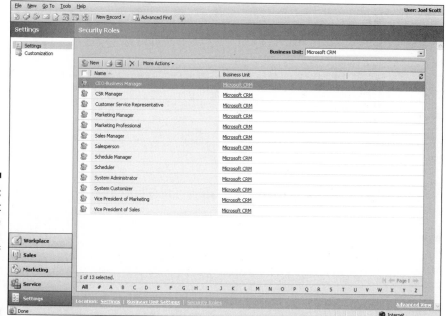

Figure 5-1: You get these standard roles out of the box, but you can add more.

4. **View the sales manager's role by clicking his or her line in the list.**

   The Role: Sales Manager window appears.

5. **Click the Core Records tab.**

   The screen shown in Figure 5-2 appears. The Core Records tab contains all the toggle switches to turn access rights on or off and is the central storehouse for role information.

6. **Click each tab in turn to see all the objects that can be accessed at various levels for the existing sales manager profile.**

7. **Click the Save and Close button to return to the Security Roles window.**

If your business has specific business rules you need to enforce, you should seek help from your system administrator or implementation partner.

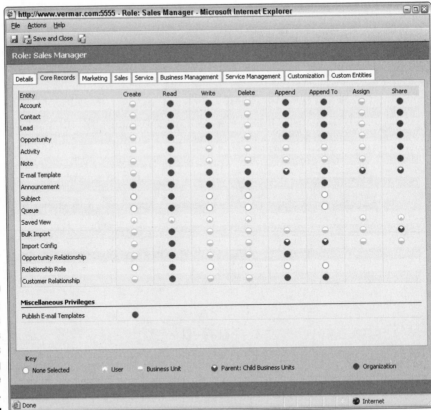

Figure 5-2: The sales manager's rights regarding Core Records.

Assigning Roles

After you have defined a role, you need to assign it to the user. Every user in the system must have at least one role to access the system.

A user can have more than one assigned role. For example, someone could have a role as a systems administrator and as a mailroom clerk. When a single user has multiple roles with different privileges and access rights, the role with the less restrictive privileges takes precedence. So, even when your systems administrator is functioning as a mailroom clerk, he or she will have the maximum levels of access rights.

If your organization is complex or you don't understand Microsoft CRM's concepts of roles, we suggest that you consult with an expert to help you in setting up your roles and assigning them to users.

To add a role to a user of the system, just follow these simple steps.

1. **At the bottom of the navigation pane, click the Settings button.**

   The Settings window appears.

2. **Click Business Unit Settings.**

3. **Select Users.**

   The Users window appears, listing all current users.

4. **Double-click a user name.**

   The User window appears.

5. **In the navigation pane, click Roles.**

6. **At the top of the Roles window, click Manage Roles.**

7. **Select the roles you want this user to have, and then click OK.**

8. **Click Save and Close.**

Sharing Information with Others on Your Team

Microsoft CRM has powerful security and record-sharing tools. If keeping certain records or data confidential is necessary for your company, that's no problem. Usually more critical than keeping data confidential, however, is your ability to share information with other members of your team.

Defining a team

Before you set up your CRM system, we suggest that you do a bit of homework and planning. So get your management staff together and order pizza, because you have got some brainstorming to do. You'll want to figure out your *business units* (think divisions or remote offices) and then assign users to those units.

Typically, the users assigned to a particular business unit are also members of a *team*. Each user in CRM can be a member of one or more teams. The concept of a team allows for a convenient sharing of records.

Sharing and assigning

You can easily *share* records and activities with members of your team — and you should. Sharing a record is like asking your buddies to help you when you need it. Rest assured: If you ask them, they will return the favor. By sharing and distributing the workload, you, your team members, and your customers all benefit. While you're on vacation, team members who have access to your data while you're away can still help *your* clients.

You can also *assign* records and tasks. Assigning is a little more like telling another user on the system to handle the assignment. (It's more like delegating than sharing.)

Unsharing

Whatever you share you can unshare. If you turned over access to your clients while you were on vacation, you can retake control upon your return. In most work environments, this is a far better solution than sending your clients an e-mail telling them you will be away for two weeks and they should just relax until you get back. And it's certainly a better approach than not letting your clients know that you'll be away at all.

Sharing and Not Sharing Data

The concept of sharing is also pertinent to security. Assuming you have sharing privileges, you can regulate who else in your organization has access to your records. By sharing your records with another user or a team, you're granting access to people who would not otherwise be able to view or modify those records.

Sharing records

Granting sharing privileges to someone who already has organizational rights (the highest level of access rights) really doesn't accomplish anything. Similarly, if you try to deny sharing rights to someone with organizational rights, nothing is going to change. That's like telling the boss he or she can't look over your shoulder.

Sharing is a good tool if, for example, you're working on a deal in New York and need to bring in a co-worker from Detroit. Under normal security, your co-worker would not be able to view your records. By sharing, you can give him or her access to the record to help work the deal.

You can share almost any kind of record, but we will use an account record as an example. Follow these steps to share an account:

1. **At the top of the navigation pane, select Accounts.**

   The Accounts window appears on the right.

2. **Select a record by double-clicking.**

   The General tab for that account appears.

3. **On the menu bar (at the top of the screen), choose Actions⇨Sharing.**

   The window shown in Figure 5-3 appears.

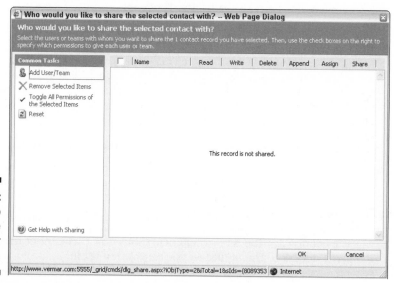

Figure 5-3:
Setting up
one or more
records for
sharing.

4. **In the Common Tasks pane on the left, select Add User/Team.**

   The Look Up Records dialog box appears, as shown in Figure 5-4.

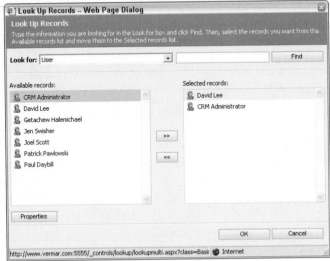

Figure 5-4:
Selecting
someone to
share with.

5. **In the Look For field, select User or Team, and then click the Find button.**

   All available users or teams are displayed.

6. **Double-click any user (or team) from the list in the left panel.**

   Another method is to highlight the user (or team) and click the right-facing arrow button. The user (or team) is transferred to the right pane in anticipation of sharing the record with that user or team.

7. **Click OK.**

   The window shown in Figure 5-5 appears.

8. **Specify which permissions you are allowing for this record.**

   To do so, check or uncheck each of the boxes that relate to the rights you are granting. As easily as you can share a record, you can also unshare it.

9. **Click OK when you're satisfied that you've shared enough rights.**

   The window for the record reappears, but now these other users have as much access to the record as you've granted them.

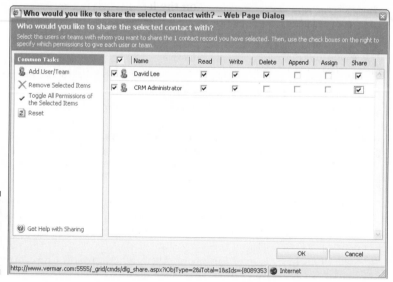

Figure 5-5:
Granting
sharing
permissions.

Unsharing records

If you can share it, you can unshare it. For example, before going on vacation, you may want to share all your records with one of your peers. When you return, you probably want to unshare them and resume your usual tasks. To unshare a record, follow these steps:

1. **Navigate to the record you want to unshare.**

2. **On the menu bar (at the top of the screen), choose Actions⇨ Sharing.**

3. **Toggle the Share check box to remove the check mark.**

   If you granted sharing rights to more than one user, you can eliminate multiple users' rights by toggling each of their Share check boxes on this one screen.

4. **Click OK.**

   The system returns to the General tab of the account record.

Streamlining the assignment of permissions

If you share with multiple people or multiple teams, you can end up having to deal with quite a few check boxes. Microsoft CRM provides two additional options in the Common Tasks panel to streamline your efforts:

✔ **Toggle All Permissions of the Selected Items:** After you've selected one or more users, this option acts like a toggle switch for all the permissions for that user. This is an easy way to grant permissions across the board for multiple users.

✔ **Reset:** This is like a do over button. Selecting Reset brings you back to the settings you had before the last time you clicked the OK button. Other systems sometimes refer to this as an *undo* button.

No form of security is ever foolproof. Although Microsoft CRM provides a sophisticated security system, this issue should remain a high priority. Security threats can come from anywhere: from your staff (innocent mistakes or not-so-innocent sabotage) and from outside hackers.

Remember, no system is foolproof (remember the *Titanic?*), but you can develop an efficient compromise and make your system user-friendly and hacker-unfriendly.

And, don't forget the Minions of Chaos and always back up your data.

Chapter 6

Managing Territories, Business Units, and Teams

In This Chapter

▶ Defining your territories

▶ Managing your territories

▶ Managing your business units

▶ Creating your teams

*T*erritories, teams, and business units are three organizational concepts that are so closely linked that you need to understand all three before deciding how to handle any one of them.

Typically, you establish territories to manage sales in bite-sized chunks. You probably want to develop a sales quota for your company in each territory and then check forecasted sales and closed sales against the quotas you've set. (We talk more about assigning quotas and forecasting sales in Chapter 15.) You may also want to use territories as a way to ensure that customers are equitably distributed among salespeople. By using Microsoft CRM, you can measure equitable distribution by geography, the number of customers, account revenue, or some combination of all three factors.

Territories come into play when assigning accounts and when reporting on them. In this chapter, we explain how to set up territories, business units, and teams.

Setting Up Sales Territories

Every account record has one field called Territory. After you define your territories, you manually enter the proper territory for each account record. You can do this from a drop-down list that your database administrator sets up, or you can use workflow rules to automatically assign an account to a territory. Assignments can be based on state, province, zip or postal code, or some combination of these.

Don't use telephone area codes for territory definitions. Area codes change too often and, in the U.S., are not geographically consistent. On top of that, with many people using cellphones or Internet phones, it's hard to relate phone numbers to geography.

Implementing workflow rules is a powerful way to have Microsoft CRM do a tremendous amount of work for you. A workflow rule can be attached to every new record, can check the physical location of that account or contact, and can assign it to a territory. Setting up such rules is appropriate for this or any kind of procedure that is well defined and frequently repeated. See Chapter 8 for a discussion of workflow rules.

Each user can be assigned to a single territory and is designated as either a territory user (a member of a team) or as the territory manager.

The task of setting up and managing territories is usually reserved for people with administrative rights. If you don't already have territories defined, this is a good time to do so. Follow these steps:

1. **At the bottom of the navigation pane, click the Settings button.**

   The Settings window with its 11 options appears.

2. **Select Sales Territories.**

   The Sales Territories window shown in Figure 6-1 appears. This is a typical view displaying the territories already in your system, presumably put there by your system administrator or by a sales manager.

3. **In the Sales Territories window's toolbar, click the New button to add a new territory.**

4. **Fill in the General tab as follows:**

   a. **In the Territory Name field, enter a unique Territory Name.**

   b. **To the right of the Manager field, select a territory manager for that territory from the drop-down list.**

   c. **If your territory names are not self-explanatory, be sure to enter a description.**

   For example, if the Territory Name is New England, you should list the individual states in the Description field. See Figure 6-2.

5. **At the top of the screen, click Save (the disk icon).**

   Note that the Members option in the navigation pane is now available. The users assigned to a territory are called *members* of that territory. After you set up a territory, you can add users to that territory.

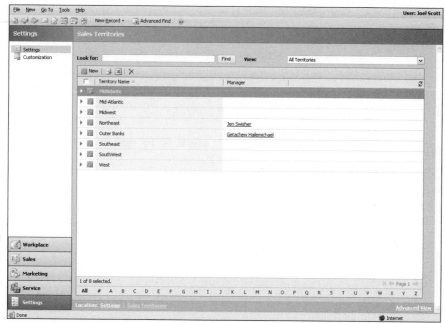

Figure 6-1:
The territories in your system.

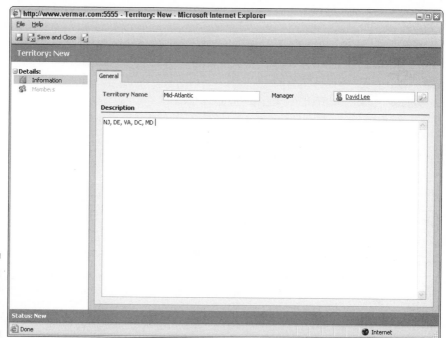

Figure 6-2:
Enter and define the territory.

6. **Add a user (member) to the territory as follows:**

   a. **At the top of the navigation pane, select Members.**

   b. **In the window's toolbar, click the Add Members button.**

   You see a list of available users in the Look Up Records window. Because an individual user can be assigned to only one territory, the available users display in Figure 6-3 shows only unassigned users.

   c. **From the available users, select one or more users (that is, members) for a territory.**

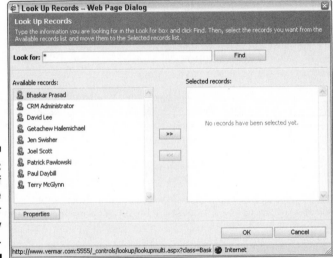

Figure 6-3: Display of available users for territory assignment.

7. **After you finish adding users to a territory, click the Save and Close button.**

   You return to the Sales Territories window.

Sometimes you may *think* that you need to assign someone to more than one territory. For example, if the Mid-Atlantic manager leaves, you may need to have the New England manager temporarily take over both territories. You do this by defining a new territory that encompasses both the New England and the Mid-Atlantic regions.

Managing Territories

If you plan to assign accounts to territories, you need to ensure that the Territory field for every account is filled in. You can do this by establishing workflow rules that automatically assign territories based on the City or State fields.

You can ensure that every account is assigned to a territory in several ways:

- ✔ Make the Territory field into a business-recommended field. (Creating Business Recommended fields is a system administrator function.) This designation turns the field label blue, indicating to the user that entering data in this field is important. The business recommended designation does not force the entry of data.

- ✔ Make the Territory field into a business-required field. (This is also a system administrator function.) With this designation, which turns the field label red, no one can save the record unless the field is filled in.

- ✔ Send missing data alerts by using a third-party alert system, such as KnowledgeSync (which is discussed in Chapter 28). An alert system sends a pop-up alarm or report to a user or manager when critical data has not been entered into a new record. These alarms work only after a record has been saved.

After you do everything possible to make sure every account is assigned to a territory, you'd think you'd be done with it. But, things change. Salespeople leave or get reassigned. New salespeople appear. Territories are merged. It's not enough to just assign a salesperson to a territory. You must be vigilant to ensure that the assignments still make sense.

When customers are assigned to a territory or reassigned, the account manager should be notified. In a perfect world, the customers should also be notified that they have a new account manager.

When one or more accounts have been added to an account manager's list, the first thing to do is to notify the account manager.

Although this seems obvious, no function is built into the software to make this happen automatically. If a salesperson already has several hundred accounts, he or she may not notice for a long time that a half dozen new accounts were just added to the list.

Workflow rules (discussed in Chapter 8) are an effective way to provide this notification. Failing that, you can resort to the old-fashioned method of either telling the salesperson or printing a report of existing customers and highlighting the new ones with a yellow marker.

The second notification needs to go to the client. Whenever an account manager changes, it is critical to inform all affected customers. With the appropriate workflow rules, you can accomplish this by an e-mail, a fax, a template letter, a scheduled phone call, or a visit.

Managing Business Units

A *business unit* is analogous to a division or a profit center in a company. But the concept of business units in Microsoft CRM allows more flexibility than the simple concept of divisions in a company. Rather, business units are more like organizational charts. They also play a large role in the security model of Microsoft CRM.

For example, suppose a software dealership has three main business units: software, hardware/networking, and professional services. One or more of these units might have subunits. Maybe the software business unit is further divided into three brands of software. Each of those three is also a business unit. The security division might be broken down into the firewall, the spyware, and the antispam units.

To set up business units, follow these steps:

1. **At the bottom of the navigation pane, click the Settings button.**

2. **In the window on the right, select Business Unit Settings.**

3. **Select Business Units.**

   The screen shown in Figure 6-4 appears.

4. **On the Business Units window's toolbar, click the New button.**

   The Business Unit: New window appears, as shown in Figure 6-5.

5. **After filling in the relevant fields (most notably Name and Division), click Save and Close.**

   The system returns to the Business Units window, where you see your new business unit.

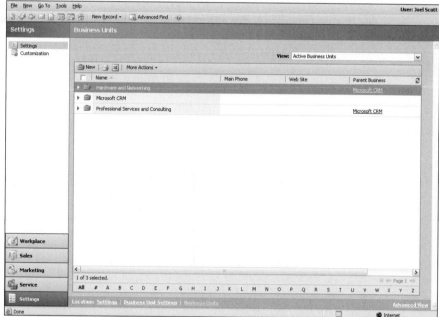

Figure 6-4:
Business
units for a
simple
technology
company.

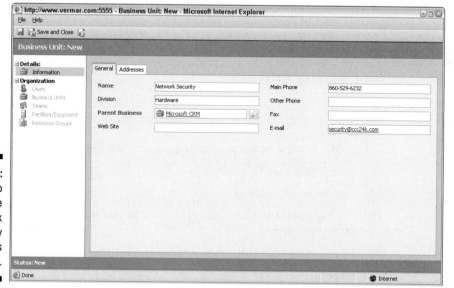

Figure 6-5:
Adding info
for the
Network
Security
business
unit.

After you create a business unit and link it to its parent unit (and maybe even give it some children), you can reorganize your business units at any time.

After you create your business units, you can assign teams of users to them. That's the topic of the next section.

Managing Teams

You might have a team of people who work together to service customers in a particular territory. Perhaps you have a separate team for each territory. Or you may have teams that are made up of users with similar skill sets. For example, you might have a sales team, a marketing team, and a technical support team. In this case, you would want to assign your teams to business units.

Unlike territory assignments, in which each user can be in only one territory, each user can be a member of many teams. In all likelihood, this will be the case, with a typical user being a member of, say, the sales team, the process brainstorming team, and the summer-picnic planning team.

The concept of sharing is also important to teams. Although you can't assign an account to a team, you *can* share an account with a team. In this section, we describe creating teams and assigning members to teams.

Creating teams

After you create a business unit, you can create and assign teams to that unit. To create a team and assign it to a business unit, follow these steps:

1. **At the bottom of the navigation pane, click the Settings button.**

2. **Select Business Unit Settings.**

3. **Select Business Units.**

4. **Double-click the business unit to which you want to assign one or more teams.**

   The Business Units window appears.

5. **In the upper part of the navigation pane, select Teams.**

6. **In the window's toolbar, click the New Team button.**

   The screen shown in Figure 6-6 appears.

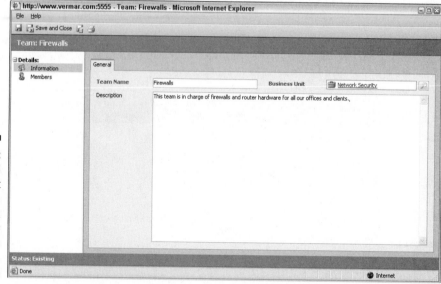

7. Fill in the Team Name field.

The business unit you selected in Step 4 is automatically filled in for you, although you can change this association by clicking the magnifying glass to the right of the Business Unit field.

8. Click Save and Close.

The system returns to the listing for that particular business unit.

If you create a team without assigning it to a specific business unit, by default it will be assigned to the overall parent unit. After a team is assigned to any business unit, you can't reassign it to another business unit. However, you can disable the team and start fresh with a new team.

Assigning users to teams

When you initially create a team, it has no members. But after the team is created, it's easy to add or later remove members.

To add one or more members to a team, follow these steps:

1. At the top of the navigation pane, select Members.

2. **In the window's toolbar, click the Add Members button and then click the Find button.**

   The Look Up Records dialog box appears, as shown in Figure 6-7.

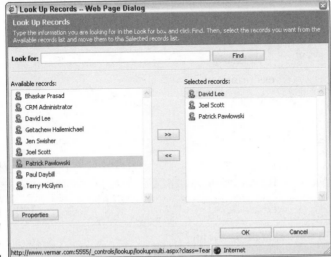

3. **In the left panel, double-click each member that you want to add to your team.**

4. **When you've finished assembling the team, click OK at the bottom of the window.**

   The system returns to that team's listing.

In this chapter, you've seen how to define and create territories, business units, and teams. Each user can be assigned to only one territory but may be a member of several teams and business units. By assigning users to teams, you can easily share and shift responsibilities between teams.

Chapter 7

Developing Processes

In This Chapter

▶ Understanding general process principles

▶ Adding and configuring sales stages

● ●

*B*usiness processes are intertwined with the workflow rules discussed in detail in Chapter 8. In this chapter, we discuss some of the basic principles involved in designing your processes and how those design principles can be implemented in Microsoft CRM.

In the almost 20 years that we have been designing and implementing CRM systems (not always Microsoft CRM, of course), it has been made clear again and again that two basic features allow CRM to earn its keep. The first is its ability to consolidate an entire organization's data into one useful, shareable place. This is not to be underestimated.

The second is its ability to automate business processes. The implementation of workflow not only forces you to think about — and then continuously rethink — your business processes but also allows you to replace notoriously inconsistent human activity with automation that always follows the rules.

Sadly, more than 90 percent of CRM implementations never achieve that automation. That initial goal seems to get lost in the effort to get the system up and running and the staff using the software. Too often, we are out of energy and money to invest further in developing the workflow that really makes the investment in CRM pay for itself. If you want to maximize the value of your system, however, do not allow yourself to run out of resources before the entire job is finished.

A good process guides your people through a series of well-documented steps for almost every type of situation. For example, although you can do a quote before properly qualifying an account, any well-thought-out system discourages this. Or you may remember to call a prospect back after sending a quote, but a good workflow-based process won't let you forget.

In this chapter, you find out how to plan your sales stages and how to relate these sales stages and other processes to your CRM system. You also discover the basic principles of process design and how these affect the design of your overall CRM system.

In the next chapter, you implement one of your well-thought-out processes in the Workflow Manager. Actually, it may not be one of *your* well-thought-out processes, but it might be similar to one of yours.

The General Principles

A good business process includes the concepts of alerts, escalation, feedback, and analysis. Each of these principles is described in this section.

Alerts

An *alert*, which is often an e-mail notice or some kind of screen pop-up, is called for when an activity should have been completed but for some reason was not. For example, if you've obtained verbal approval and the prospect promises a written PO within a week, the system should alert the account manager 10 days later if that PO has not arrived. (If you're a Type A personality, you may want to adjust your waiting period to 10 minutes.)

Alerts are appropriate also as a warning that an upcoming activity is almost due. For example, you might want a polite warning 30 days before a client's annual contract needs renewal.

Depending on the number of alerts you anticipate, you may decide on individual e-mail notices for each alert, or you may want a single e-mail or report that contains all the alerts. A typical sales alert might be to let a manager know on the 18th of the month that a forecasted sale that was slated to close on the 15th has not closed yet. If you expect more than two or three of these alerts, you will be better off planning to put them in a consolidated report that the manager receives. Otherwise, you risk clogging up your manager's in box with dozens of these warnings, which he or she will soon learn to ignore.

Escalation

When something doesn't get done on time, someone needs to know. Now, you can do this properly, or you can do this in a way that gets everyone upset.

Escalations are typically done by e-mail notices, by automatically scheduling activities, or by some combination of the two.

Typical activities that deserve escalation are sales that haven't closed when predicted or customer support issues that haven't been resolved in a timely way.

To be fair, the first step in escalating any issue is to notify the person to whom the issue was originally assigned. There might be a perfectly valid reason why the issue hasn't been resolved, and you should allow the original person to resolve it.

If the task or issue still hasn't been resolved within a few days, a notice should go to the original person's manager.

CRM can't send a notice to the manager unless it knows who that person is. Each user's record has a field for the user's manager's name. Escalating issues is probably the best use of this field.

The typical steps of an escalation plan are as follows:

1. Test to see whether an alert is required.

2. Send an initial alert to the primary user.

3. Wait a reasonable period (one to seven days, for example) and test again. If the issue is still not resolved, escalate to the primary user's manager.

4. Test again a reasonable time later. If the issue is still not resolved, notify the manager's manager. Continue this notification until you run out of management levels. Adjust the waiting period between notifications as appropriate.

Each time a manager is notified, all users who received prior notifications should be copied.

Feedback and analysis

It's not a good process unless you can measure it. Losing weight is a process. Before you start that process, you undoubtedly weigh yourself and continue to do so as you work toward your desired weight. Without measuring, you don't know how well you're doing, and you can't make midcourse corrections. Business processes are the same.

If you're implementing a sales process whose focus is to move each sale from one stage to the next, you want to measure a number of factors. You probably want to know:

- ✔ **Where and when the lead originated.** The purpose of tracking the source of each new record is to be able to better allocate your marketing dollars by determining which lead sources are best.

- ✔ **Who is working on the lead.** Aside from wanting to give credit where credit is due — that is, commissions, bonuses, or a pat on the back — you also want to identify salespeople who may be having problems with particular types or stages of sales so you can correct these problems.

- ✔ **How long it takes to get from each stage to the next.** If your sales are being bogged down at a particular stage, you want to know that and make corrections to your process or workflow.

Planning Your Sales Stages

Microsoft Corporation and Microsoft CRM both follow the sales process called Solution Selling, which was originated by Sales Performance International. If you haven't taken one of the classes, read one of the books that provides an overview of this sales philosophy. We are partial to *Solution Selling: Creating Buyers in Difficult Selling Markets,* by Michael T. Bosworth.

If your company already has a sales process other than Solution Selling in place, that's okay. Microsoft CRM has enough flexibility to allow you to configure almost any kind of process.

Your organization undoubtedly needs more than one process. For example, if you sell software and technical support, the associated sales cycles and techniques will be different, and you'll want a process for each type of sale. Also, you may need a different sales strategy just based on the size of the potential deal or even the size of the prospect. You would sell 2 pounds of nails to a homeowner in a different manner than you would sell 200 tons of nails to a home improvement store.

In CRM, sales processes are associated with opportunity records. Although you may consider the sales process to begin when a lead is entered, this isn't the case. The process can't begin until you convert a lead to an opportunity. We distinguish a lead from an opportunity the same way we distinguish a suspect from a prospect. It's not an opportunity or a prospect until this potential customer has expressed some interest in your products or services. After that has happened, you may have an opportunity, and it's time for the sales process to begin.

No immutable laws govern the development of a sales process. The sales process police won't be knocking at your door if you have too few or too many stages, but sales processes do have a few guidelines.

The more complex or the longer your sales cycle is, the more stages you'll need to describe where the deal is in your pipeline. However, the more stages you program into the cycle, the more likely your salespeople will object to being forced to enter unnecessary data or take unnecessary steps. So, the simpler, the better — with an eye toward gathering good information about where sales bog down or at what point a particular salesperson begins to struggle.

In Table 7-1, we present a typical sales cycle. Before you can begin to implement CRM's workflow rules, you must define your process. Start with the table and compare it with your own existing sales steps. Chances are, you don't even have a well-documented set of steps. Now's the time to begin creating that system.

Table 7-1		**Typical Sales Cycle**	
Stage	*Description*	*Probability*	*Comments*
1	Prequalify	10	Make sure it's the right kind of client
2	Initial meeting	20	A phone call or a physical appointment; probability increases to 25 if the prospect comes to your office
3	Qualified	30	Not only are they interested, but their timeframe and financials make a deal possible
4	Demonstration	40	Show and tell at their place or, even better, at yours
5	Quotation or proposal presented	60	There may be several of these, and you may go back and forth from stage 6 to 5 more than once
6	Negotiating	75	Always be ready for some give and take
7	Verbal approval obtained	85	Not as good as a written PO or a signed check
8	Purchase order received	99	It's not a done deal until the money arrives

Select your simplest product or service and compare the steps you use to the steps in Table 7-1. Then create a table that best follows either the steps you are taking today or, better yet, the steps you think you should be taking.

Before you just jump in and begin programming the workflow rules described in Chapter 8, you need to organize your thoughts. Convene a brainstorming session with the users who are involved on a day-by-day basis with each process you want to automate.

The result of that brainstorming session should be a detailed outline or diagram of the process. Each outline needs to include, for each step:

- ✔ The action that will be taken
- ✔ Who will be responsible for that action
- ✔ What will trigger the action (for example, a change in the data or a missed appointment)
- ✔ How to escalate if the action is not completed

After you have this set for each step of the process, it's time to go to Chapter 8 and begin making your new process happen.

Chapter 8

Implementing Rules and Workflow

*W*orkflow — I know what you're thinking. Workflow? What is that? Well, as one of the most powerful functions of Microsoft CRM, workflow is the nearest thing you'll find to a money machine.

The Workflow Management System takes your manual business rules (or procedures) and turns them into an automated system. Without workflow, you'd have a database with names, addresses, and a schedule, but the database by itself wouldn't do anything. With workflow, Microsoft CRM becomes a system that farms your existing accounts for additional business, helps you hunt for new accounts, and ensures that important tasks do not slip through the cracks. Whooaa. That's a pretty hefty statement, isn't it? However, by providing you with electronic business alerts, Microsoft CRM can step beyond being your contact/account database and become an important part of your business and corporate culture.

You probably have many business rules already in place, even if they aren't set in writing and mentioned all the time. For example, do you return a phone call to a client who asks you to call him back? That's a business rule, and workflow might automate that business rule by sending you an electronic reminder message — again and again — until you actually make the call. Your business rule has now become a workflow rule. I like to call this one "auto-nag."

Now, before you go and start plugging in workflow rules, we recommend that you review all your current business processes. This may take some time. You should consult with the CEO, his or her assistant, the sales department, the marketing department — you get the idea. This is also the best time to do spring cleaning. Get rid of business rules that worked before the advent of the Internet, and update others or make new ones. Automating an ineffective procedure is like building a faster Edsel. The speed is there, but it's still an Edsel.

In this chapter, we touch on the general principles of implementing workflow rules and then provide you with an example of a typical rule. You also find the background and basis to design and implement at least some simple workflow rules of your own. However, keep in mind that the creation of complex workflow rules is probably best left to professional Microsoft CRM consultants or dealers.

Describing the Limitations of Workflow

Let's start from the beginning. Workflow may sound complicated, but once you get the knack of it, it's fairly simple. Workflow has two main modules: Manager and Monitor. Manager enables you to develop and use workflow rules, which is nothing more than a system to automate the business processes you already have and use. Monitor provides a display of the current status of each rule. You can see exactly which processes are running and which ones may be waiting for a triggering event.

Although Workflow is a powerful utility, it's not Super Program and does have some limitations. For example:

- Workflow can monitor data and events within the Microsoft CRM database but not outside it, unless you write a custom .Net assembly. (More on .Net assembly in a moment.)

- A workflow rule can't check for data in more than one object (accounts or contact records or case records) at one time. For example, a workflow rule can look through all your accounts to notify you of any that are missing telephone numbers, but a single workflow rule can't check for accounts that are missing phone numbers *and* have open cases more than two weeks old.

- Workflow rules have difficulty checking for the absence of an event, meaning they can alert you to an open or uncompleted appointment but don't tell you about stuff that wasn't scheduled but should have been. (It's a software program, not a mind-meld machine.)

Microsoft CRM allows you to write a small piece of code called a .Net assembly that does some custom functions. For example, if you want Microsoft CRM to check the credit on one of your customers and update the customer record with their FICO score, you could write a small .Net assembly that calls another application to get that information and then updates Microsoft CRM. Based on the returned score, Microsoft CRM could then finish processing the rest of the rule you set up.

A third-party business alert system, KnowledgeSync, enables you to look at multiple databases and multiple types of records. We describe KnowledgeSync in Chapter 28. If you anticipate the need to build sophisticated rules and alerts, and you don't want to write any custom code, you may want this add-on program.

An important step in creating your workflows is to think through the flow itself carefully. What are the exceptions? What conditions should terminate the process? For example, if someone buys something, workflow should start treating the person as a new customer and not as a prospect.

Creating Workflow Rules

For creating your workflow rules, we recommend that you use members of your staff who work with the product on a daily basis, both on the administrative side and the operations side. This way, you cover your business processes from all angles.

Now, we do suggest letting your company's system administrator be the only person to set up workflow rules. Not only is Workflow Manager accessed directly from the Microsoft CRM server, those sys admins can be territorial!

One of the most common tasks your company may want to automate is the assignment of an account manager to a newly created account. We use that as our example for creating a workflow rule:

1. **Choose Start⇨Programs⇨Microsoft CRM⇨Workflow Manager.**

   This particular feature is not accessed from the open Microsoft CRM program. The Workflow Manager Log On dialog box appears.

2. **Enter the name of the Microsoft CRM server you want to target, and then click OK.**

   The name you enter is the server your Microsoft CRM is on. When you click OK, the Microsoft CRM Workflow Manager window appears, as shown in Figure 8-1.

3. **Choose an entity type and a view.**

   The Entity Type option is the type of record (account, contact, lead, and so on) that your workflow rule focuses on. Click the down arrow to the right of the field to open the drop-down box and choose the entity you want to work with. Just a quick note, as our underpaid office manager discovered, if you shrink this window, the drop-down arrow disappears. If that happens, just click inside the Entity Type field to open the drop-down box.

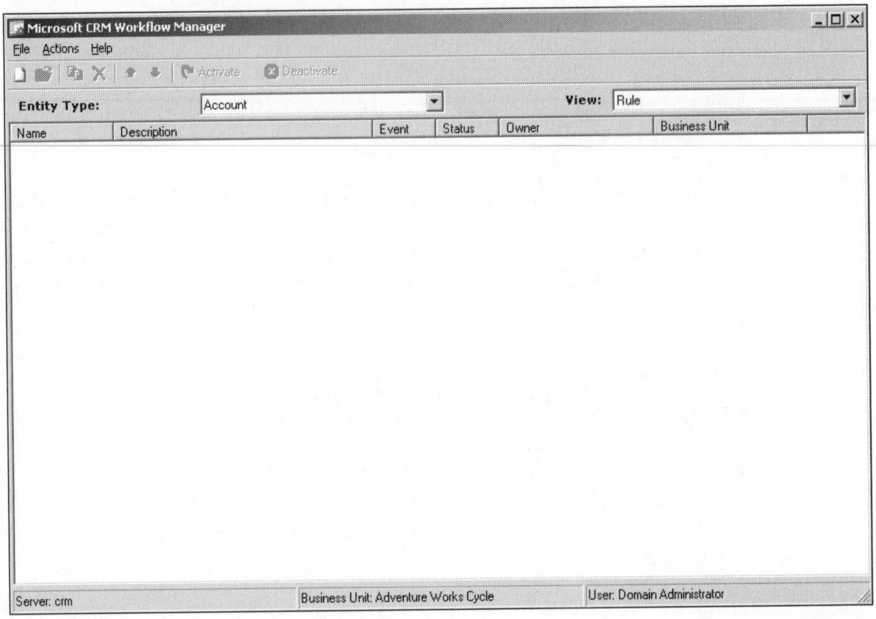

Figure 8-1:
The
Workflow
Manager.

Over in View, click the down arrow to the right of the field to open the drop-down list and choose to make a rule or a rule template (workflow rule templates are discussed later in this chapter).

For this exercise, we chose Account for Entity Type and Rule under View.

4. **In the menu bar (at the top of the screen), choose File⇨New.**

You can also click the little blank paper icon in the toolbar. The Create Workflow Rule dialog box appears, as shown in Figure 8-2. Note that the Entity field is already filled in with your choice from the preceding step.

5. **Enter a name, description, and event for your rule.**

Keep in mind that the Name field is required but the description field is not. In the Event field, click in the field or click on the drop-down arrow next to the field. A list appears with the following choices: Manual, Assign, Create, and Change Status. (We provide a description of these at the end of the chapter.) For our example, we're going to choose Create, because the creation of a new record will trigger this workflow rule. If you want to use this rule for the creation of a subprocess later, be sure to mark this one Manual.

6. **Click Next.**

The Select Behavior window appears, as shown in Figure 8-3, with a Common Tasks pane and a workspace.

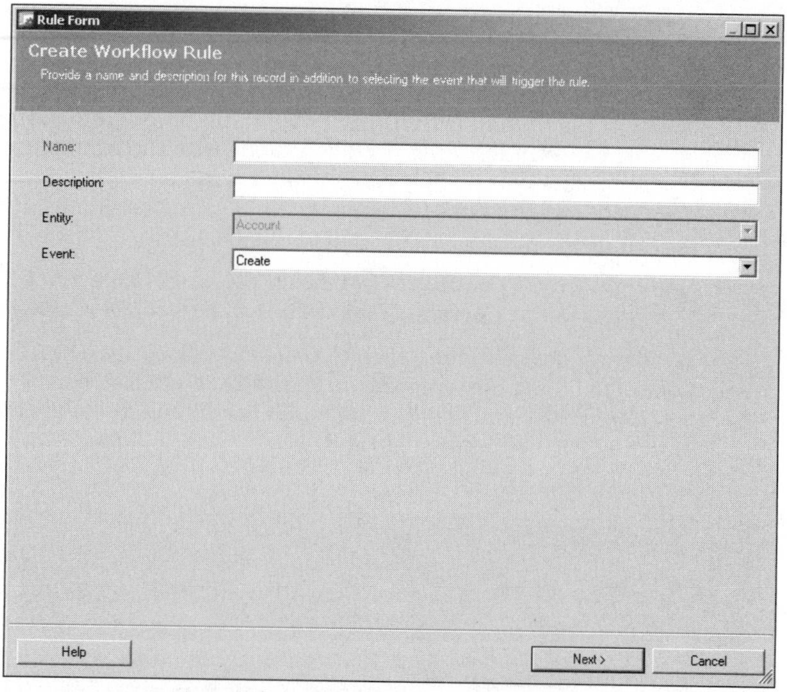

Figure 8-2:
Create your workflow rule — don't go wild now!

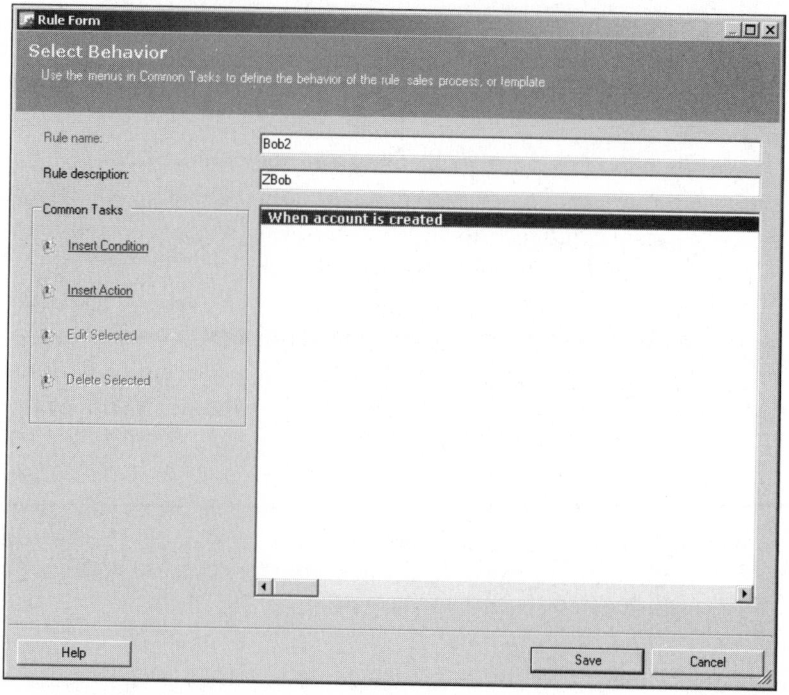

Figure 8-3:
Everyone needs a Select Behavior option.

7. **In the Common Tasks pane, click Insert Condition, and select a condition.**

   When you click Insert Condition, a small submenu appears practically on top of the option, with three choices: Check conditions, Wait for conditions, and Wait for timer. To follow along with the example, select Check conditions, which automatically inserts an If/Then clause in the main window with options to add conditions and actions. For a description of these options, see the end of this chapter.

8. **Highlight <<add conditions here>> in the workspace, click Insert Condition in the Common Tasks window, and select a condition.**

   To follow along with the example, select Check entity. The Check Entity Condition dialog box appears, as shown in Figure 8-4. The two named fields are Entity and Field; the two unlabeled ones become activated based on what you select in Field.

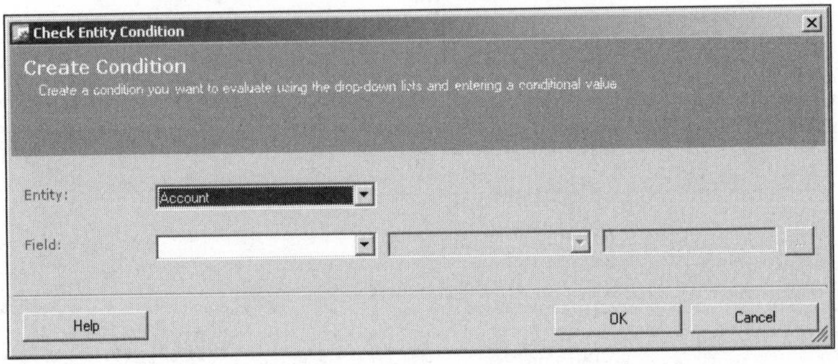

Figure 8-4:
Check it out!

9. **Click the down arrow by Field and select an option.**

   Just about every field in Microsoft CRM is available here. If you wanted to assign only records in Massachusetts to your account manager, Ted, for example, you would choose any of the fields for State.

10. **In the unlabeled field in the center of the window, click the down arrow and select an option among the many choices.**

    The null operator allows you to test whether a field is blank or empty. You would use null to test, for example, whether a phone number or an e-mail address exists. The combinations of =, <, and > operators can be used equally well with text and date fields.

    The Contains, Begins with, and Ends with operators can produce surprising results if you don't carefully consider what data these expressions might find. For example, if you search for records containing *East*, you also get records containing *beast*.

11. In the next unlabeled field, click the ellipsis button (the three dots).

The Select Value dialog box appears, as shown in Figure 8-5.

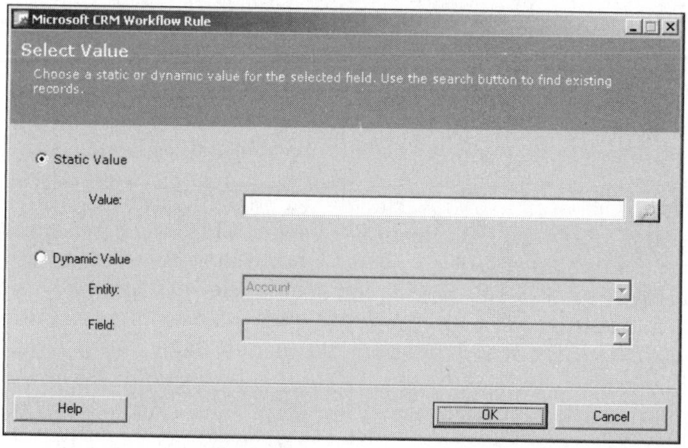

Figure 8-5:
Where
would you
rather go?
AK or HI?

12. Enter the data the rule should search for, and then click OK.

For example, if you selected State in Step 9, you could put the state here in the Static Value field. If you wanted to compare two fields, you could select Dynamic Value.

13. Click OK in the Create Condition dialog box.

You return to the Select Behavior dialog box.

14. Highlight <<add actions here>> in the workspace, click Insert Action in the Common Tasks pane, and select an action.

The action you select tells the program what you want done when the condition you set in Steps 11–13 is met. A list of actions and their descriptions is at the end of this chapter.

15. Click OK or Close to return to the Select Behavior dialog window.

16. Click Save to save the new rule.

The Select Behavior window closes, taking you back to the Microsoft CRM Workflow Manager, where your rule should now be listed.

17. To activate the new rule, click the Activate button in the toolbar.

If you forget to do this, your perfectly good new rule will sit there forever, forlorn and lost.

Testing a new rule

Throughout this book, you will find reference to our office manager's arch nemeses, the Minions of Chaos. They love to sneak inside your database and wreak havoc. Remember this because they can make an appearance at any moment, now that you've created your workflow rules.

Back to the workflow rules. They're complete and ready to go, so you load them up and awwaayy you go, right? Negative, databoy.

Loading an untested workflow rule on your active database is an invitation to the MoC, who want nothing more to get in and show you any errors or glitches that are on your live system — by bringing your system to a grinding halt as that workflow rule runs amok on your data. Okay, this is dramatic, but we must stress the importance of testing your workflow rules *before* you make them live features of your Microsoft CRM.

The good news is that testing your workflow rule is easy. Here's how:

1. **Now that you've created your workflow rule, go ahead and start Microsoft CRM.**

2. **Create a condition in your database that should trigger the workflow rule.**

   For example, if you set your workflow rule to trigger on every new account created in the system, go ahead and create an account and remember to save, Save, SAVE and Close the record.

3. **Reopen the record you just created so you can check for the intended result.**

   If the rule said to assign every new account to Bob, you would check to see whether Bob was listed as the owner.

If you don't see the desired result, you either failed to activate your rule, or you need to review the rule criteria and specifics to determine the cause of the problem. Always go back and check out how you built the workflow rule first before assuming there's a bug in the program, because most computer errors are the result of operator error.

Creating a manual rule

Manual rules are just what the title claims. Sort of. A *manual rule* is a rule that can only be invoked manually and not automatically (at least not directly). For those of you designing complex workflow rules, manual rules can be called by another rule. By *calling,* we mean that each rule should do one or two simple things and should then trigger, or call, another rule if more functionality is needed.

Speaking of calling, try to avoid creating a giant workflow rule Godzilla. Instead of one massive process, it may be easier to put together a series of simple manual rules that call each other. You could also do what computer programmers do (no, not change people's passwords for fun) and create small modules of code, or in this case, workflow rules that can be reused for many different applications.

Remember how we activated the workflow rule we just created, as the last step? Manual rules, just like all the other rules, must be active before they can be invoked or called.

Workflow rules are great if everyone remembers to invoke or trigger them. The key word here is *remembers*. In today's offices, most people are so busy answering the phone, dealing with customer service issues, and making sales calls that things are bound to slip through the cracks. We suggest that you create a system with a master workflow rule that automatically attaches to every new record and begins a sequence of calling additional rules as conditions in that record warrant.

Creating follow-up rules

Almost every business does some sort of follow-up with its customers, and yours is probably no exception. You may want to send a thank-you e-mail for a recent purchase, or you may want a call scheduled for accounts that have had no activity for 60 days. This is called a follow-up rule, and it's usually a manual one. The steps are similar to creating a rule in the first place, so we'll just touch on them here and make sure we point out the variations.

To create a manual rule that assigns a follow-up activity to the owner of an account, follow these steps:

1. **Choose Start➪Programs➪Microsoft CRM➪Workflow Manager.**

2. **Enter the name of the Microsoft CRM server you want to target, and then click OK.**

   The Microsoft CRM Workflow Manager main window appears.

3. **Select an entity type and a rule from the view drop-down lists, just as we did earlier.**

   No changes here. You still want your entity type and rule for your selections.

4. **Choose File➪New.**

   The Create a Workflow Rule Template window appears.

5. Enter a name, description, and event for your follow-up rule.

Here's a slight variation. Choose Manual from the Event drop-down box and click Next to open the Select Behavior window. Now you can begin building the conditions and actions of your new manual rule.

6. Follow Steps 7–14 under "Creating Workflow Rules."

As mentioned earlier, the steps mostly mirror the ones you use to create a workflow rule. You should be in the Select Behavior dialog box to continue with Steps 7–14.

7. In the Common Tasks pane, click Insert Action. From the pop-up menu, select Create activity.

The Create Activity window appears, as shown in Figure 8-6. Here, you can specify what tasks the follow-up rule should perform when it is called, or triggered.

8. Enter a subject and a description for this new activity.

For example, in the Subject field, you might enter New Account or Assigning an Account Manager to a new Account.

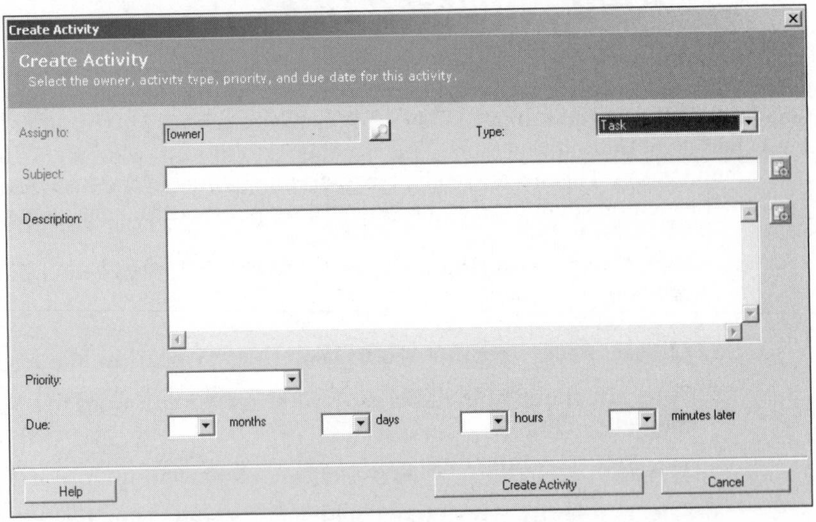

Figure 8-6:
This activity can create a task, phone call, fax, or letter.

9. Enter a priority and a due date.

The due date isn't so much an actual date but a length of time you want the system to wait before it sends the letter or fax or prompts you to perform the task or make the phone call. The priorities are low, normal, and high.

10. **Click the Create Activity button.**

    You return to the Select Behavior dialog box.

11. **Click Save and then Close.**

    You can return to the Workflow Manager window, where your follow-up rule is now listed.

12. **Right-click the rule and choose Activate.**

    Remember, rules do nothing unless you activate them.

Testing a manual rule

Remember the Minions of Chaos mentioned earlier? They do not discriminate between automatic rules and manual ones, so you'll want to test these as well.

The steps for testing follow-up rules are different than those for testing automatic ones:

1. **Create a condition in Microsoft CRM that triggers the original rule.**

    A good example is the New Account workflow rule we just created.

2. **In Microsoft CRM, use the navigation page to find and highlight the account.**

3. **In the window's toolbar, click More Actions and choose Apply Rule.**

    The Apply Rule dialog box appears.

4. **Select your workflow process from the pull-down list, and then click OK.**

    The process begins to run invisibly.

5. **Go to the workplace and click Activities in the upper part of the navigation pane.**

    You should see the follow-up activity listed there (if the activity was assigned to you, anyway).

Monitoring Your Workflow

Now that you have all those workflow rules processing merrily away, you want to see them all on one screen, without having to go to every account or contact to see whether a rule has been applied. You can do this through the Workflow Monitor. Like Workflow Manager, Workflow Monitor is a separate program that operates outside the Microsoft CRM program. It also keeps a log of processes that are currently active and records which ones have already been run. This application, like Workflow Manager, can be accessed only from the Microsoft CRM Server.

Here's how you access the Workflow Monitor:

1. **Choose Start⇨Programs⇨Microsoft CRM⇨Workflow Monitor.**

   The Workflow Monitor Log In window appears.

2. **Enter the name of your CRM server and then click OK.**

   The Workflow Monitor window appears, as shown in Figure 8-7, open to the Process tab. In this display, you can see which processes are active and paused.

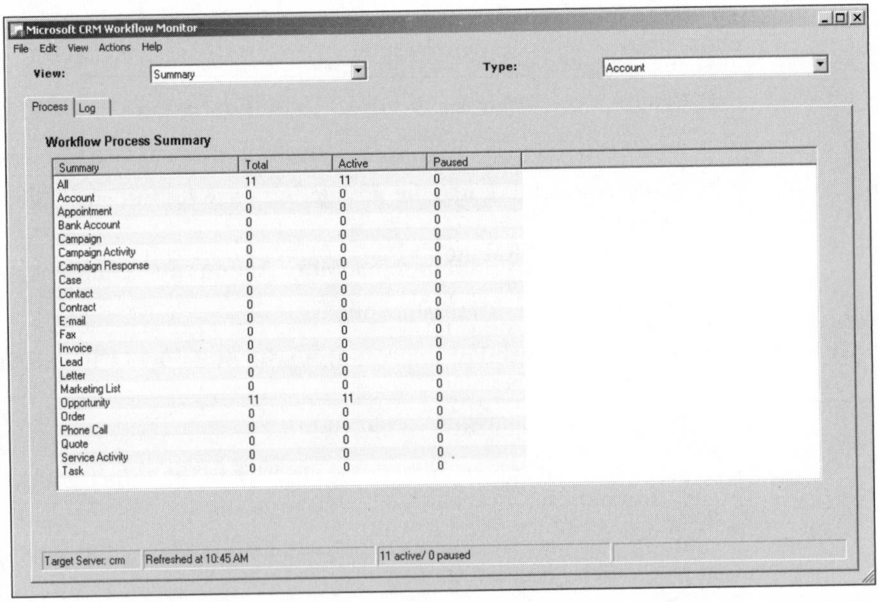

Figure 8-7:
Look at those processes go!

3. **To see what processes have been run, click the Log tab.**

   You can sort the items by clicking the header for each column. You can also export the log to save it (click Actions⇨Export Log).

The Workflow Monitor only shows workflow rules that have been triggered. Even though you may have additional rules activated, they remain invisible to the Monitor when an event triggers them.

Workflow Glossary

Throughout this chapter, we tell you to select an event, or choose an action, or set a condition. Maybe you're wondering what, exactly, constitutes an event, action, or condition. Well, we list them all here, in a one-stop, look-see that's easy to find.

Events

In Microsoft CRM, an *event* is the trigger condition that initiates a workflow rule. For example, you can set a workflow rule for Assign, and anything that is assigned has that workflow rule applied to it. Microsoft CRM has four events:

- ✔ **Assign:** Assigns (or reassigns) a record to a different user or team. CRM e-mails the new user, notifying him or her of new tasks.
- ✔ **Create:** Enter a lead, and CRM assigns the account to the appropriate account manager and notifies him or her of that assignment.
- ✔ **State change:** CRM monitors whether records have changed state from active to inactive.
- ✔ **Manual:** All workflow rules can be invoked manually. Workflow rules can also be categorized as specifically *manual,* in which case they can be invoked only manually. To perform this invocation, select Apply Rule from the Actions tab of the Workflow Manager window.

Conditions

Every business process is triggered by some change in a *condition.* That condition might be a change in a data field, a due date being passed, or a record being created. The Conditions section of the Workflow Manager enables you to initiate an action based on a field or an activity that has changed or based on an amount of time that has transpired.

The options for possible conditions are as follows:

- **Check Object Conditions:** This enables you to drill down to a specific field in a record. For example, if the State field is New York, an action can be taken to assign the New York sales rep to the account. Based on the type of field (whether it's a numeric, text, or date field, for example), various operators are available.

- **Check Activities:** By checking activities, you can initiate actions based on scheduled or completed activities.

- **Else if:** This enables you to nest additional condition statements saying that if the first condition is false, evaluate the second condition.

- **Wait for Conditions:** Workflow can wait for a specified amount of time until the specified criteria becomes true before the rest of the rule is completed. This can be the cornerstone of an activity escalation plan. For example, if a lead is assigned to a sales rep, the system can be instructed to wait for three days before checking to see whether an appointment has been created. If the system finds no evidence of an appointment, a message can be automatically sent to the sales rep or the sales rep's manager could be notified.

- **Wait for Timer:** This is similar to Wait for Condition, but this condition can be used to make sure that an assignment is handled within a specified time limit. For example, a high-priority tech support call that must be returned within an hour can be monitored by using Wait for Timer.

Actions

Actions are a series of operations performed after conditions have been evaluated as true. Nine activities can be enacted:

- **Create activity:** This is used to schedule a task, phone call, fax, or appointment.

- **Send e-mail:** This powerful utility enables you to send a confirming e-mail to a customer who has just placed an order or to notify a sales rep when a lead has just been assigned to him or her.

- **Create note:** A note can be attached to a record. For example, you could create a note that places an account on hold when payment becomes overdue.

- **Update entity:** You can use the Update Object action to modify individual fields in records. Many fields in each record are not, by default, displayed on the screen. You can use Update Object to modify visible as well as invisible fields.

✔ **Change status:** Different types of records are assigned different types of status. The Change Status action enables the workflow system to change a record's status automatically based on conditions being met.

✔ **Assign entity:** Workflow can automatically assign cases to customer service reps based on a topic, or it can assign an account to a sales rep based on a territory. For example, if a customer calls about a malfunctioning transporter, the case can be assigned to Molly, your most experienced customer service rep.

✔ **Post URL:** This action sends a web site address of another business to a data field. For example, when a new account is created, you can post the web site address in the Web site field.

✔ **Run subprocess:** Basically, this is one process or rule calling another one. By using this technique, you can program a large number of simple workflow rules, with each rule potentially calling another rule.

✔ **Stop:** This brings your process to a halt.

✔ **Call assembly:** This option contains any custom .Net assemblies that your administrator or implementation partner have registered with Microsoft CRM. Refer to the SDK documentation to add your own assemblies here.

We hope you now have a definitive and solid base from which to build your workflow rules. As mentioned, once you get the knack of it, building rules is fairly simple — after a few weeks, you'll probably wonder how you managed without them.

Chapter 9

Creating and Using the Knowledge Base

*O*nce upon a time, a person had a dream . . . and that dream was called a database. Actually, it was called a library — a giant room filled with books upon books, information stored in a central location. With the advent of the computer, such libraries can be stored with much less space and transmitted with ease.

Based on templates and articles, Microsoft CRM's database, or library, is called the *knowledge base* (also referred to as *KB*) and is a powerful model for sharing information across your organization and with your customers.

Templates determine how information is formatted, found, and presented. *Articles* are the products created when information is applied to a template.

In this chapter, you find out how to create knowledge base templates and articles. You also discover how to search the knowledge base and associate relevant information with other sections of Microsoft CRM.

Organizing Information for Your Knowledge Base

The key to the knowledge base is organization. So announce a staff meeting and order pizza, the ultimate brainstorming food, because that's what this meeting is about. Brainstorming and organizing your documentation and processes. If you have a whiteboard (complete with the permanent-marker line that can't be removed), make sure you use it to record ideas and thoughts for the stuff you want to put in the KB, so everyone can keep track of what's been brought up. Next, give everyone a notepad, sit them down, and get ready to organize.

Your task is to take the sales and service documents your company uses and put them together in some form of order.

Let's say you have sales documents and service documents. Your sales documents could include features and benefits of your products, pricing, system requirements, availability, delivery timelines, and fancy marketing advertisements.

On the service side, you have things like schematics, maintenance requirements, warranty information, and installation procedures. Ultimately, these topics become the building blocks for your knowledge base.

Remember to keep your topics and titles in plain, easily discernible language because, after you're finished here, you're going to put all your notes together in Microsoft CRM to create your company's knowledge base.

Creating Article Templates

The knowledge base contains articles built on templates. By using templates for the foundation of a new knowledge base article, all of your company's articles will be easy to enter and have a uniform layout, regardless of whether Jane from Accounting or Clean-o-matic Bob is creating the article.

Microsoft CRM comes with a collection of default article templates: General Use, Procedure, Question & Answer, Solution to a Problem, and Standard KB Article, as shown in Figure 9-1. And those of you who like to think outside the box can create your own templates.

The Procedure template is laid out using a standard format of three sections: Purpose & Scope, Procedure, and Additional Comments.

Normally, you create a new article within an existing template. But we're going to walk you through the creation of a new template, just in case none of the standard ones fit what you're looking for. Later in the chapter, you create a new article based on an existing template

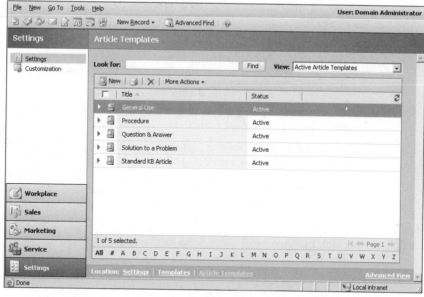

Figure 9-1:
The Article
Templates
window
displays
a list of
all current
article
templates.

To create a template, follow these steps:

1. **In the lower part of the navigation pane, click the Settings button.**
2. **In the Settings window, select the Templates option.**
3. **Select Article Templates.**

   The Article Templates window appears, displaying all available article templates (refer to Figure 9-1).

4. **In the Article Templates window's toolbar, click the New button.**

   The Article Template: New windows opens and, right on top of that, the Article Template Properties dialog box appears, as shown in Figure 9-2.

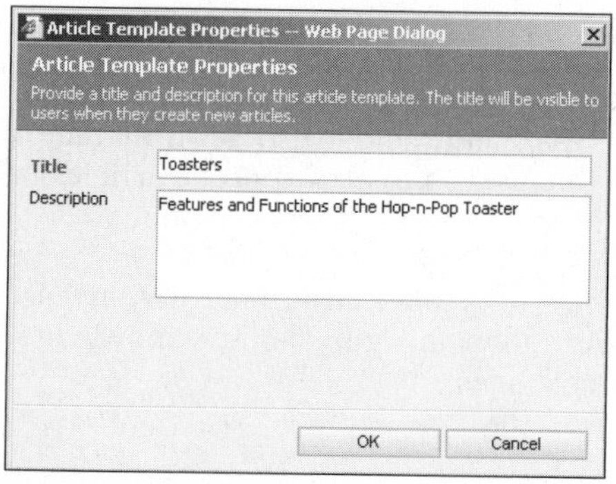

Figure 9-2:
This
window is
your first
step in
creating a
template.

5. **Enter a title and a description of the article template, and then click OK.**

   The description is optional, but we suggest you include it because it offers one more way (in addition to the title) to describe the template you're creating. When you click OK, you return to the Article Template: New window to design the template.

6. **On the right of the Article Template: New window, in the Common Tasks pane, click Add a Section.**

7. **In the Add a New Section window, enter the title and a description or instructions for the section, and then click OK.**

8. **If you want to add another section, repeat Step 7.**

   You can add as many sections as you want to the template. These sections will appear when you create articles (later in this chapter).

9. **Click the Save and Close icon in the upper-left corner of the Article Template: New window.**

   The window closes, the new template is saved, and you return to the Article Templates window.

Creating a Knowledge Base Article

The knowledge base acts as the staging area for all your company's articles. This is where you store, edit, and publish articles, and also where your staff finds the finished product.

Imagine that your company doesn't have an assigned editor and this happens: Bob from Washing Machines adds an article regarding a quick blurb he heard on the news about the competitor's washing machine. Stan from Refrigerators adds a comic strip about refrigerator repair guys. Anne from Accounting adds instructions on placing orders and taking credit cards. Thomas the CSR adds one about what to do with irate customers. John from the mailroom . . . well, you get the picture.

Microsoft takes another step in preventing chaos by enabling your company to choose who can add articles to and remove articles from templates. We recommend that you set up this person to also approve articles before they are published, checking for format, accuracy, and continuity.

The next few pages explain how to create and submit draft articles as well as approve and publish them. As shown in Figure 9-3, the knowledge base categorizes articles in one of three stages:

✔ **Draft:** Your works-in-progress, that is, composed articles that have not been submitted for approval and drafts. Drafts are visible only to their respective authors, and users can't search for them in the knowledge base.

✔ **Unapproved:** Store your articles pending editor approval here. Users can't search for these in the knowledge base.

✔ **Published:** Your finished, editor-approved articles ready for the general public. Published articles are read-only (so they can't be edited), but users can search for them in the knowledge base.

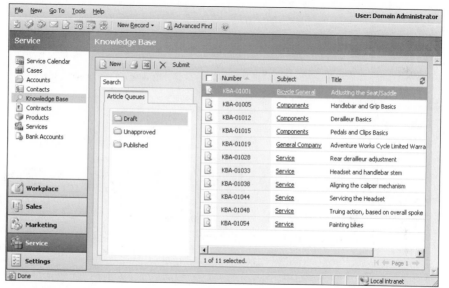

Figure 9-3:
The Knowledge Base workspace.

Follow these steps to create a new article:

1. **In the lower part of the navigation pane, click the Service button. Then, in the upper part of the pane, select Knowledge Base.**

    The Knowledge Base window appears (refer to Figure 9-3). You can view articles (based on their status) in the main part of the window, on the right.

2. **In the Knowledge Base window's toolbar, click the New button.**

    The KB Template Explorer appears, listing all the templates currently available in your system. Find the template you created earlier. Template information (title and type, creator, and description) will appear on the right of the KB Template Explorer window as you highlight a template.

3. Highlight your template and click OK.

The Article: New window appears, as shown in Figure 9-4. The sections and instructions you created earlier appear here.

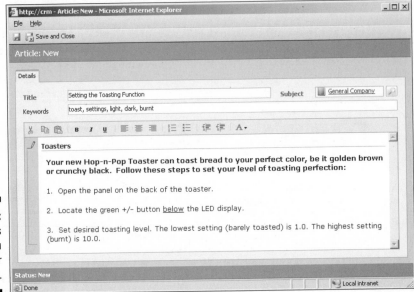

Figure 9-4:
This is
where you
build your
article.

4. Enter a title.

Required fields are Title and Subject; they must be filled in before you can save the article.

5. Link the article to a subject.

To do so, click the magnifying glass to the right of the Subject field. The Look Up a Subject window appears. Use the plus signs to open and collapse the subjects to specify a section within the subject. When you find your subject, highlight it and click OK.

6. In the Keywords field, enter words that will help your staff find this article.

Much like a search on the Internet, you can enter words here to search for articles pertaining to certain subjects. For example, if I were the CSR on the phone with Mrs. Reynolds and her Hop-n-Pop Toaster, I could search for *settings* and this article would show up in my search results. Separate each of your keywords with a comma. Another suggestion for your article keywords is the model number of your product.

7. **Click inside the text area and enter your information.**

   The instructions disappear and you're ready to type. Microsoft CRM's predefined templates are already formatted with specific information. For example, if we had chosen the Procedure template to create our article, the following section headings would be in the template: Purpose & Scope, Procedure, and Additional Comments. When you created your template (earlier in the chapter), this is where the sections you created are used.

   The sections allow you to create an easy-to-read, informative article for your CSRs and your customers. You can write step-by-step instructions, create question-and-answer scripts, or even make a Frequently Asked Questions (FAQ) section.

   Use the toolbar under the Keywords field in the Article: New window to do basic editing of your article and even add color text for emphasis.

8. **Click the Save and Close icon.**

   The article goes into your Draft folder for further editing and, ultimately, submission for approval.

Although this publishing process may seem overwhelming and (in some cases) unnecessary, maintaining the process is important. Carefully managing information stored in the knowledge base guarantees that you're providing the latest, most accurate information to your sales and service staff and, even more importantly, your customers.

Submitting a draft article

Now is the moment every writer dreads: time to hand over your masterpiece to the person your company designated as editor (when your business units were defined in Chapter 6).

To submit a draft article for approval, follow these steps:

1. **In the navigation pane, click the Service button. Then in the upper part of the pane, select Knowledge Base.**

   The Knowledge Base window appears on the right

2. **On the left side of the Knowledge Base window, click the Draft folder to access your drafts.**

3. **On the right side of the window, highlight the article you want to submit.**

4. **In the Knowledge Base window toolbar, click the Submit button.**

The dialog box shown in Figure 9-5 appears.

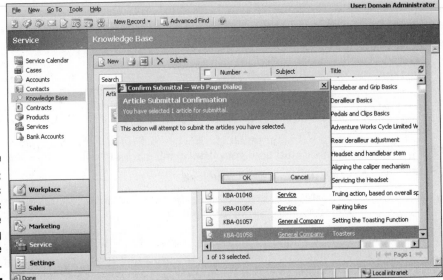

Figure 9-5:
This
appears
when you're
submitting
an article
for approval.

5. **Click OK.**

The article you submitted has now moved from the Draft folder to the Unapproved folder.

You can check that your article has been moved by clicking the Unapproved folder on the left side of the Knowledge Base window. All the articles pending editor approval are here. Just a reminder: These are not searchable.

Approving an article

Editors, break out your virtual red ink pens. All those articles in the Unapproved folder are yours to check, edit, correct, and otherwise make your high school English teacher proud (or cry).

Articles in the Unapproved folder can be opened and edited by anyone with editing rights. After all appropriate changes have been made, the editor has the ability to approve the article and add it to your company's knowledge base.

Follow these steps to approve an article:

1. **In the navigation pane, click the Service button and then select Knowledge Base.**

2. **On the left side of the Knowledge Base window, click the Unapproved folder**

   All the articles awaiting approval are displayed.

3. **On the right side of the window, find your article, highlight it, and double-click to open it.**

   This opens right to the article itself so you can make changes or return it to the author. If you make changes, make sure to click Save (the disk icon) in the upper-left corner of the screen.

4. **In the Knowledge Base window toolbar, click Approve.**

5. **In the confirmation window that appears, click OK.**

   The Article is automatically moved to the Published folder and is now searchable in the knowledge base.

In the event you have to reject the article, you would click Reject instead of Approve in Step 4. You will be given the option to add comments explaining your rejection in the Provide a Reason dialog box, as shown in Figure 9-6.

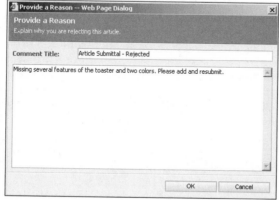

Figure 9-6:
Enter your
suggestions
and reasons
for rejecting
an article.

Let's say you've approved the article, but a week later, someone finds an error in it. For example, the Hop-n-Pop toaster's reddish color isn't called Cinnamon. It's called Beauty Red. In this situation, you (with the appropriate rights) can unpublish an article. To do so, follow these steps:

1. **Click the Published folder in the Knowledge Base window.**

2. **Click the article you want to unpublish.**

3. **Click the Unpublish button.**

   The article is automatically moved to the Unapproved folder for revisions.

Now let's say you have found an article that is out of date and you need to delete it. Again, you'll need the appropriate rights to complete this two-step process: Unpublish the article first and then delete it.

1. **Click the Published folder in the Knowledge Base window.**

   All published articles are displayed.

2. **Click the article you want to unpublish.**

3. **Click the Unpublish button, and then click OK.**

   Your article is moved to the Unapproved folder. When you return to the Published folder, the list will be refreshed automatically.

4. **Click the Unapproved folder.**

5. **Highlight the article you want to delete, and then click the Delete button.**

   The Delete Confirmation dialog box appears.

6. **Click OK.**

   Goodbye out-of-date article. The Unapproved folder refreshes automatically.

Because all articles and subjects in Microsoft CRM are related, you will be warned that deleting an article will also cause Microsoft CRM to remove any records attached to the article. Normally, this is not a problem because the only attachment an article can have is to a subject, but we recommend that you and your staff use the delete feature sparingly. For those of you who don't want to delete the article and start over, you can simply add a comment to it on the Comments tab in the open article window.

Searching the Knowledge Base

Mrs. Reynolds is on the phone again and you need to find the article you read aloud to her last week. Problem is, you don't remember the article's name. That's right, retreat to your trusty knowledge base and take advantage of the search function. Like a card catalog in a library, the knowledge base is the warehouse of information for your company (as is Abby, the Admin Assistant).

With Mrs. Reynolds in one ear, here's how you search the knowledge base:

1. **At the bottom of the navigation pane, click the Workplace button.**

2. **In the upper part of the navigation pane, select Service and then select Knowledge Base.**

   All of your company's published articles are displayed. You can reach this section also by clicking the Service button at the bottom of the navigation pane and then selecting Knowledge Base at the top of the pane.

3. **On the left side of the Knowledge Base window, click the Search tab.**

   The Search pane appears, as shown in Figure 9-7.

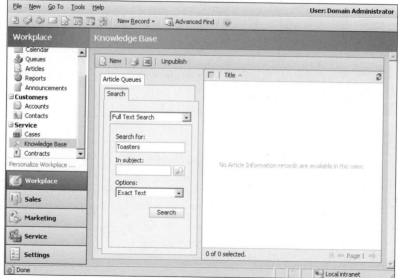

Figure 9-7:
Use the
Search
pane to zero
in on the
article you
want.

4. **Fill in the following fields to define your search criteria:**

   • **Unlabeled field:** Use the drop-down menu in the first field to tell your search engine which fields to search. Full Text searches the title, case number, and body of every article. It does not search for keywords. Keyword searches only the keyword field of every article. Title searches the title field of every article. Article Number searches for a specific article number (probably that number on the Post-It stuck to the monitor).

- **Search for:** This is where you enter your search words. For our example with Mrs. Reynolds, you might enter *toaster* and the model number. If you remember only part of the model number, you could use a wildcard character. For example, entering *1138 will return every article with the numbers 1138 in the field you search.

- **In subject:** Narrow your search even more by selecting the subject you want to search. This is especially helpful if you have, say, several hundred articles..

- **Options:** Another drill-down feature, this option allows you to search for the exact text you entered in Search For or choose a broader search with Use Like Words. An Exact Text search is quicker but less forgiving; you'll need the exact wording to ping the articles you want. Use Like Words takes longer but allows you some freedom if you can't remember whether Mrs. Reynolds has, say, the Model 1138 or the Model 1138A.

You can use the * wildcard only with Options: Exact Text. Using the wildcard character with the Use Like Words option results in an error message.

5. **Click the Search button.**

   All articles that match your search criteria appear on the right side of the window.

Just a note on searching for articles: When you add a new article to the knowledge base, you'll be able to view it from the Published folder, but you will not be able to search for it until the catalog's index is updated. Microsoft CRM does this automatically every 15 minutes (unless your administrator changes this value).

Chapter 10

Setting Up the Product Catalog

In This Chapter

▶ Understanding the product catalog

▶ Getting to the Product Catalog screen

▶ Setting up a discount list

▶ Creating unit groups

▶ Formulating your price lists

▶ Adding products to the catalog

*P*roduct catalogs, whether they're the paper version or a virtual one, are a great invention. And product catalogs aren't just for consumers! They also make excellent reference tools for your sales and customer service staff.

With Microsoft CRM, your company can create a brawny, capable, all-inclusive computer-based product catalog. That way, you can quickly and easily find all the items and services you sell (nix thumbing through pages). This chapter shows you how to set up this valuable resource.

Overview of the Product Catalog

Within a product catalog, you can create pricing schedules and assign them to your customers as default schedules. This way, Bob's Big Discount Warehouse gets the wholesale pricing schedule, and the National Organization for Toasters gets nonprofit pricing. Using these assigned pricing schedules and the quote generation feature of Microsoft CRM (refer to Chapter 18), your salespeople can generate accurate quotes quickly. Quotes beget orders and orders beget invoices and invoices beget bucks (most of the time).

You can create a number of pricing schedules, for any reason. These schedules could be as simple as retail, wholesale, and nonprofit pricing or as complex as seasonal pricing or tiered membership pricing. Chapter 18 details how to create and use the pricing schedule to your company's advantage.

The product catalog can link to opportunities, competitors, and product literature. In fact, the product catalog has its tentacles into virtually every aspect of the system.

If you're integrating with one of Microsoft's Dynamics back-office accounting systems, you set up the product catalog in Dynamics and link to it rather than setting up the catalog in Microsoft CRM. If you're integrating with an accounting system other than Dynamics, you can upload that system's product list directly into the CRM product catalog. When integrating with these systems, any data from the accounting side normally overrides what you entered previously in the CRM product catalog.

If you use an accounting application other than one from the Microsoft Dynamics family, there are solutions for you too. See Chapter 28 for some add-ons that simplify this work.

It's a good idea to read the entire chapter before you build your product catalog. This will give you an overview and allow you to do some planning.

When you're ready to start building your product catalog, we recommend that you use the order suggested by Microsoft, which we follow too:

- ✔ Discount lists
- ✔ Unit groups
- ✔ Price lists
- ✔ Products

To start your planning, categorize your products and services and organize and simplify your pricing schedules. This is also a good time to check and update your inventory lists. Take out products you haven't sold since President Nixon was in office. And while you're at it, update your pricing. Remember, the cost of living has increased considerably since you founded the company (36 cents for a gallon for gas, anyone?).

Getting to the Product Catalog Window

You create a product catalog in the Product Catalog window of Microsoft CRM. You won't have to venture out of this section while creating your catalog — though we recommend venturing out of your cubicle for a leg stretch once in a while.

Now that you've stretched your legs and shared the latest rumor, it's time to get to work. Start by going to the Product Catalog window, as follows:

1. **At the bottom of the navigation pane, click Settings.**

   The Settings window for all Microsoft CRM functions appears on the right.

2. **In the Settings window, click Product Catalog.**

   The four components of the product catalog appear in the Product Catalog window.

As mentioned, we recommend that you create your product catalog in the order that Microsoft indicates. So that's what you do next.

Creating a Discount List

Discount lists control how prices change based on the quantity of the product or service being purchased. You can set your discounts in two ways:

- ✔ By percentage
- ✔ By reduction according to a set dollar amount

For example, a seasonal sale in which you offer a 10 percent discount on all purchases calls for a percent discount list. Offering $5 off for every touchdown the high school team makes during the weekend game is a set dollar amount discount.

To set up a discount list, you first need to get the Product Catalog window, as explained in the preceding section. Then follow these steps:

1. **In the Product Catalog window, click Discount Lists.**

   All existing discount lists are displayed, as shown in Figure 10-1.

2. **In the Discount Lists window's toolbar, click the New button.**

   The Create Discount List window appears.

3. **In the Name field, enter a title for your new discount list.**

   We recommend a unique and self-explanatory title so that others will be able to identify the list. In our example, we entered "Summer Special Discount."

4. **Choose the type of discount that you want to offer your customers.**

   The Percentage option is based on a percentage of the regular price. The Amount option is based on a set dollar amount deducted from the regular price. To follow along with our example, select Percentage.

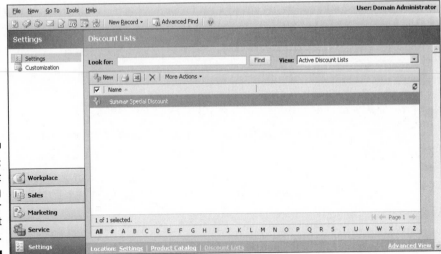

Figure 10-1:
Start
building
your
discount
lists here.

   5. Click OK.

   The Information window for your new discount list appears. (The top of the navigation pane has two options: Information and Discounts. The Information display is the default display.) Note the top of the window; whatever you named your discount list appears here.

   At this point, you can continue with creating the discount list, or you can exit the discount list by clicking Save and Close.

   6. Enter a note for the discount list.

   For example, you can add a note about the limitations of the discount (such as "limit 4").

   7. In the navigation pane, select Discounts.

   The Discount section of your discount list appears, as shown in Figure 10-2. This is where you begin entering the details for this discount.

   8. Now to make your discounts: Click the New Discount button on the toolbar.

   9. In the Discount: New window that appears, enter the following information for your discount:

   a. **The beginning and ending quantity:** The program calls these Begin Quantity and End Quantity.

   b. **Your discount amount:** If you chose Percentage in Step 4, this line will say Percentage. If you chose Amount in Step 5, this line will say Amount ($). When entering the amount, don't enter the symbol (% or $).

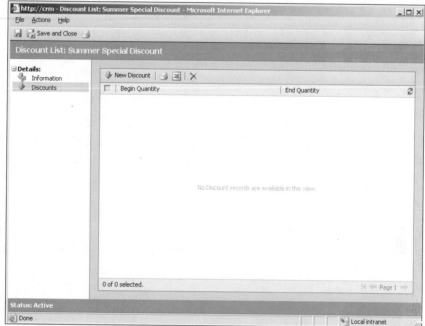

Figure 10-2:
The
discount
workspace
of your
discount list.

10. **Click the Save and Close button to return to your discount list.**

11. **To enter another line item, go back to Step 8.**

    You can enter as many line items as you want to establish the necessary price breaks for this discount list. For example, if you want to offer price breaks for quantity purchases, you might create a line item for a discount for 1–10 items purchased and another one to assign a price for 11–20 items.

12. **To save this list, click Save and Close in the Discount List window.**

Make sure that you don't overlap quantity ranges. For example, suppose your first discount covers the first nine items sold, and you have a larger discount for ten items and above. You enter 1-9 for the first discount and 10-99 for the second discount. But what if you sell time and break it down in 15-minute increments? The undefined quantity between 9 and 10 could be an issue. We suggest that you break down time increments into decimals when entering quantities for time.

Creating a Unit Group

A *base unit* is the smallest or most common means of tracking an item sold. Typical base units are pounds, gallons, hours, days, and tons.

A *unit group* defines how individual items are grouped into larger quantities. For example, suppose that you sell books individually, by the case, and by the pallet. A unit group of books shows how a book relates to a case and a case to a pallet. Using this example, if you sell 2 cases of books, with 20 books to a case, the system knows that you sold 40 books.

To create a unit group, follow these steps:

1. **In the Product Catalog window, click Unit Groups.**

   If you need help finding the window, see the earlier section titled "Getting to the Product Catalog Window." The screen shown in Figure 10-3 appears.

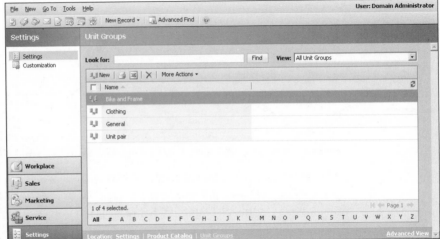

Figure 10-3: This is your main Unit Groups display.

2. **In the window's toolbar, click the New button.**

   The Create Unit Group dialog box appears.

3. **Enter the following information for your unit group:**

   a. **Name:** The name of your unit group. For our example, we're calling this unit group Books.

   b. **Primary Unit:** This is the smallest unit by which the product can be sold. The primary unit is also known as the base unit.

4. **Click OK.**

   The Information window, which is the default display, appears.

5. **At the top of the navigation pane on the left, click Units.**

   The Unit Group: Books window appears. (If you named your unit something else, that name would appear instead of *Books*.) This is where you'll add your units to your unit group.

6. **In the toolbar of your new Unit Group, click New Unit.**

   The Unit: New window appears.

7. **For each of the three units (book, case, and pallet), do the following:**

   a. **Enter the name.**

      This is where you enter the name of each unit. To follow along with the example, enter Book (the first time through), then Case, and then Pallet.

   b. **Enter the quantity.**

      Again, to follow along with the example, enter a quantity of 1 for Each because this is our base unit. The Case quantity is 20, meaning that each case contains 20 base units. The Pallet quantity is 10, meaning that each pallet contains 10 cases.

   c. **Enter the base unit.**

      The base unit is the smallest increment of this new unit you are creating. Continuing with the example, you can see that Each has no base unit (because it *is* the base unit and was determined in Step 3 to be the Primary Unit). Case has a base unit of Each, and Pallet has a base unit of Case. Use the magnifying glass to browse for the unit you want to set as the base unit. All units, with the exception of the primary unit, must have a base unit.

   d. **Click the Save and Close button.**

   A quick note for those keeping score: The columns in the Unit Group workspace are listed in a different order than those in the Unit: New window.

8. **Click the Save and Close button.**

   You are returned to the unit group you are working on, as shown in Figure 10-4.

9. **To save the unit group, click the Save and Close button again.**

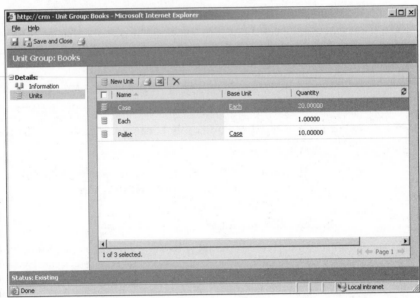

Figure 10-4:
We've
added units
to the group.

Creating a Price List

Price lists are the backbone of all your opportunities and quotes. Your company may have more than one price list, such as a retail price list and a wholesale one. You could also have separate price lists for government and nonprofit customers. You can add a default price list to each contact or account, but this can be overridden when you create quotes and invoices (see Chapter 18).

Here's how you create that price list:

1. **In the Product Catalog window, click Price Lists.**

   The Price Lists window shown in Figure 10-5 appears.

2. **In the window's toolbar, click the New button.**

   The Price List: New window appears. The navigation pane displays two choices: Information and Price List Items. Price List Items is not available until you've saved the price list.

3. **Enter a name for your price list.**

   Required fields are in red. The Name field is required, but the start and end date fields are not. In our example, we created the "It's Too Cold!!" price list to offer special prices to match the dropping temperatures. However, winter lasts only so long, so we've set the price specials to end in February.

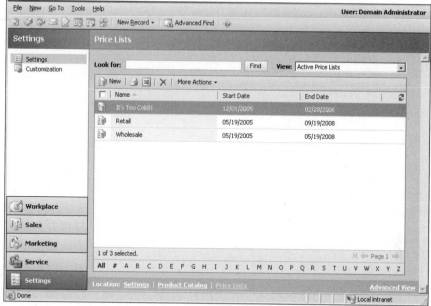

Figure 10-5:
Manage
and create
your price
lists from
this screen.

4. **Click Save (the disk icon next to the Save and Close button).**

   Clicking Save allows you to continue with the next part of the process, adding price list items. However, if you aren't ready to enter your price list items or need to get out of this window for some reason, just click the Save and Close button.

5. **In the navigation pane on the left, click Price List Items.**

6. **On the Price List Items toolbar, click the Add Price List Item button.**

   The Price List Item: New window appears, as shown in Figure 10-6.

7. **Enter your price list information in the available fields.**

   Some fields must be filled in by using the magnifying glass to the right of the field. The magnifying glass opens a Look Up window. Other fields can be filled in freehand or by using the drop-down boxes. As with other screens in Microsoft CRM, the fields in red are required.

   a. **Price List:** This is filled in automatically by the program. However, you can change the price list using the magnifying glass.

   b. **Product:** Use the magnifying glass to find the product you want in this price list. Microsoft thwarts the Minions of Chaos by allowing your staff to enter only predefined choices from the product list.

   c. **Unit:** Use the magnifying glass to make your selection. This field is not enabled until you select a product.

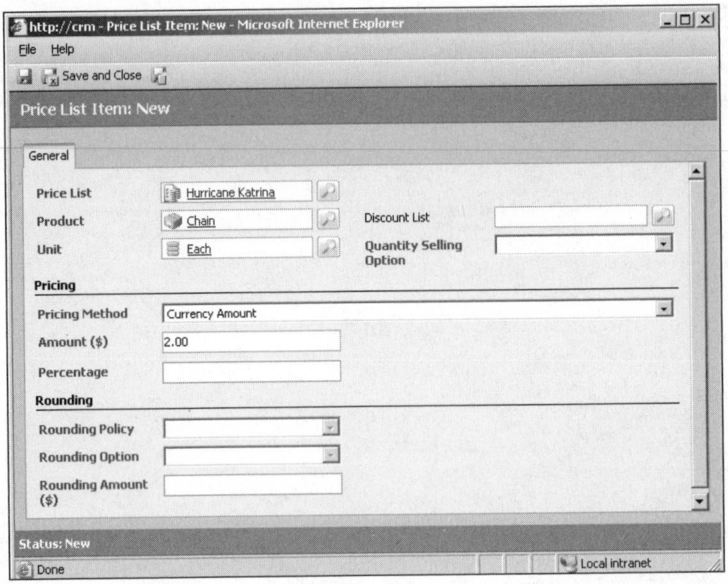

Figure 10-6:
Enter the
information
about your
item here.

   d. Discount List (optional): Use the magnifying glass to find the discount list you created earlier in the chapter and link it to your price list. By adding a discount list to work in tandem with the price list item, your staff can create thorough pricing to quote your customers. (See Chapter 18 for details on generating quotes.)

   e. Quantity Selling Option: This is where you define the quantities your product will be sold in. Choose No Control, Whole, or Whole and Fractional. This feature really comes in handy if you sell fractional services such as help desk or prorated time products.

   f. Pricing Method: Six options are available: Currency Amount; Percent of List; Percent Markup — Current Cost; Percent Margin — Current Cost; Percent Markup — Standard Cost; Percent Margin — Standard Cost.

   g. Amount ($): Enter the dollar amount for the price list. The Amount option is available only if you chose Currency Amount under Pricing Method. Don't include a dollar sign.

   h. Percentage: Enter the percentage for the price list. Don't include the symbol (%).

   i. Rounding Policy: Your rounding policy tells the system how to round percentage calculations to arrive at a specific price. Your options are None, Up, Down, and To Nearest. Rounding applies only when the pricing method is based on percentage. If you selected Currency Amount for the Pricing Method, this field is not available.

j. Rounding Option: This option works with the Rounding Amount field. For example, select Ends In here and .00 in the Rounding Amount field if you want to round to the nearest dollar. Select Multiple Of here and enter .05 in the Rounding Amount field to round to the nearest nickel. If you selected None for the Rounding Policy or Currency Amount for the Pricing Method, this field is not available.

k. Rounding Amount: Fill in the amount on which you want to base your rounding, as described in the preceding entry. If you selected None for the Rounding Policy or Currency Amount for the Pricing Method, this field is not available.

8. **Click Save and Close to save your price list items to your price list.**

   As mentioned, the fields in red are required. If you've missed one (due to excessive caffeine intake or hunting down who burned the popcorn), the program will remind you.

By creating price lists, you build an easy-to-use system to generate price quotes for your customers. Microsoft CRM uses the price lists, discount lists, and price list items to automatically calculate client costs, so your salespeople can focus on selling and not math.

If your company uses an accounting system and wants to integrate it with Microsoft CRM, keep in mind that the interface will normally provide all this information and will overwrite your price lists with the information from the accounting system. With the integration provided to Microsoft CRM, much of this functionality is disabled because it is controlled by the accounting application.

Adding Products

Your products — without them, you wouldn't have a business, right? From the first entrepreneurial caveman, businesses are made because someone had a product to sell. We use the term *product* as a general term to encompass products, services, the help desk — basically whatever you build your business around.

Now, because the Minions of Chaos love mischief, Microsoft has taken a smart step in preventing them from running amok in your system: Only system administrators are allowed to add new products. That means if Sam the Salesman can't find the entry for the Hop-n-Pop toaster, he won't be able to add entries that could create confusion when you want a report or when other salespeople are looking for the Hop-n-Pop. Can you imagine if he added the product as hopnpop, Mary in the next cube added it as HnP, and then Carey added it by the model number X900? How could you run a report on how many of those have been sold?

Another function of Microsoft CRM allows you to group products to be sold as a *kit*. Take your Hop-n-Pop toaster, sell it with bagels and organic preserves, and you have the Bagel Buff Gift Basket. You could also create special kits to simplify your sales and ordering processes or to get rid of some stuff that you don't want anymore — clearance, anyone?

You can also *relate* individual products to substitute products. This is a handy function for your salespeople when Mrs. Reynolds wants a Hop-n-Pop toaster, but you sold the last one two days ago. By relating this product to a substitute, your salesperson can easily recommend the equivalent HotHopPop toaster.

If you're a system administrator, follow these steps to add a new product to your product list:

1. **In the Product Catalog window, click Products.**

   A list of your active products appears, as shown in Figure 10-7.

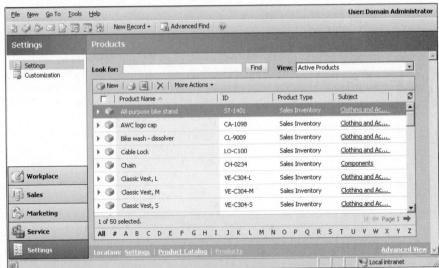

Figure 10-7:
The active products screen.

2. **In the Products window's toolbar, click the New button.**

   The Product: New window appears with three tabs, as shown in Figure 10-8.

3. **Fill in the General tab.**

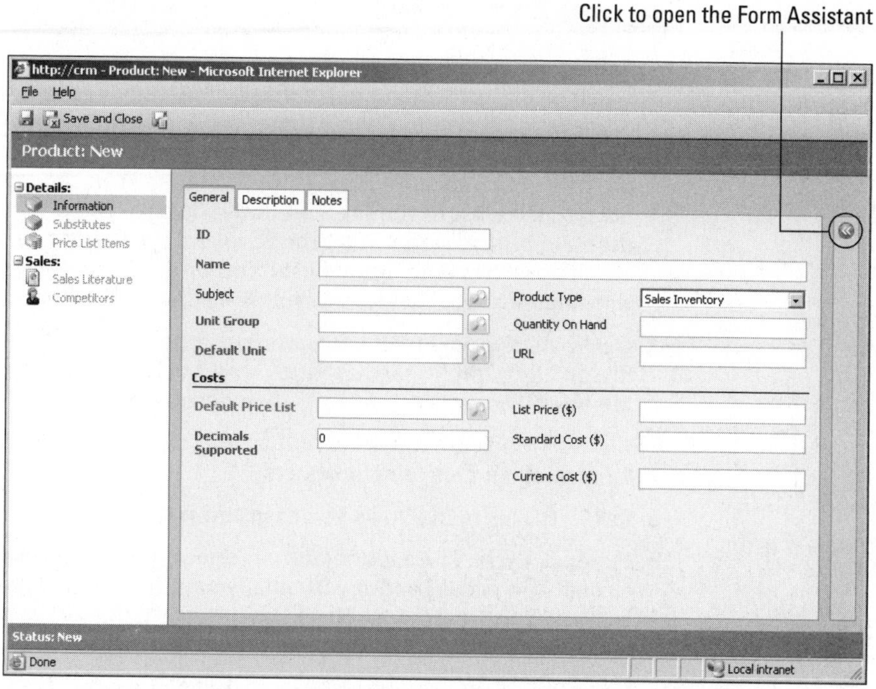

Click to open the Form Assistant

Figure 10-8:
Enter
your new
product
information
here.

The General tab, which is the default tab, is where you'll enter most of the information for your product. You can fill in some fields freeform, others using the magnifying glass (thwarting those Minions of Chaos), and still others with the Form Assistant. (In Figure 10-8, the Form Assistant has been collapsed. To open it, click where indicated in the figure.) For details on using the magnifying glass and the Form Assistant, see Chapter 2.

The following fields are mandatory:

a. **ID:** If your system is integrated with your accounting system, the ID is the item number used by the accounting system. It is through this field that the accounting system updates (and overwrites) information in each product record.

b. **Name:** This is descriptive text entered freehand. But it can also be populated by your accounting system if it is integrated.

c. **Unit Group:** If your system is not integrated with accounting, select the unit group that includes the units by which this product will be sold.

d. **Default Unit:** This is the unit you would typically sell the product as. For example, if you sold the book, *Toasting the Night Away,* as a single product, the default unit would be Each. If you were selling nails, the default unit might be Box.

    e. Default Price List: Earlier in the chapter, we discussed price lists. This field relates an individual product to a default price list (wholesale, retail, dealer, government, and the like) you've set up. When salespeople go to make that quote, they'll actually get the price list attached to the customer record. However, if no price list is attached to the customer record, the system defaults to the price list indicated for the product itself. You can't assign a default price list to the product until you save the product (use the Save button rather than the Save and Close button) and associate the product with a price list item. Until you do this, you see a warning message that the default price list has not been set.

    f. Decimals Supported: If your product (books, for example) can't be divided into fractional quantities, enter 0. If fractional quantities are possible, you can use up to five decimal places.

The following fields are optional, but we find them helpful in building a product catalog and entering products:

    a. Subject: This field allows you to group your products for reporting.

    b. Product Type: The four default product types are Sales Inventory (usually physical goods); Miscellaneous Charges (fees, such as for restocking); Services (such as consulting or annual maintenance fees); and Flat Fee (for example, handling or shipping charges).

    c. Quantity on Hand: The number of items in stock. This field is controlled by the back-office system if you have integrated it.

    d. URL: The Web address related to this product. This is a handy place to get up-to-date product information.

    e. List Price, Standard Cost, and **Current Cost:** The price on a generated quote is based on these fields.

4. **On the Description tab, you can enter vendor and part number information.**

   Having the vendor and part information can be helpful, especially if you sell similar products with similar names. Entering information on this tab isn't mandatory, but it does offer you another opportunity to identify your product.

5. **The Notes tab is for freeform notes and information about your product.**

   Suppose that your product comes in other colors. Instead of making the salesperson back up a few screens to see what colors you offer, you can list the colors here too.

6. **After you've entered all your product information, click Save and Close to return to your product catalog (refer to Figure 10-7).**

   Remember the motto of computer users everywhere: save, Save, SAVE!

Ta-dah! Now you've entered your product into your product catalog! Give yourself a pat on the back.

Chapter 11

Running Reports

"**W**here's my report?!" How many times do you hear that one! Or this one: "I need that report yesterday, Smith!!" Microsoft CRM has a huge set of built-in reports. Those report-happy folks (every office has at least one) will be in seventh heaven, especially when they discover that they can also design custom reports in SQL Reporting Services or Microsoft Excel and add them to Microsoft CRM. For those upgrading from the older 1.0 or 1.2 versions, which used Crystal Reports as the primary reporting engine, Microsoft includes options for system administrators to upgrade their Crystal Reports. Your consultant or value-added reseller can help you with this.

To some, reporting is an art form; creating appropriate reports to view activities, details, and dollars across the database is to them what painting was to Vincent van Gogh (with the exception of that whole ear thing, thank goodness). For management folks, reporting is even more compelling, because they can slice and dice to get a detailed picture of who's selling and serving and who's not.

On the flip side, reports can do a lot for your sales staff. Say they have ten phone calls to make that day and a report on their prospects to prepare. Which would you rather have them do? Sell. Yes, we thought so too. Right there is where Microsoft CRM reporting functions pay off. Instead of wasting time fiddling with the report, your sales staff can come up with a report in a few clicks and spend the rest of their time selling. Of course, the report has to be set up ahead of time, but you get the picture.

In this chapter, we show you how Microsoft CRM organizes its many reports and how you can customize the data and the report appearance. We also go over exporting and printing your reports.

Identifying Report Categories

Microsoft CRM contains predefined reports and charts separated into four major categories — sales, service, administrative, and marketing. Each of these categories contains reports that display information related to that specific area of Microsoft CRM. Keep in mind that some reports can be hidden from certain users, depending on their security roles, and some are just not assigned to a category or entity:

- **Sales reports:** Collect all the activities associated with a sale, from the lead through the actual sale. These reports can also provide statistical information about accounts, lead sources, competitors, and products.

- **Service reports:** Provide statistical information related to contracts and cases and summaries of knowledge base articles. These reports provide quick analyses of which products require the most support and where your service representatives are spending the most time.

- **Administrative reports:** Provide summary information about your Microsoft CRM users. This section is a logical place to store custom reports related to company-wide information, such as a list of all employees who participate in your 401(k) plan.

- **Marketing reports:** Describe accounts, campaigns, lead source effectiveness, and other areas of interest to the marketing department. The reports provide summary and detail information across accounts, campaigns, and lead sources.

Your system administrator, consultant, or value-added reseller can create custom reports and can make a report available in one or more categories, as well as from forms for related record types or from lists for related record types.

Reports can also be assigned to an entity (case, contact, account, activity, and so on) and may be viewed from that entity by clicking the Reports button on the toolbar. Entity options are listed in the "Accessing Reports" section.

If your security profile prevents you from accessing data in Microsoft CRM, you will not be able to see that data in any report you run. The reporting feature respects security settings.

Accessing Reports

"Where's my report!?" "Coming right up!" Now you can say that with confidence because it won't take you long to bring that report up.

Remember, however, that the settings in your security profile determine which reports you can see. This is another area where Microsoft CRM stands out, by allowing you to set up multilayered security access for your staff. For example, you can give only your Human Resources department access to reports containing confidential information such as salaries and commission rates. Or perhaps your system administrators could restrict access to resource-intensive reports to keep the reports from being launched by mistake during the day, when the system is already busy.

Next up, how to access reports.

You can access reports in the Reports window or, for those reports linked to specific entities as noted, from within the entities.

We also touch on how to drill down the report search results (which comes in handy for those needle-in-the-haystack searches).

1. **At the bottom of the Navigation pane, click the Workplace button. Then, at the top of the pane, click Reports (under My Work).**

    The Reports window appears, as shown in Figure 11-1. Remember, you'll see only the reports that your security profile allows you to see.

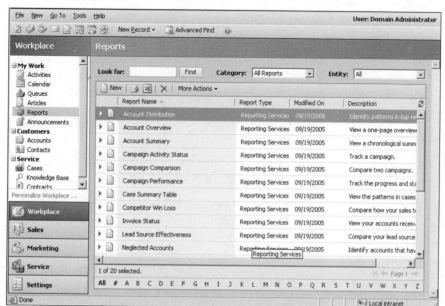

Figure 11-1: Lots of reports.

2. **Fill in the Look For box and click the Find button.**

   This is the first method we're using to reduce the size of the list. By entering text in the Look For box, only reports with that text anywhere in the display (that is, in the Report Name, Report Type, Modified On, or Description column) will be listed.

3. **Click the arrow next to the Category box and select a category.**

   This is another way of narrowing the reports listed and comes in handy if you're a report-heavy company.

4. **Click the arrow next to the Entity box and select an entity.**

   Choosing an entity allows you to find reports connected to that entity. You can choose from accounts, cases, campaign responses, marketing lists, quotes, and more.

5. **When you find the report you're looking for, click it to highlight it.**

6. **To run the report you just highlighted, click More Actions in the window's toolbar and choose Run Report.**

   This opens the Report Viewer screen, where you'll see a notification that your report is generating. Then you see the report itself. Figure 11-2 is an example of one report.

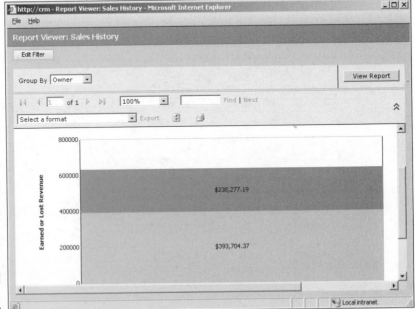

Figure 11-2:
Let's hope that's earned revenue and not lost revenue.

You can also view reports from inside an entity. For example, click Workplace in the navigation pane and then click Contacts under Customers. In the Contacts window, click the Reports icon. In the drop-down list, choose Records by Contact, or choose Run Report to go to the Report Viewer screen (refer to Figure 11-2). If you choose Records by Contact, you'll be asked to select the records in a dialog window before continuing.

Report Filtering

Let's say you have your report, but even though you chose a category and an entity, you still have too much information. By using filters, you can customize and narrow down that information to make a report that shows only the information you want.

You can set filtering options by clicking the Edit Filter button at the top of the Report Viewer screen (refer to Figure 11-2). This gives you the option to edit your original filter criteria or add new criteria to the filter.

So, using the account distribution report (part of the Sales category), let's see how to filter a report:

1. **At the bottom of the navigation pane, click the Workplace button. Then, at the top of the pane, select Reports (under My Work).**

2. **In the Reports window, double-click the Account Distribution report.**

   The Report Viewer: Account Distribution window appears, as shown in Figure 11-3. The Report Filtering Criteria section has two subsections (Accounts and Opportunities), where you can enter values. In some other reports, this area may be blank or may have different options.

 If you click Help in the main menu and choose Help on This Page, you get a description of this report, where the data comes from in Microsoft CRM, suggestions for ways to use the report, and how to handle problems with the report.

3. **Click the Edit Filter button (in the upper-right corner of the screen) to display the filter criteria.**

   A criteria selection area pops up in the workspace of the Report Viewer window.

4. **Edit the filter.**

   To do so, place the cursor on the first field to select the option and click once to display all the categories your company uses. What you see in the remaining two fields depends on what you choose in the first field.

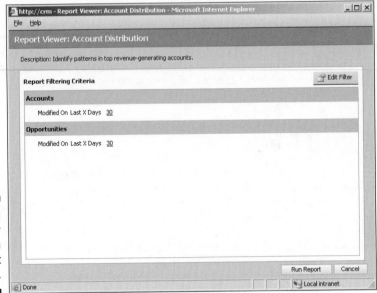

Figure 11-3:
Another
report in
Microsoft
CRM.

5. **Click the Run Report button (at the bottom of the screen).**

This opens the Report Viewer screen (the report itself and the editing screen are both called Report Viewer), which shows the new, filtered results. The next steps involve detailed filter editing, so you can either read on or skip to the next section, "Using Viewing Options." If you want to continue in this section, continue to Step 6.

6. **Click the Edit Filter button again.**

This expands the level of detail for editing, as shown in Figure 11-4. You enter data into the fields exactly as you did in Step 4. However, you now see arrows to the left of the line items, and you see a new option called Select.

7. **In the first line below the Clear button, click the arrow to open a drop-down menu and choose Hide in Simple Mode (to follow along with the example).**

As shown in Figure 11-4, *(Hidden)* pops up on the far right.

8. **Click the Hide Details button.**

You return to the Report viewer screen (refer to Figure 11-3), but the Accounts area has disappeared. To get it back, click the Edit Filter button, click the arrow below the Clear button, and choose Show in Simple Mode.

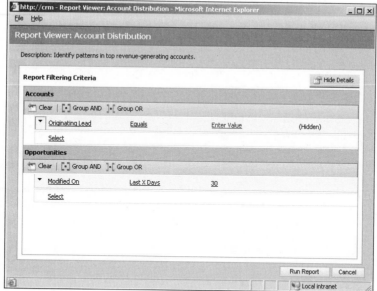

Figure 11-4:
You'll see
this filtering
ability again
in other
chapters.

9. **For practice, let's group and ungroup some of the options.**

    a. **Use the Select option to select two or more rows.**

    b. **Click the Group AND or the Group OR button.**

    AND means that all the lines must be true (this is the default if you do no grouping). OR means that any one of these lines must be true. This allows you to build sophisticated logical expressions.

    c. **Click the arrow inside the AND or OR box and see your further options.**

    d. **Click Ungroup.**

Be careful when selecting criteria. If you set up the filter to look for a record with the owner as, for example, Bob AND Stanley, you'll get zero results because a record can't have two owners. You'd want to use OR in this case.

10. **In the Accounts section, click Select, click the arrow to the right of the box to open the drop-down box, and choose a field from Accounts.**

    The Select list under the Opportunities section will give you different options. The drop-down box will not appear until you mouse over or click the word *Select*.

11. **Click the condition drop-down list, select Equals, and then click the arrow to the right of the box.**

    Take a look at the other options here to get an idea of the kinds of filtering you can perform.

12. To continue adding conditions, click Select again and repeat the process.

As an exercise, click Select again and scroll down to the Related section (under the bold Related header) to see the separate lists of items related to the Accounts list. Select one of them to create a new section. Then click the arrow to the left of that section and delete it.

The Clear button in the Edit Details screen in the Report Viewer clears all the changes you made and returns the filter to its original state. This way, you save a step by not having to close the filtered version of the report and reopen the full version.

After showing you all the great things that Microsoft CRM can do, we hate to bring up bad news, but this is something you have to know. Microsoft CRM does not save filters. However, there is an add-on product that will save filter criteria, as we describe it in Chapter 28.

Using Viewing Options

Okay. You have your spiffy report, built with your new filter, and now you want to look at that baby. You want to customize it, giving it the virtual equivalent of a metallic flame job. At the top of each report window (see Figure 11-5) are the tools you can use to customize the report.

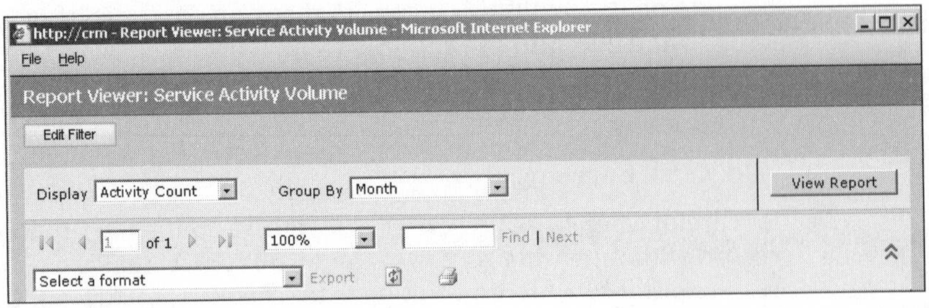

Figure 11-5:
No option
for a
metallic
flame job.

http://crm - Report Viewer: Service Activity Volume - Microsoft Internet Explorer

File   Help

Report Viewer: Service Activity Volume

Edit Filter

Display [Activity Count ▾]   Group By [Month ▾]   [View Report]

|◀ ◀ [1] of 1 ▶ ▶| [100% ▾]   [   ] Find | Next

[Select a format ▾] Export 📄 🖨

Let's take a look at all those options:

✔ **Display:** Choose to display Activity Count or Activity Duration.

✔ **Group By:** Sort your report by these options, such as by day, month, user, or status.

✔ **Page navigation:** If your report has more than one page, you can move through using these VCR-type controls. From left to right, the first button (First Page) takes you to page one of the report. The next button (Previous Page) takes you back one page from the page currently displayed. The third button (Next Page) takes you to the next page. The last button (Last Page) takes you to the last page of the report. The display between the second and third button tells you the page you're on and the total page count.

✔ **Display size:** Next to the navigation options is a box showing the size of the display. Click the arrow for the drop-down box to modify the size of the report.

✔ **Find | Next:** This field enables you to search for specific text in the report. You can use * as a wildcard to search partial text. (For example, typing **Mart*** will find Martin.) Just fill in the Find field and click Find. You'll be taken to the first result. To move to the second result, click Next.

If the text you enter in the Find field appears in the report on a page previous to the one you're viewing on the screen, the search will come up empty. So, when conducting a search using the Find field, always jump to the first page of the report before clicking Find.

✔ **Report-specific parameters:** Below the main options line, there may be a row containing report-specific options. The labels for the fields and the field arrows should explain the use of each field. At the right of the main options area is a button with two chevrons. This is a toggle that shows and hides these parameters.

You can drill down on summary reports (or graphs) to see the underlying detail. For example, if you opened the Case Summary Table report, you'd see a table with summary data for each user. If you click one of the summary items, you get a detailed line-item breakout. Click the Original Report button at the top of the screen to return to the summary report.

Exporting and Printing Your Report

Exporting report data is just what it sounds like — the movement of data from inside Microsoft CRM to outside Microsoft CRM. Let's look at exporting your spiffy report.

Printing is a form of exporting. To print your report, just click the little printer icon in the line above the report. You'll get the basic Print dialog window, where you can make the usual selections.

For the most part, when we use the term *export* in this business, it's describing sending the data to another application. In Microsoft CRM's case, the data doesn't export to just Microsoft products. You can create your report in HTML (good for display on your company web site) or export it to an Adobe Acrobat file.

Follow these steps to export a report:

1. **With the report on the screen in the Report Viewer window, click the arrow by the Export box, and select the application from the drop-down list.**

   Your choices are HTML, Excel, Web Archive, Acrobat, TIFF, CSV (comma delimited), and XML.

2. **Click the word *Export*.**

   You see a familiar screen, asking whether you want to open the file or save it to disk. Your computer thinks you're downloading a file from a Web site; so you're asked whether you want to open it or save it. If you choose to open it, you will have the option to save it from the report window.

3. **Decide whether to open or save the file, and then click OK.**

   After a moment, your report opens in the format you selected.

When you select one of the export formats, the associated application opens and displays the report. Interestingly, no matter which selection you make, the report opens in a browser window (remember that Microsoft CRM is browser based). So, for example, if you select Microsoft Excel as the export format, the report opens in what *looks* like Excel, but it's inside a browser. All of Word's menus will be available.

Microsoft CRM uses SQL Server 2000 Reporting Services as its primary reporting tool (replacing Crystal Reports in Version 1.2) If you want to create your own custom reports, you must install (and learn) SQL Server or work with your consultant or value-added reseller to help you create reports.

Exporting Records to Excel

In our officer manager's opinion, Microsoft Excel is right up there with Velcro and peanut butter. What's more, it is easy to use but can still handle tons of data. We think it's the best way to create quick and efficient reports, whether those reports are static worksheets, dynamic worksheets, or pivot tables (consult your friendly *Microsoft Excel For Dummies* for more on Excel).

Dynamic worksheets offer some big advantages, mostly because you don't have to re-enter data and run the risk of making mistakes. When a worksheet is dynamic, the data in Excel changes automatically every time that same data is updated in Microsoft CRM. Another advantage is that if you share that report, Microsoft Excel checks with CRM and adjusts the content of the document based on the security rights of the user running the report.

To export your report to Excel, follow these steps:

1. **Go to an area in Microsoft CRM that shows a workspace (or listing).**

2. **Click the Export to Excel icon.**

   The Export Data to Excel dialog box appears, as shown in Figure 11-6.

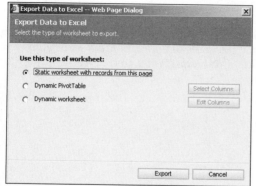

Figure 11-6: Getting ready to export.

3. **Choose one of the following:**

   • **Static worksheet with records from this page:** Select All records on current page or Records from all pages in the current view (10,000 records at a time is the maximum export limit). Then click Export. This simply gives you an Excel worksheet with the same data in the columns as appears in the Microsoft CRM grid.

   • **Dynamic PivotTable** or **Dynamic worksheet:** Click the Select Columns button (for Dynamic PivotTable) or the Edit Columns button (for the Dynamic worksheet option). In the dialog box that appears, choose the columns you want in your report and then click OK. You return to the Export Data to Excel dialog window. Click Export. You are asked whether you want to save or open the report. If you choose Save, you can save the file and then open it. If you choose Open, you can later save the report after it's opened. The report is generated in Microsoft Excel format (in a web browser window), and the Query Refresh dialog box appears with the following choices: Enable Automatic Refresh or Disable Automatic Refresh (Figure 11-7). After you make your choice, you have access to the report.

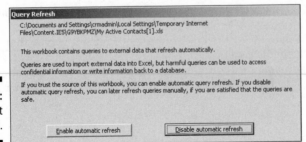

Figure 11-7:
The text
says it all.

Voilà! Isn't that report pretty? Now when you hear your boss bellow "Where's my report?" you can proudly offer your masterpiece. The next step is to show your boss how invaluable you are by arranging the data so you're the only one who can interpret it.

Seriously, as you can see, the reporting function of Microsoft CRM is a full-on, serious tool that can analyze loads of data and provide, at your demand, accurate captures of data, products, clients, and more.

Chapter 12

Sending Announcements

In This Chapter

▶ Writing an announcement

▶ Checking announcements

Announcements are internal messages that you can put into everyone's workspace in Microsoft CRM. Let's say you want to announce the upcoming maintenance and downtime planned for the system, or the yearly company picnic, or that Bob's wife just had her baby. Creating an announcement in Microsoft CRM is how you would inform everyone in your company. You don't even have to be an IT guy to do this.

Creating an Announcement

So, you want to announce the meeting with the IRA/401(k) representative, or maybe your company is hosting a blood drive. In this section, we show you how you can let everyone know using Microsoft CRM (with the exception of the actual wording — that you have to do yourself!). Take a look at the following steps:

1. **At the bottom of the navigation pane, click the Settings button. Then, at the top of the pane, select Announcements.**

   The Announcements window appears, as shown in Figure 12-1.

2. **In the Announcement window's toolbar, click the New button.**

   The Announcement: New window appears, as shown in Figure 12-2. The Title and Body fields are required. (Remember, anything bold in the pictures or red on your screen is a required field.) The More Information URL and the Expiration Date fields are optional.

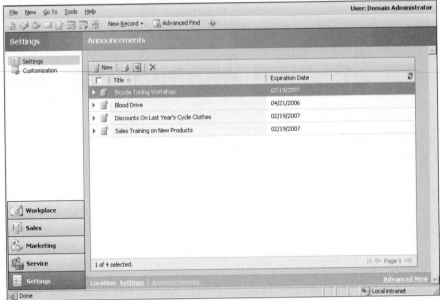

Figure 12-1:
Reach
out and
announce it!

Figure 12-2:
Go ahead —
tell every-
one!

3. **Fill in the Title field.**

4. **In the body field, type the announcement.**

   Remember, what you put in the body is what will go out to everyone.

5. **In the More Information URL field, you can enter a web site where your staff can go for more information.**

   For example, let's say you're announcing the annual American Red Cross blood drive. You can include the Web site of the Red Cross here.

6. **Set the expiration date for the announcement.**

   This tells Microsoft CRM when to remove the announcement from the system, therefore doing a bit of housekeeping. You can enter the date free-form or use the calendar at the end of the field. You can also delete the announcement manually, as described in a moment.

7. **When you're finished, click the Save and Close button**

Remember, the Minions of Chaos are lurking out there, so make sure you save!

To delete an announcement manually, simply highlight it and then click the black X in the toolbar. You will be prompted to confirm the deletion. Just click OK and it's gone.

You can preview the first few lines of each announcement. Click the right-pointing arrow at the far-left side of the entry in the Announcements window. A small drop-down window appears with the first few lines of the announcement.

Viewing Announcements

All right, let's go to the flip side. You're Bob the sales guy, and you want to check the announcements because you want to include a screen shot of the birth announcement for little Eunique's baby book. Or maybe you were jawing about the company picnic at the scuttlebutt (that's water fountain for you civilians), but no one could remember the date and you want to check.

Here's how you view announcements:

1. **At the bottom of the navigation pane, click the Workplace button.**

2. **At the top of the pane, choose Announcements under My Work.**

   The Announcements options should be at the bottom of the My Work choices.

> The My Work section might be collapsed, depending on the work you're doing. If it is, simply click the plus sign beside My Work to open the section.

3. Read the announcements (see Figure 12-3).

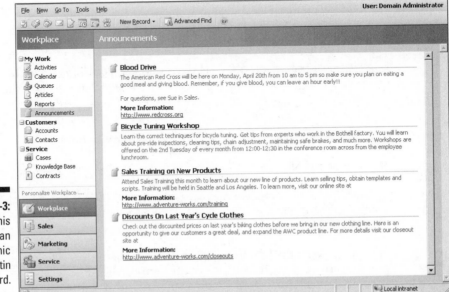

Figure 12-3:
Think of this
as an
electronic
bulletin
board.

See? It's simple to create announcements in Microsoft CRM. Plus, this sure beats an overloaded corkboard in the lunch room. We recommend you save that spot for Federal notices that must be posted in conspicuous places.

Part III
Managing Sales

The 5th Wave — By Rich Tennant

In this part . . .

This part deals with the sales side of your organization. CRM has four types of customer records: leads, opportunities, accounts, and contacts. This part explains all four and shows you how to enter and manage them.

Activities, which are tasks such as appointments and phone calls, are associated with each of these record types, and are discussed in Chapter 14. Managing sales quotas and forecasts is the turf for any sales organization and is detailed in Chapter 15.

E-mailing to prospects and to customers is detailed in Chapter 16. Leads and opportunities, near and dear to every salesperson, are discussed in Chapter 17. As an opportunity matures to a closed deal, you need to know about generating quotes, orders, and invoices — and these are the topics in Chapter 18.

Setting up what is essentially a knowledge base of sales literature and tracking your competition are both covered in Chapter 19, followed by a discussion of documenting everything you do with notes and attachments.

Chapter 13

Working with Accounts and Contacts

In This Chapter

▶ Adding accounts — and subaccounts

▶ Finding information on your accounts

▶ Assigning accounts

▶ Adding contacts

*A*ccount and contact records, as well as related lead and opportunity records, hold much of the primary information that your team has or will collect. Depending on the nature of your business, you may use one or both types of records. Microsoft CRM continually refers to accounts, contacts, and customers, so it's important to keep the terms straight. *Accounts* are companies, *contacts* are people, and *customers* can be either companies or people.

Assuming for the moment that you sell to other businesses and that you use account records, you'll also need to use contact records. Each account record can have multiple people (contact records) associated with it. The larger the account, the more people you likely need to track.

If you sell only to individuals, you may never actually use account records to track your customers. In all likelihood, however, you will want to track more than just your customers in Microsoft CRM. For example, keeping track of your company's vendors in the same database is useful. Your competitors may also be candidates for their own account records if you don't create actual competitor records for them. If you are strictly a B2C company, you will probably still encounter situations like these where you need the account record.

In this chapter, we describe how you add new accounts and contacts and how best to use and access those records after you create them.

Adding and Editing Accounts and Subaccounts

The first step in getting started with CRM is to stock it with all the organizations and people you deal with. If you already have the information organized in data files (in Excel, other CRM systems, or accounting data files, for example), you will be doing some importing. If the data is stored in your head (or, worse, someone else's head), you're in for some typing. The basic entities into which this data will go are accounts and contacts.

As mentioned, *accounts* are companies. *Subaccounts* may be divisions of the main company or separate physical locations of the same company. Anything you add in Microsoft CRM, you can edit. And anything you add can be deleted, but a better practice is to deactivate an account rather than delete it. Deactivating an account is like making it go dormant. If you deactivate an account, you can always resurrect the information later if you discover you need it. Deletion is forever.

Old-timers who used Version 1 may be looking for the Quick Create function — the lazy person's way to create new records using only required fields. This function has bitten the dust in Version 3.

Every account you add will almost always be associated with one or more contacts (people), so you will find it easier to create the contact records before you create the account record. You can then easily link the two.

Account records and their four sections

You can get to your account records from each of the three application modules and even from the Workplace. In each of those modules, Accounts appears up at the top of the navigation pane.

Each account record has four related tabs: General, Details, Administration, and Notes. You can access these tabs, or create a new account, as follows:

1. **At the top of the navigation pane, select Accounts.**

   The Accounts window appears on the right.

2. **In the window's toolbar, click the New button.**

   The Account: New window appears, as shown in Figure 13-1.

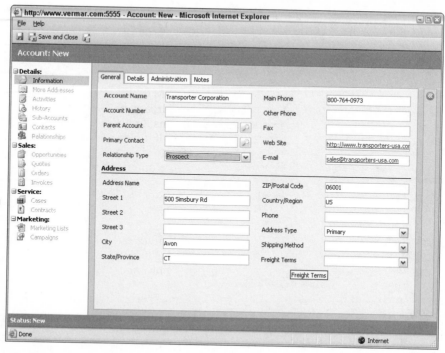

Figure 13-1:
The General tab is where you begin entering information about the account.

The General tab

The General tab has most of the critical contact information for your account, including the required field Account Name. Most of the fields on the General tab are self-explanatory, but the other three tabs deserve a little discussion.

When filling in data fields in the various tabs, you could click the Save and Close button when you've finished with each tab. But you can often save some steps by just clicking Save (the disk icon), which activates related actions on the navigation pane.

The Details tab

The Details tab contains mostly financial information, such as annual revenue and its stock symbol if the company is publicly traded. It's the kind of stuff you'll get if you receive data from Dun and Bradstreet or other similar services or list providers. This provides useful demographic information about the account, assuming someone in your organization does the research to fill in the information and keeps it current. The Details tab is shown in Figure 13-2.

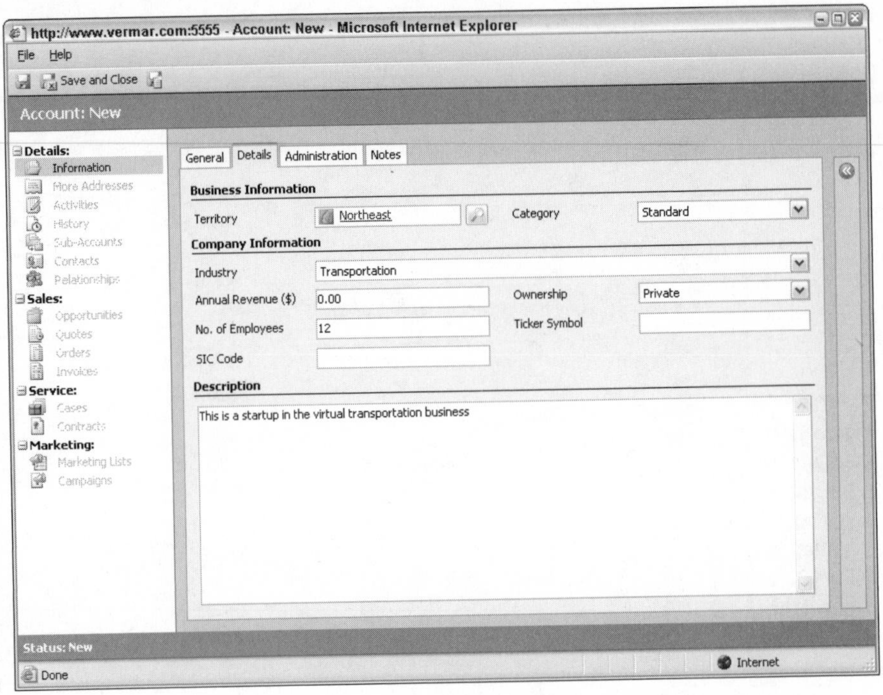

Figure 13-2:
The Details
tab of the
Account
window,
housing
basic
company
demo-
graphics.

The Territory field on the Details tab is one of the most important. Many companies, particularly national or international ones, divide their business into territories usually based on geography. Salespeople, or teams of sales-people, are assigned to each territory and their revenue is tracked.

Territories should be set up in the Settings module (see Chapter 6 for more information). Then you can manually select a territory for an account by clicking the magnifying glass to the right of the Territory field and selecting the appropriate territory.

You can also customize the system so that each new account is automatically assigned to a territory or so that accounts are reassigned automatically when it's time to reorganize your territories. This may require the services of an experienced dealer or developer though.

The Administration tab

The Administration tab, shown in Figure 13-3, is a catchall for accounting and marketing and service information. The Owner field is the only required field and is filled in automatically with the name of the user creating the record. So, by default, the record owner is the person who enters the information. If that's not the way it works in your organization, you can reassign the record to another user by clicking the magnifying glass to the right of the Owner field and selecting the proper user.

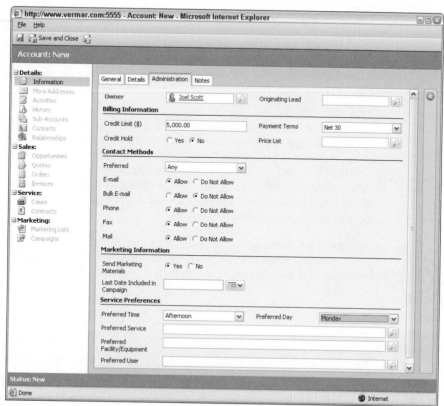

Figure 13-3:
You can add
all sorts of
information
here.

The Originating Lead field automatically keeps track of the source of this account record if it came from a converted lead record. Your marketing department will definitely want this field filled in accurately so that they can understand which marketing efforts are generating revenue.

The Originating Lead field is a system-generated field, so you can't enter anything into it. To be filled in, the account must be generated from a lead when it is qualified.

It's a great advantage for salespeople to know at least a little bit about their clients' billing and credit situation. The fields in the Billing section are prime candidates for integration with whatever accounting system is being used at your company. This integration will probably require some custom work and is usually the domain of the business partner who sold you the software.

The fields in the Contact Methods and Marketing Information sections regulate how you market to and correspond with this account. Keeping track of this is increasingly important as more and more laws go into effect regulating how we market to prospects and clients.

Even if you aren't using the Service module, the Service Preferences section contains basic service-related information that will help you tailor manual or automatic responses to service requests. For example, this is a simple place to keep track of the equipment your customer has and who your preferred technician is whenever service is needed.

The Notes tab

The Notes tab starts out as a blank slate: a large area where you can begin typing. You should use the Notes section to record general information about the account. After you finish typing your notes, just navigate to another section. This is one of the few areas in CRM where you do not have to tell the system to save your work. It does so automatically. In fact, CRM also records who created the note and timestamps the note. Figure 13-4 shows a Notes Tab after a few notes have been entered.

Everything you write in the Notes section is public information — and CRM does not have a spell checker or grammar checker. Pay attention to your writing style, and don't enter anything that you wouldn't want a client or a judge to see.

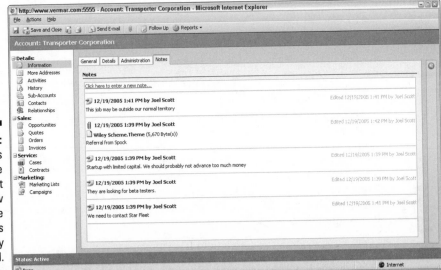

Figure 13-4: The Notes tab of the Account window with some Notes already entered.

Setting up subaccounts

An account record may be the *parent* of other account records, and those other account records are called *children*. A *child* record is also referred to as a *subaccount*. Typically, you use the subaccount system to subordinate one record to another. An example is when you're dealing with a company that has multiple locations. The headquarters would be the parent account, and each regional location would be a subaccount. By relating the accounts this way, you can use the reporting system to consolidate, subtotal, or total revenue for all the related accounts.

The General tab (refer to Figure 13-1), which is the default window when you are creating a new account record, contains the field that relates one account to another. This field is labeled Parent Account and has a list containing all account records in the system. There is no limit to the number of levels of parenting. In other words, every parent account can have multiple children, grandchildren, and great-grandchildren, and so on.

As you create this structure, the best approach is to map out the relationships between the accounts and begin at the top. First enter the parent account and then enter the children. As you enter each child account, click the magnifying glass next to the Parent Account field and select one parent to connect each "generation."

Finding and Viewing Account Information

No matter what your role is, as a user of CRM you'll find yourself looking up accounts, contacts, leads, and opportunities on a regular basis. You can locate records in Microsoft CRM in two basic ways: the Find function and the Advanced Find function.

Find

You can access the Find function from any of the main windows. Using Find is the simplest and fastest way to locate a record. Figure 13-5 shows a typical list view.

At the top of the window is a field labeled Look For. The Find button, which actually sets this function in motion, is to the right of the field. You can locate an account in several ways:

✔ Enter the first few letters of the account name in the Look For field and click the Find button. All the accounts beginning with those letters appear in the list. Click the account in the list to go to that account record.

The Find function is not case sensitive, so you needn't worry about uppercase and lowercase.

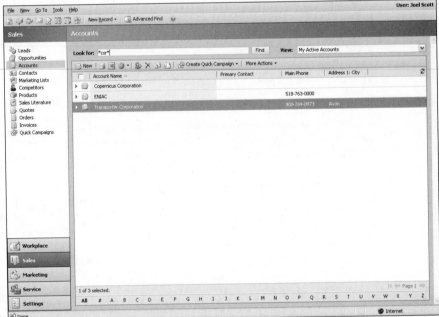

Figure 13-5:
The Find
function
makes it
easy to find
records.

✔ Enter part of the account name preceded or followed by an asterisk (*). If you want to locate all the companies that have LLC in their name, you could enter **LLC** in the Look For field. This locates all the accounts that start with LLC. If you think LLC may occur in the middle or at the end of the name, however, you can generalize your search by using ***LLC***.

✔ Click a letter of the alphabet at the bottom of the grid and scroll through the listing of all companies that begin with that letter. This approach is useful if you have a small database, but if you have hundreds of accounts that span multiple pages, one of the other techniques is easier.

Advanced Find

The Find function enables you to locate an account record quickly if you know the name of the account and that's the only criterion by which you're searching. Advanced Find, however, provides a more powerful search capability, enabling you to locate specific records (and activities) based on multiple fields. When you use Advanced Find, you can specify one or more search conditions. For example, you can find items by account name, city, and the name of the salesperson responsible for the account. You may want to find all the A-level accounts in your city and send them an invitation to a seminar.

Your search can contain Boolean operators, such as AND or OR. While using Advanced Find, you can also enter an asterisk when performing a search (for example, when you are searching for an account, a user, or a contact).

The values you enter are not case sensitive. For example, if you are entering a state code, Microsoft CRM will find the same records whether you enter **CT** or **ct**.

Boolean logic dictates that conditions within parentheses are evaluated before conditions separated by ANDs. ANDs are evaluated before ORs. The Advanced Find function does not have parentheses and evaluates expressions in the order in which they appear in your search.

To do a search with Advanced Find, follow these steps:

1. **On the main toolbar, click the Advanced Find button.**

   The window shown in Figure 13-6 appears.

2. **In the Look For drop-down list, select the appropriate choice.**

   In this example, the Look For list allows you to specify which record type Advanced Find will focus on. After you select the record type (in this example, Accounts), all related fields are available to you. You now proceed to the selection of specific fields, conditions and values.

3. **In the first row, select a field (in this example, City) from the drop-down list by clicking the down arrow to the right of the field name.**

   Based on the field you choose, the system selects your available choices for conditions. You can see all the possible conditions by clicking the down arrow to the right of the Condition field.

4. **Choose a condition.**

   The most commonly used conditions are Equal, Does Not Equal, Contains, Begins With, Contains Data, and Does Not Contain Data. Click the condition you want from the drop-down list. In the example, we chose Equals.

5. **Enter a value in the Value field.**

   Microsoft CRM allows you to have multiple values in this field. If you separate individual values with a semicolon (;), the system treats that semicolon as if it were an OR condition. We chose Avon.

6. **Continue to the next row to add additional search criteria.**

   If you run out of rows, click the Select button to begin another row of criteria.

7. **Click the Save as button if you'd like to name your query and retain it for future use.**

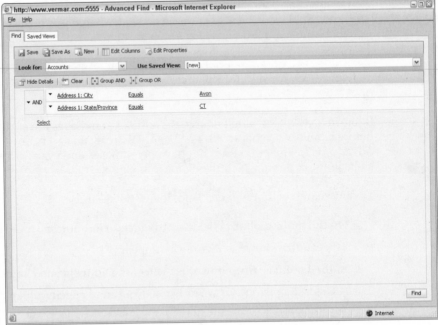

Figure 13-6:
A sample
search is
already
entered.

Assigning and Sharing Accounts

The toolbar in every account window enables you to assign or to share your accounts. You can also delete or deactivate an account.

Deleting accounts is usually a bad idea because any records attached to an account, such as contacts or opportunities, also go away. After you delete an account, you can never retrieve the information, and you can't undo the action. Deletion is forever. However, if you had previously set up a subaccount, that subaccount remains.

Deactivating an account turns it off, rendering it inactive. An inactive account can't be edited or have other types of records associated with it. It disappears from your usual lookups and is visible only if you specifically search for inactive accounts. The advantage of deactivating over deleting is that you can restore a deactivated account to active status should that become necessary.

Assigning accounts to users

If you go on an extended vacation, you may want to assign an account to another user. Or perhaps the territories your company covers are being realigned, and many accounts need to be tended to by other managers. If you assign one of your accounts to another user, that new person becomes the account owner, and you are removed from that position.

To assign one or more accounts, follow these steps:

1. **In the upper part of the navigation pane, select Accounts.**

   The Accounts window appears.

2. **Choose the accounts you want to reassign by clicking (highlighting) each account listing.**

   You can select multiple accounts by using the Shift key or the Ctrl key. The Shift key selects all the accounts from the first one you selected to the one you are currently positioned on. Hold down the Ctrl key and click to select noncontiguous accounts.

3. **Click the Assign icon.**

   The Assign Accounts window appears.

4. **Click the radio button next to Assign to another user.**

5. **Click the magnifying glass at the end of the User field.**

   A window opens for choosing the new user.

6. **Select the new user and click OK.**

   The system returns to the Accounts window. You will no longer be able to see the reassigned account in the list unless you change the View to Active Accounts.

Sharing accounts

Sharing is a little different from assigning. *Sharing* one of your accounts doesn't remove you from ownership; it merely adds additional users to the team servicing that account.

To share one or more accounts, follow these steps:

1. **Go to the Account List View and select all the Accounts you want to share.**

   You can select multiple Accounts at one time by using the Shift key or the Ctrl key. The Shift key will select all the Accounts from the first one you selected to the one you are currently positioned on. The Ctrl key allows you to randomly select individual Accounts.

2. **In the window's toolbar, select More Actions and then select Sharing.**

   The Who Would You Like to Share the Selected Account With window appears.

3. **Choose the users or the team from the Who Would You Like to Share This Account With dialog box.**

   After you select the users or teams, the system returns you to a List View with check boxes for the security privileges assigned to each user or team. By default, none of these privileges are assigned.

4. **Select the security privileges you want to give to each of the users with whom you are sharing by checking all the appropriate boxes.**

5. **To save these sharing specifications, click OK.**

Adding and Editing Contacts

You can add a contact record that stands alone, or you can add one that is associated with an account record. Adding or editing contact records is almost identical to the process you follow for account records.

Contacts have a list view just as accounts do. This view can be accessed from the Sales, Marketing, or Service area. The Contact database is the same for all three areas of CRM, so all your users access the same contact records.

Individual contacts can be added or edited manually in the same way that account records are handled. Contact records have a Parent Account field just as account records do. If you do business only with individuals, you may never need the Parent Account field. You should use it, however, if you need to associate a person with a company. Note that you can associate many different people with the same company (account record).

In addition to the manual entry of contact records, Microsoft CRM also comes with an automated wizard-based system for importing contact records. Although the wizard was designed with Outlook files in mind, the import facility can handle other types of data, such as text (.TXT) files.

Some of the more standard file types, such as .XLS, .MDF, and .DBF, don't work with the Import Wizard. And, although you can do at least a limited import of contact records, you're going to have trouble if you want to bring in associated activities for your contacts. If you need to perform a significant amount of importing, investigate the third-party import products discussed in Chapter 28 or check the Microsoft CRM Data Migration Framework.

Chapter 14

Managing Your Calendar

. . . .

In This Chapter

▶ Displaying your calendar

▶ Checking out your activities

▶ Making an appointment

▶ Scheduling others

▶ Assigning activities

▶ Completing activities

. . . .

*M*icrosoft CRM comes with a basic activity management system that enables you to schedule or log activities associated with the various records in the database, such as opportunities, leads, contacts, accounts, or cases.

Your calendar is a subset of your activities and displays only appointments. Your activities show a wider assortment of things that take up your time, such as phone calls and miscellaneous tasks such as meeting with your boss or coordinating the company golf outing. In addition, only the appointments on your calendar are coordinated with Outlook. Phone calls and tasks never show up in the main area of Outlook.

Aside from the obvious practice of entering all your activities in the system to ensure that they are properly documented and that you don't forget to do them, workflow rules can also have an important role with activities in your business processes. Workflow rules can look for overdue activities and alert you to them. They can look for activities that should be scheduled (such as following up on a quote that was sent out a week ago or an annual mainte- nance contract that is coming due next month) and send a series of alerts to the right team members. This is a powerful use of scheduling, but it works well only if everyone on the team is consistently logging his or her activities. (We discuss workflow in detail in Chapter 8.)

The ingredients essential to activity management include viewing existing activities, entering new activities, delegating activities, the inevitable rescheduling of activities, and completing activities. In the next few pages, you'll find out how to manage your activities and, to the extent possible, the activities of others as well.

No Outlook Here

Microsoft designed its CRM product assuming that most users would also be using Outlook. In this chapter, we discuss how to use Microsoft CRM's activity management system assuming that you're *not* using Outlook. This is a big assumption, but it helps simplify the discussion of calendar usage.

If you're not going to use Outlook, you'll want to look at the Service Scheduling calendar as a way to keep you and your team members on the same page. You won't be getting any alarms about appointments or due dates. (Maybe you view this as a good thing!)

Chapter 3 covers using Outlook with Microsoft CRM. If you're an Outlook user, consider reviewing Chapter 3 next. Doing so will fill in the holes created in this chapter.

If you're coming to Microsoft CRM with experience using another CRM system, you may wonder where some of the more advanced teamwork functionality is hiding. So, before you start looking around, here are some of the program's shortcomings:

- ✔ To look at everyone else's activities, you have to go to the Service Scheduling area. Using Outlook provides some assistance here, though, in that it allows for shared calendars.

- ✔ You can schedule other users to do something, but no convenient, automatic way exists to notify them that you did the scheduling. And because you can't see their calendar easily, you may end up scheduling them into a conflict. Outlook's Meeting Request is the answer to this situation. (And Outlook Meeting Requests can be linked to CRM, so this is a viable workaround.)

- ✔ You can't set an alarm on any kind of activity to alert you to an upcoming event. Therefore, Microsoft also doesn't have a snooze button.

- ✔ The system doesn't automatically roll over activities from one day to the next if you don't complete something when you're supposed to. Activities do remain on your calendar as past-due activities and will show up on your activity list as long as you fail to complete them.

Some of these oversights are resolved if you're using the remote, Outlook-like version of the system. More on that in Chapter 3.

Having now finished our complaints, we must say, in all fairness, that Microsoft CRM enables you to schedule and track all the important activities associated with customers. If you use this feature consistently, you'll always be organized. You'll never forget to do the important things. You'll make more money, live long, and prosper. But we do still need to easily see and share our staff's calendars.

Viewing Your Calendar

To display your calendar, click the Workplace button at the bottom of the navigation pane. Then, at the top of the pane, click Calendar, which appears under My Work. (If nothing appears under My Work, click the plus sign next to it to display the list.) The Calendar window appears on the right, as shown in Figure 14-1.

The calendar displays the weekly view of appointments and service activities. Note that service activities are activities associated with the Service module that have not only a user but also company resources. The information is available also in the Service Scheduling window, which allows users to see other user's calendars and activities.

The area on the far right of the screen contains a calendar you can use to change the date or date range of the calendar display. You also can select from three display modes, month, week, and day.

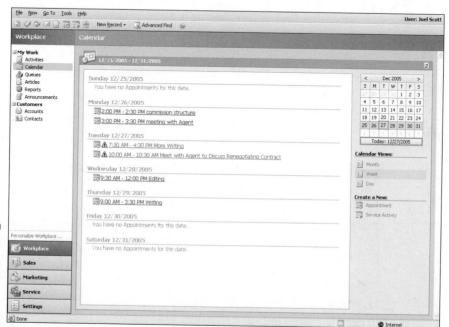

Figure 14-1: A typical week in the life of a writer.

The calendar is just a subset of your activities (only appointments and service-related activities) with a more graphical view of them.

Viewing Your Activities

If you really want to know what's on your agenda, the Activities window is the place to go. To get there, select Activities under My Work at the top of the navigation pane. Figure 14-2 shows a typical Activities window. This is probably where your day should begin and where you should spend much of your professional life.

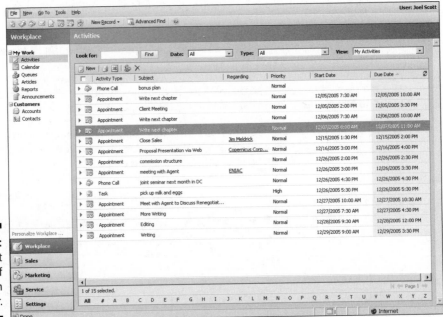

Figure 14-2: A snapshot of the life of a certain writer.

Figure 14-2 shows the Activities window for appointments, but remember you can manage eight types of activities in Microsoft CRM:

- ✔ Tasks
- ✔ Fax
- ✔ Phone call
- ✔ E-mail
- ✔ Letter

✓ Appointment

✓ Service activity

✓ Campaign response

Clicking the column title re-sorts your activities by that column, from ascending to descending order. Activities are sorted within each day's display. If you want to adjust the width of a column, drag the border between the column titles. You can change the columns displayed by saving your own Advanced Find searches, or your system administrator or implementation partner can create customized views.

At the top of the window, the Look For field allows you to locate scheduled activities based on the subject. Although you can use the alphabetical listing bar at the bottom of the window to locate Subjects beginning with a particular letter, the Look For field is more flexible. For example, you can enter consecutive characters, such as flor, to find activity subjects starting with, say, Florida. You can also use the wildcard character * to match any sequence of characters.

If you are trying to find all your activities, enter * in the Look For field and then click the Find button. This will display both open and closed activities. You might think by just choosing My Activities in the View drop-down list, all your activities would be displayed. But you'd be missing the closed activities with that method of searching.

You can use the View menu (in the upper-right corner of the Activities window) to select from one of several views. Your selection of a view works with your Find Activity selection. These views are

✓ **All Activities:** This comprehensive list displays open and completed activities no matter whose they are.

✓ **Closed Activities:** These are all the completed activities the system contains — yours and everyone else's.

✓ **My Activities:** These are the activities on your schedule. This is probably the most important view and the one we use most often.

✓ **My Closed Activities:** These are all your completed activities that the system contains.

✓ **Open Activities:** These are all open activities, whether they belong to someone else or to you. Unfortunately, the default view does not show to whom they belong.

✓ **Scheduled Activities:** These are all your scheduled appointments.

Of course, there are no activities to view if you don't enter some in the first place. Creating these activities in CRM is the subject of the next section.

Creating an Appointment for Yourself

You can create an appointment for yourself directly from the Workplace, which Microsoft online help suggests. This method is quick, but you can easily cause yourself problems by flippantly agreeing to some appointment without first checking your calendar — or better yet, your activity list.

The calendar shows only appointments, not tasks or phone calls. If you want to avoid scheduling two conference calls at the same time, for example, use the Activities window instead of the calendar.

You are always better off checking before you schedule appointments. For that reason, we recommend another approach to scheduling your appointments *when working online* in Microsoft CRM:

1. **At the bottom of the navigation pane, click the Workplace button. At the top of the pane, select Activities (under My Work).**

   Review your schedule here before committing to another appointment or activity.

2. **In the Activities window's toolbar, click the New button.**

3. **Select an activity (such as Appointment) and then click OK.**

   Figure 14-3 shows a typical window for entering appointment details. We describe this screen in detail in a moment.

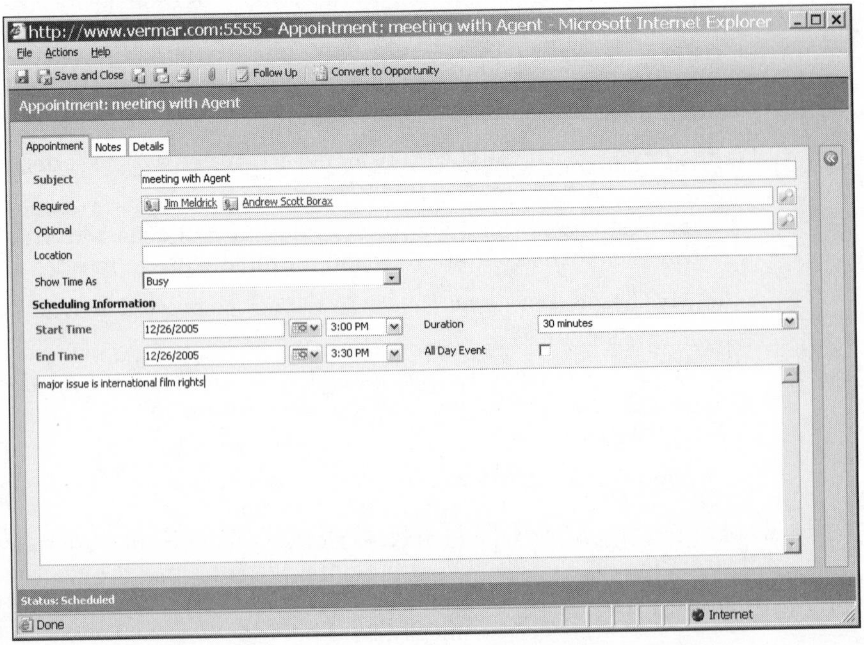

Figure 14-3: Planning to meet with your agent.

4. Fill in the details.

5. When you're finished, click the Save and Close button.

You return to the Activities window.

The Appointment window is divided into three tabs: Appointment, Notes, and Details. Several fields deserve clarification or further elaboration:

✔ **Organizer:** This field is on the Details tab. The Organizer is the person coordinating the activity and is not necessarily one of the attendees. This is the person you blame when the meeting is messed up.

✔ **Required** and **Optional:** These are two fields on the Appointment tab. When you click the magnifying glass to the right of each of these fields, CRM presents a window allowing you to specify one or more people involved in the meeting. The first field, Required, is for those people for whom attendance is mandatory. The Optional field is for people not quite so important.

✔ **Subject:** The text you enter in the Subject field appears in the Activities window and the Calendar window. In the weekly view of the calendar, the text wraps so you can see it all. In the daily view, if the text is too long, it is cut off.

✔ **Start Time and End Time**: If you don't enter a start and end time, particularly for appointments, the times will not be displayed on your calendar.

✔ **Event:** By default, an event is a day-long activity. When you select an All Day Event, you no longer have the option of selecting specific times. However, you can specify the dates; if the end date is different from the beginning date, you've created an activity that spans multiple days. Vacations are a good example of an appropriate use of events.

✔ **Notes:** The Notes section is an unlabeled free-form text area that appears on the lines just below the time span and subject on the calendar.

✔ **Regarding:** This field enables you to attach an activity to one or more records, such as contacts, accounts, or leads. By associating the activity with more than one record, you can then see the activity from any of those records.

That's what it takes to schedule something for yourself. One of the more powerful features of CRM systems is the ability to schedule activities for other people — that is, to delegate. That's what we discuss next.

Scheduling for Other People

How you use Outlook determines how you can best schedule activities for others on your team. Specifically, if calendar sharing is enabled in Outlook, scheduling is easy. Even if sharing is not enabled, you can use Outlook's meeting request functionality to assist in setting up activities for other people. Outlook is discussed in detail in Chapter 3. Assuming you're not using Outlook, you still have a few options.

Because you can't actually see anyone else's complete schedule using Microsoft CRM, it would be improper to even try to put anything directly on someone else's calendar. You are left with two options when attempting to schedule the activities of others: e-mail requests and instant messaging.

You can use Microsoft CRM's e-mail system to send an activity "suggestion" to one or more users on your team. You can attach the e-mail to the appropriate record and request that the other users schedule that phone call or appointment.

The second method for coordinating your activities with other members of your team is to use one of the instant messaging systems. They're free, which makes them even more appealing. The most common ones are Microsoft's Instant Messenger, Yahoo!, AOL, and ICQ.

Everyone in your user group must use the same instant messaging system.

Several compelling reasons exist for implementing such a system. You can see who is online and available at any given moment. You can coordinate with users who are widely separated geographically. We like the instant part of the equation also. In addition, some instant messaging systems keep a history of your messages. You could, when the conversation is over, cut and paste the message history into the Notes section of the appropriate record.

In a flash, you can ask another user to call a client and get a confirmation that that task is going to happen. This is an ideal way to respond to a client call requesting service or support.

Assigning an Activity to Someone

When you create an activity, you can assign it directly to yourself (by default) or to another user or a queue. Similarly, you can reassign an activity to another user or a queue. When you do reassign an activity, the ownership of that activity doesn't change until the intended user or queue accepts the assignment. Activities may be assigned from anywhere but can be accepted only from the Queues area of the Workplace.

Assigning an activity is our favorite. We love to delegate. To do so, follow these steps:

1. **At the bottom of the navigation pane, click the Workplace button. At the top of the pane, under My Work, click Activities.**

The Activities window appears on the right. Based on your selection in the View field, you see some or all of your scheduled activities.

2. **Select one or more activities that you want to assign to someone else.**

   In Figure 14-4, we've selected two activities.

   You can select one or more activities by highlighting those activities and using either the Shift key (for contiguous activities) or the Ctrl key (for noncontiguous activities).

3. **Click the Assign icon in the Activities toolbar.**

   The Assign to Queue or User dialog box appears to lead you through the sequence of actions to delegate all the activities you highlighted in Step 2.

4. **Click the magnifying glass at the end of the field to see the entire list of users to whom you might assign these activities.**

5. **Select one or more users from the list.**

6. **Click OK.**

   CRM returns to the Activities window.

You can also choose to delete activities, but this is generally a poor choice because you can't undo a deletion. If an activity is being cancelled, you should complete it (see the next section) and include a note that the activity was canceled by the client or by a user.

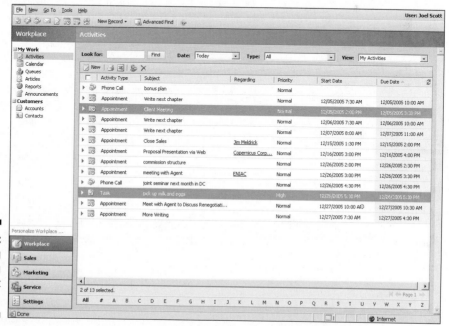

Figure 14-4:
Delegating everything you don't want to do.

Completing an Activity

Nothing is as satisfying as getting things off your activity list. To complete, or close, an activity, follow these steps:

1. **At the bottom of the navigation pane, click the Workplace button. At the top of the pane, under My Work, click Activities.**

   The Activities window appears on the right.

2. **To follow along with the example, select an appointment that you want to mark as completed.**

   The Appointment window appears, with three tabs: Appointment, Notes, and Details.

3. **Click the Notes tab and create a note that will be attached to the record.**

   A typical Notes screen is shown in Figure 14-5. Documenting what you do is important so the historical trail for this record is complete.

4. **Click the Save and Close button.**

We have a saying in our office: "If it's not in CRM, you didn't do it." A rough translation is that unless you enter your activities and close them when you've completed them, there's no evidence that you did anything. Later, you'll be explaining to a skeptical boss that you really did make those follow-up calls but just didn't bother completing them in CRM. Complete every activity immediately afterwards. Then there's no doubt.

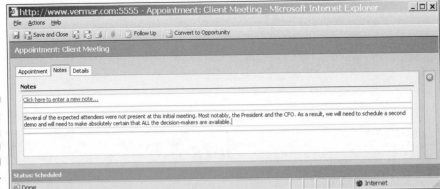

Figure 14-5:
Adding notes when completing an activity.

Chapter 15

Setting Sales Quotas and Generating Forecasts

*T*oward the end of every year, our sales team sits down and develops a plan for the coming year. That plan includes the products we will sell, who will sell those products, and a guideline for how much of each product our account managers will sell (we hope). That guideline translates into a quota in Microsoft CRM.

The quota not only helps us budget for the coming year but also gives us a series of monthly or quarterly milestones. Failure to meet quotas or milestones causes midterm reevaluations or sometimes something worse. Meeting or exceeding our goals is what keeps our company healthy and happy.

In this chapter, you find out how to set quotas for salespeople, how to log forecasted sales against those quotas, and how to adjust these forecasts and quotas as you go along.

How a Manager Sets Up Quotas

Quotas relate to your company's quarterly fiscal periods. Before you can set up a quota for anyone, Microsoft CRM needs to know your company's fiscal periods. Fiscal periods may be set only once, and the task should probably be performed by someone with a title like CFO.

Fiscal year settings

Quotas are usually related to the time period in which accountants measure profits and losses, that is, the fiscal period. Accountants have devised a variety of fiscal years. They can be based on calendar years or can end on other seemingly random dates. A fiscal year can be semiannual or divided into quarters.

You can set the fiscal year options only once. You cannot change these settings after you have set them.

To set a fiscal year, follow these steps:

1. **At the bottom of the navigation pane, click the Settings button.**

   Eleven customization topics appear on the right.

2. **In the Settings window, select Organization Settings.**

   The Organization Settings window appears.

3. **Select Fiscal Year Settings from the list.**

   The Fiscal Year Settings window appears, as shown in Figure 15-1.

4. **Enter the starting date for your fiscal year as well as the periods you use for measuring revenue.**

   The required Template field allows you to specify your fiscal periods. The rest of the fields in this window allow you to specify the naming conventions your company uses and the formatting of the periods.

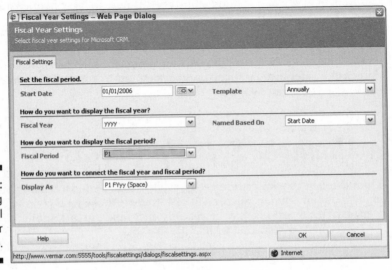

Figure 15-1: Creating your fiscal year information.

You need to enter the fiscal year information carefully and correctly because you get only one shot at it. The system displays a warning message to this effect. You also can't enter sales quotas until you've entered the fiscal year settings.

5. Click OK to save your entries.

Setting up a salesperson's quota

After the fiscal year information is set, you need to establish quotas. Of course, before quotas can be entered into the system, your management team must develop a business plan and sales plan and coordinate the quotas with that plan.

To set up the quota for a user (salesperson), follow these steps:

1. At the bottom of the navigation pane, click the Settings button.

2. In the Settings window, select Business Unit Settings.

This selection brings you to a window with eight topics.

3. Select Users.

A list of all available users of the system appears.

4. Select one or more salespeople.

Although *users* is a more general term than *salespeople,* usually only salespeople have quotas. To select more than one salesperson, hold down the Ctrl key while clicking with the mouse. If a group of salespeople have the same quota, you can set quotas for the group all at once.

5. From the menu bar (at the top of the screen), choose Actions⇨Manage Quotas.

The Manage Quotas dialog box appears, as shown in Figure 15-2.

If you have selected more than one user, you may get a warning message. If this is the case, the new quota you are about to enter will override any existing quota. If that was not your intention, you can cancel the operation; you return to the list of users (Step 3), where you can make another selection.

6. On the right side of the window, fill in each period's quota.

These quotas will apply to every salesperson you selected in Step 4. However, nothing happens until you click the Apply button.

7. Click the Apply button at the bottom of the dialog box.

Your quotas are saved. This is an important step. If you click OK without applying your changes, nothing is saved.

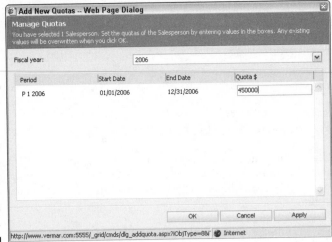

Figure 15-2:
Entering
a sales-
person's
quota.

8. **Click the OK button at the bottom of the dialog box.**

   You return to the Quota window.

9. **If you want to enter a quota for another salesperson, repeat Steps 4 through 8.**

Entering Sales Forecasts

Anyone who's been in sales for more than a day has wrestled with sales forecasting in some fashion. This wrestling match may have been with some formal system or may have been a manager demanding to know when that big deal is going to finally go down. Without reasonably accurate sales forecasts, it is difficult for management to steer the boat.

Forecasts in Microsoft CRM are part of the Opportunities section of the program (in the Sales module). The words *forecast* and *opportunity* are nearly synonymous in this system.

To enter a new opportunity, follow these steps:

1. **At the bottom of the navigation pane, click the Sales button. At the top of the pane, select Opportunities.**

   The Opportunities window appears on the right, as shown in Figure 15-3.

2. **In the Opportunities window's toolbar, click the New button.**

   The Opportunity: New window appears, as shown in Figure 15-4. On the General tab, the Topic and Potential Customer fields are both required fields.

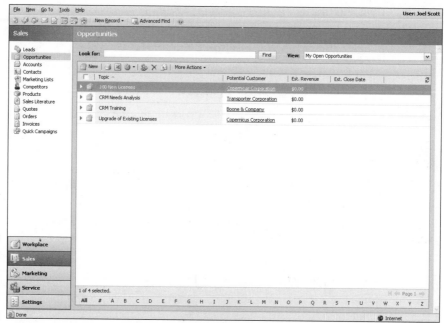

Figure 15-3:
The Opportunities window.

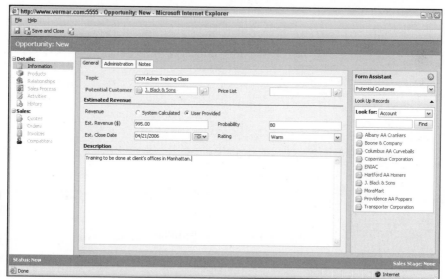

Figure 15-4:
Entering a new opportunity.

3. In the Topic field, enter a general description of the product or service you're selling.

For example, you might type Residential Swimming Pool Installation or Client Retention Consulting Engagement.

4. Fill in the Potential Customer field as follows:

a. Click the magnifying glass to the right of the Potential Customer field so you can link the opportunity.

Every opportunity should be linked to an account or a contact.

b. In the Look For field, select Account or Contact.

To follow along with the example, select Account.

A customer can be either an account (a business) or a contact (a person).

c. Enter a portion of the potential customer's name and then click Find to locate the specific account or customer to which you are linking this opportunity.

(We discuss the Find function in detail in Chapter 2.) The Look Up Records dialog box appears, as shown in Figure 15-5.

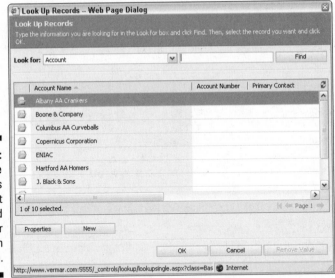

Figure 15-5: The accounts that correspond to your search criteria.

d. In the Account Name field, select an account.

The General tab of the Opportunity: New window reappears.

5. For the Revenue option, select User Provided.

If price lists have been set up, you may be able to have the system calculate the price of your list of products and services. In this example, we are assuming you don't have price lists that apply, so a manual entry of the price is needed.

6. **In the Est. Revenue field, enter the estimated revenue from this opportunity.**

7. **Fill in the Est. Close date field using the calendar at the end of the field.**

8. **In the Probability field, enter the probability of closing the deal.**

   If your company uses a sales process automated by workflow rules, this field may be autopopulated.

9. **If you want, make a selection in the Rating drop-down list.**

   You can rate the deal Hot, Warm, or Cold, but the Probability field covers this.

10. **In the Description field, add any comments.**

   You might notice that a Notes tab is associated with this new opportunity. There is no rule for using the Description field versus the Notes tab. However, for complex sales that take a long time to close or involve a team of people, we use the Notes tab so that each note can be time stamped and date stamped. For simpler and shorter deals, we use the Description field.

11. **Click the Save and Close button.**

   You return to the Opportunities window.

Updating Your Forecasts

Forecasts have a tendency to get stale quickly. We recommend that you review and revise your forecasts at least once a week. These revisions need to focus not only on the estimated close date but also on every field that may have changed.

To update a forecast, follow these steps:

1. **At the bottom of the navigation pane, click the Sales button. Then at the top of the pane, select Opportunities.**

   The Opportunities window appears on the right. If the opportunity you need to check doesn't appear, check the View menu in the upper-right corner to make sure you're looking at My Open Opportunities or Open Opportunities.

2. **Select the opportunity in question.**

   The detailed information for the opportunity appears, as shown in Figure 15-6.

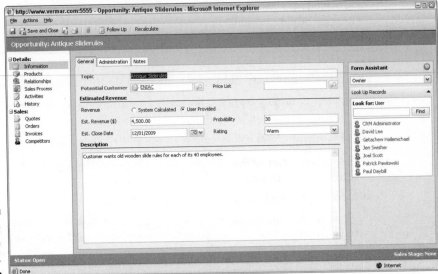

Figure 15-6:
It's all in the
details.

3. **Make your modifications.**

   Although much of the forecast is for your own benefit and is meant to
   keep you on track, the forecast is also probably being reviewed by the
   sales management team. Reasonable and realistic estimates are always
   better than pie-in-the-sky guesses.

4. **Click the Save and Close button.**

   The Opportunities window reappears. From here, you can review or edit
   another opportunity that needs attention.

Examining Your Forecast Data

Microsoft CRM has built-in reports that focus on opportunity management:
opportunity reports and pipeline reports. These can be customized by your
dealer or by a knowledgeable systems administrator. Additional custom
reports can also be added. However, that customization is outside the scope
of this book.

Opportunity reports are typically simple line reports with subtotals or totals.
They can be filtered and sorted by territory, potential revenue, closing probability, salesperson, and many other fields.

Pipeline reports and charts generally involve a little math. If you are a sales manager, you may want to see how much each salesperson is likely to close this quarter. A pipeline report can show this to you, either in tabular or graphic form, by multiplying the potential revenue by the probability.

Printing a report

To select a report for printing or saving, follow these steps:

1. **At the bottom of the navigation pane, click the Sales button. Then, at the top of the pane, select Opportunities.**

   The Opportunities window appears.

2. **In the View drop-down list, select the opportunities you want to report on.**

   For example, choose My Open Opportunities if you want to see only your own deals, or choose Open Opportunities if you want a more company-wide report (assuming you have the rights to see these).

3. **In the window's toolbar, click the Reports button.**

   The system displays a list of all available reports. Our copy of the software lists just two reports: Competitor Win Loss and Lead Source Effectiveness.

4. **Select a report from the list.**

   After the system processes all the data, the reports appears on your screen.

5. **Print or save the report.**

Using Excel

You can export your forecast data directly to a local copy of Excel on your own computer. Then, if you have even a little facility with Excel you can manipulate the data and look at it in a tabular or in a graphical presentation. (If you need help with Excel, get a copy of *Excel 2003 For Dummies*.)

To export your forecast data to Excel, follow these steps:

1. **At the bottom of the navigation pane, click the Sales button. At the top of the pane, select Opportunities.**

   The Opportunities window appears.

2. **In the View drop-down list, select the types of opportunities you want in your Excel export.**

3. **In the window's toolbar, click the Excel icon.**

   A screen appears with several worksheet choices.

4. **For the simplest kind of export, select the first option, and then click Export.**

   CRM loads your data into a local copy of Excel. You can then calculate totals, add columns with calculated values, or even create graphs.

5. **For more sophisticated dynamic Excel tables, select the second or third choice.**

   Dynamic worksheets automatically update their data as you change the data in another application.

Sales forecasting is one of the most critical aspects of the sales process at our company. It allows each salesperson to track his or her progress, and the information in the combined sales forecasts gives management a view of coming attractions. Most importantly, this same information allows workflow rules to ensure that no sale falls through the cracks.

Chapter 16

Using E-Mail

*F*ifteen years ago, believe it or not, the world operated without e-mail (no, it wasn't the Bronze Age). Our office manager twitches when she remembers the good ol' days (but it could be the caffeine). Try and run your business without e-mail today and you probably wouldn't get very far. E-mail is now an essential part of your relations with your customers or, rather, your CRM.

With e-mail becoming such a large part of your contact with customers, the concern arises about documentation. With no paper trail, you have no leverage when and if you need it. On the not-so-dramatic side, it's just good business practice to keep track of everything between you and your customers. In Microsoft CRM, you can do this by linking, or associating, e-mails with your clients, so that Mrs. Reynolds's e-mail thanking the Toaster Man for all his wonderful help gets put in her record and not on the record of, say, Acme Credit Collections. No one would be able to find it! Any good CRM application, Microsoft CRM included, allows you and your staff to link e-mails to accounts and activities.

You send two basic types of e-mail messages: one to individuals (such as the Toaster Guy thanking Mrs. Reynolds for those brownies) and one to groups of people. Some call the latter an e-mail blast, others call it a marketing campaign or mass mailing, and yet others call it spam. The legality issues of lunchmeat aside, Microsoft CRM calls it *direct e-mail*. With direct e-mail, you can send an e-mail to a group of contacts. And although these mailings can go to hundreds of people, each recipient receives an individualized e-mail message with no hint that he or she was included in a larger group. We'll cover direct e-mail later in this chapter.

For right now, we'll stick with plain ol' e-mail and show you how to send and receive e-mails and link them to contacts and activities using the Microsoft CRM interface. (For information on working with e-mail offline using Outlook, see Chapter 3.)

Microsoft CRM also lets you do the following:

✔ Create and preview e-mail messages from within other activities, such as an account or a case.

✔ Link e-mail messages to activities, contacts, or accounts.

✔ Receive and reply to e-mail messages.

✔ Create and use personal and public e-mail templates.

✔ Receive your e-mail in the Microsoft Office Outlook mailbox or in Microsoft CRM as an e-mail activity. Note that if you receive all your e-mail as a Microsoft CRM e-mail activity, the e-mail can be accessed by anyone who can open your activities.

Setting Up Your E-Mail Options

The first thing you'll need to do to get your e-mail working is to set up your e-mail options. Microsoft CRM logs incoming and outgoing e-mail messages as records. Each e-mail record contains the content of the message as well as associations with other records in CRM, such as accounts, contacts, cases, and opportunities.

Converting an e-mail message to a record can occur only if one of two conditions exists:

✔ The Microsoft CRM Exchange Connector recognizes the e-mail as a reply to an e-mail that was originally sent from Microsoft CRM.

✔ You define a personal option to convert *all* incoming e-mail messages to CRM records.

Here's how you set those personal options:

1. **On the menu bar (at the top of the screen), choose Tools⇨Options.**

   The Set Personal Options dialog box appears, as shown in Figure 16-1. (You can set all your personal options in this dialog box. For more on these other options, see Chapter 4.)

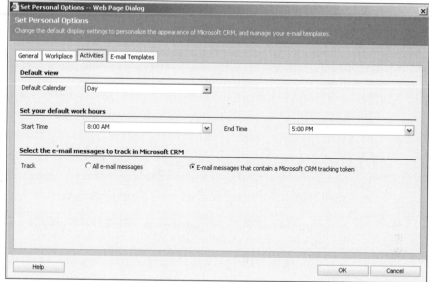

Figure 16-1:
The Set
Personal
Options
dialog box
open to the
Activities
tab.

2. **Click the Activities tab.**

   On this tab, you have three areas, but we are concerned only with the last area.

3. **Make a selection in the Select the e-mail messages to track in Microsoft CRM area.**

   If you select All e-mail messages, all e-mail messages are linked to Microsoft CRM records. If you select E-mail messages that contain a Microsoft CRM tracking token, only those messages that are replies to messages that you have sent (sometimes called a thread) are linked to Microsoft CRM records. Regardless of which option you select, the linked records become activity records that are seen as history in Microsoft CRM.

4. **Click OK to close the dialog box.**

   Your changes are saved automatically.

Out of the box, Microsoft CRM e-mail supports only Microsoft Exchange Server e-mail. Your administrator or implementation partner must link Microsoft CRM and Microsoft Exchange Server using the Microsoft CRM-Exchange Server Connector. If you do not have that installed, no e-mail is linked to CRM. So if you want e-mail in Microsoft CRM, make sure that this piece gets installed on your system.

Viewing E-Mail

Now that you've set up your e-mail preference, go get your coffee because it's time to get to work. There are two basic types of e-mail that you'll be dealing with. Your personal e-mail (meaning mail coming directly to you) in the Activities window and e-mails associated with queues, which can be found in the Queues window.

Viewing your personal e-mail

First, we'll look at your personal e-mail. Follow these steps:

1. **At the bottom of the navigation pane, click the Workplace button. At the top of the pane, select Activities.**

   This view shows all your activities, including e-mails, as shown in Figure 16-2.

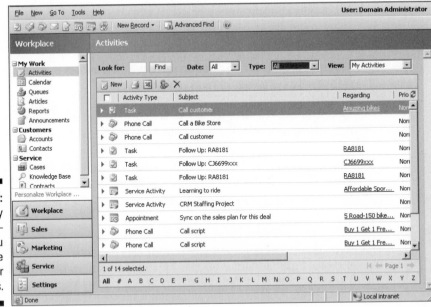

Figure 16-2:
Activity
central —
where you
can manage
your
activities.

2. **In the Type field, click the arrow to open the drop-down list, and select E-mail.**

   Now you've weeded out all activities except your e-mail.

3. **In the View field, click the arrow to open the drop-down list and make your selection.**

   You have yet more options here: All E-mails; My Draft E-mails (draft e-mails are those that you've created but not yet sent); My Received E-mails; or My Sent E-mails. You can choose any of these, depending on what you want.

Use the Look For and Date fields to further narrow the list of displayed activities.

Viewing queue e-mail

As we mentioned, queue e-mail is the other type of e-mail you can view. An example of queue e-mail is e-mail that arrives through your Web site. You know those forms where a visitor fills out some information, types a message, and clicks Submit? The Web site generates an e-mail that comes straight into the designated queue. Another example is the e-mail that goes to a generic e-mail address, such as sales@acme.com. All e-mail to that address goes into a queue and is assigned from that queue to the customer service staff.

To see all e-mails associated with queues, follow these steps:

1. **At the bottom of the navigation pane, click the Workplace button. At the top of the pane, select Queues.**

   The Queues window appears, as shown in Figure 16-3. The window has its own navigation pane, which contains two main folders to hold your work: My Work and Queues.

2. **In the Queue workspace, double-click an e-mail to open it.**

My Work (Assigned and In Progress) shows everything (e-mails included) assigned to you and stuff that you're working on. The Queues area displays a folder for each queue your username is assigned to. Chapter 26 covers managing and creating queues. Each folder under Queues holds e-mails (and other activities) assigned to that.

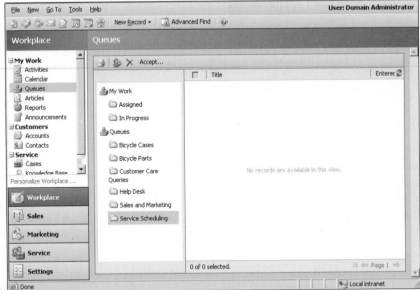

Figure 16-3:
Take a look
at your work
and all the
queues to
which you
are
assigned.

Creating Outgoing E-Mail

Alrighty, now that you can find and view your e-mail, it's time to create an
e-mail, maybe thanking Mrs. Reynolds for those brownies she sent. Microsoft
CRM has creating e-mail down to a science and that's a good thing, especially
for those who process a hundred e-mails or more a day (don't laugh, it
happens).

Microsoft CRM defines e-mail as an activity, just like a task, a call, or an
appointment.

Here's how you create an e-mail message:

1. **From the menu bar (at the top of the screen), choose New⇨New
    Activity⇨E-mail. Or click the Create New E-mail icon below the
    menu bar.**

    The E-mail: New window appears, as shown in Figure 16-4. You can start
    a new e-mail from anywhere inside the program. Lots of fields are avail-
    able, but only the Owner is required.

2. **Select a recipient of your e-mail as follows:**

    a. **Click the magnifying glass icon to the right of the To field.**

        The Look Up Records dialog box appears, and you can look for
        accounts, contacts, leads, queues, or users. Your search results
        appear to the left, under Available Records.

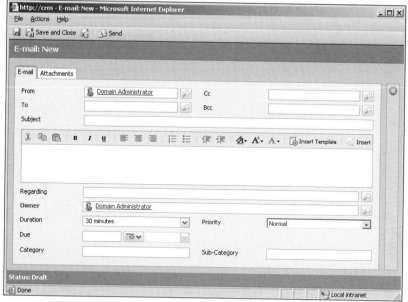

Figure 16-4:
This is
where you
address and
compose
your
messages.

b. Highlight the record you want.

You may select multiple names or names from a combination of lists by pressing the Ctrl key as you highlight each name.

c. Click the >> button to move the recipient(s) to the Selected Records pane.

d. Click OK to close this window and return to your e-mail.

If you add several recipients, each one will be able to see all the names. You can use the BCC function if you want to blind-copy recipients on this e-mail or use Microsoft CRM's direct e-mail feature (as described later). You can also choose to CC someone (such as when you're sending an e-mail to a client and want your boss to see the e-mail too).

CC means carbon copy; all recipients see the names on the e-mail. BCC means blind carbon copy; recipients will not see the names or addresses on the e-mail.

3. Enter a subject.

The Subject field is free-form, so you can type anything here. Whatever you type in the Subject field replaces the word *New* at the top of your E-mail: New window. Keep in mind that sending an e-mail with no subject is usually considered bad e-mail etiquette. It also increases the chances that your e-mail will be considered spam and will be filtered out by the recipient's spam filter.

4. **In the open text box below Subject, type your message.**

You have typical formatting options — cut, copy, paste, alignment, specify fonts, sizes, styles, colors, indents, bullets, numbering, and the like. You can also insert templates or knowledge base articles. (Knowledge base articles are covered in Chapter 9. Templates are covered later in this chapter.)

5. **To associate, or link, the message to a record, do the following:**

   a. **Click the magnifying glass icon to the right of the Regarding field.**

   The Look Up records dialog box appears.

   b. **Search for your contact, and then click to highlight it.**

   c. **Click OK.**

6. **Add other options as desired.**

The remaining optional fields are Duration, Priority, Due, Category, and Sub-Category. Duration and Priority use drop-down boxes. The Due field offers you a calendar, but you can also enter the date free-form. Category and Sub-Category are also free-form fields.

7. **To add an attachment to your e-mail:**

   a. **First click Save (the disk icon).**

   b. **Click the Attachments tab.**

   c. **Follow the directions in the next section.**

   We cover attachments next, in "Adding attachments to e-mail messages."

8. **To send your message, click the Send button (next to Save and Close).**

   Voila, the e-mail is on its way.

To find a record of your e-mail, go to the account (or record) to which the message was associated and select History in the navigation pane. E-mails displayed there have a status of Sent.

Saving an e-mail message doesn't send it. Instead, the e-mail is assigned a Draft status. To view and edit the message, click the Draft E-Mail folder under Activities in the Workplace tab, and then click the e-mail you want to review.

Adding attachments to e-mail messages

Just like in Microsoft Outlook, in Microsoft CRM you can attach pretty much anything to an e-mail. Here's how you add that attachment:

1. **With your e-mail message appearing in the E-mail: New window, click the Save icon (if you haven't done so already).**

2. **Click the Attachments tab (see Figure 16-5).**

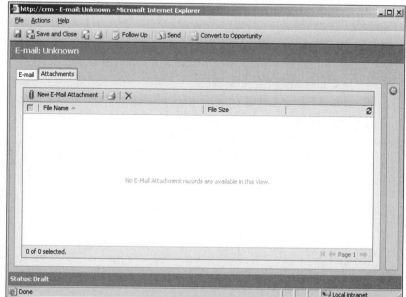

Figure 16-5:
Here's where you add attachments.

3. **In the window's toolbar, click the New E-Mail Attachment button.**

   The Add Attachment dialog box appears, as shown in Figure 16-6.

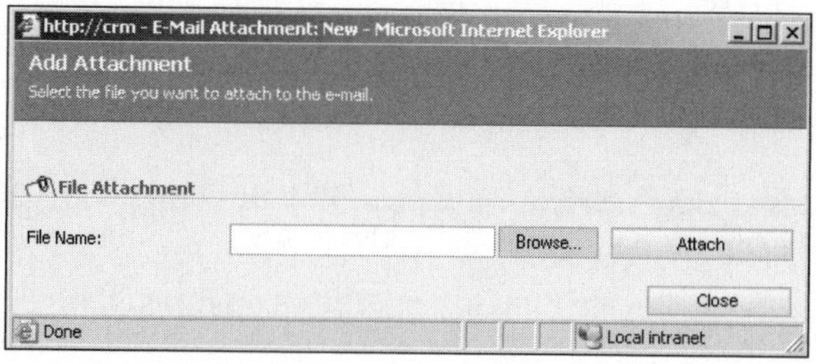

Figure 16-6:
Search for and attach files from this window.

4. **Click the Browse button to search for the file you want to attach.**

   A standard Microsoft window appears, so you can browse to the location of your document.

5. **After you've found your document, click OK.**

   You return to the Add Attachment dialog box, and the document path is now in the field to the left of the Browse button.

6. **Click the Attach button.**

   The text in the Add Attachment dialog box changes to the document path in the File Name field. A Remove button appears, replacing the Browse and Attach buttons.

7. **Click Close to add the attachment to the message.**

   The Add Attachment dialog box closes and you're returned to the Attachments tab of your new e-mail. If you want to add more attachments, repeat Step 3–5.

    If you want to delete an attachment from the e-mail (you had too much caffeine and got carried away with that Control-select function), just highlight the document and click the X next to the printer icon.

8. **Click Save (the disk icon).**

   After you click Save, the e-mail (with the attachment) is saved as a draft in the My Draft E-Mails view in the Activities window.

9. **You can either send the e-mail by clicking Send or continue working on the message by clicking the E-mail tab.**

Viewing your sent e-mail

Let's go back to that e-mail you sent Mrs. Reynolds, thanking her for the brownies. Maybe you attached a coupon to the e-mail, and you want to make sure you attached the right one. Reading your sent e-mail is simple. Just remember that sent e-mail can't be edited, except to change the owner of the e-mail, but it can be replied to or forwarded.

That said, here's how you would check out a sent e-mail:

1. **At the bottom of the navigation pane, click the Workplace button. Then, at the top of the pane, select Activities.**

2. **In the Type field, choose E-mail from the drop-down list.**

   This narrows the activities in your workspace to your e-mail.

3. **In the View field, choose My Sent E-mails from the drop-down list.**

   All your e-mails are weeded out, except the sent ones. You can see e-mails sent to clients in other ways to, but we find that this method is the simplest.

You can click at the top of any column to reorganize your sent e-mail, and you can also search by date and by the Find field.

4. **After you've found the sent e-mail you want to view, double-click it to open it.**

   The e-mail dialog box appears. In the bottom-left corner of the window, the status is Sent. The only field that you can edit in this window is the owner. All the other fields are either unclickable or the magnifying glass is dimmed.

To forward a message, make sure the e-mail message appears on the screen. Then, in the menu bar, click Forward. Note that the Forward option is available only after the e-mail window is open.

You can also go to the history of the account or contact to whom you sent the e-mail to view it and forward it, if necessary. That account's or contact's completed activities are listed, and you can search for them by using the Filter On options or by clicking the label of a column to sort by that column.

Assigning and Accepting E-Mail

As you know by now, e-mail is one of the most popular forms of communication. In Microsoft CRM, you can assign and forward e-mails. You can also easily accept e-mail. As mentioned earlier in the chapter, you can work on two basic types of e-mail: your personal e-mail and e-mail in the queues. In this section, we look at both types.

Assigning e-mail

So, let's go to Mr. Wayne and his Cobweb Catchers business. He uses your Heavy-Duty Super-Sucker X1138 model vacuum, and it's making a funny noise (kind of a WANG! thwip-boop). He's e-mailed you because you're his sales rep (and therefore omnipotent).

You have no clue what's causing that noise, but you do know that your troubleshooting team will be able to help. So you assign his e-mail to the troubleshooting queue. That way, the right people can give Mr. Wayne the right answers. (For more on creating and managing queues, see Chapter 26.)

To assign an e-mail to a queue, follow these steps:

1. **With the customer's e-mail open, choose Actions⇨Assign from the menu bar (at the top of the window).**

   The Assign to Queue or User dialog box appears.

2. **Under Assign to a User or Queue, click the magnifying glass to the right of the field.**

    The Look Up records dialog box appears.

3. **Find the record you want as follows:**

    a. **In the Look for field, choose Queue or User.**

    b. **Either navigate to the record using the arrows at the bottom or type your selection in the field next to Find and then click Find.**

    c. **When you've found the record you want, highlight it.**

    d. **Click OK.**

    You're back at the Assign to a Queue or User dialog box. The field now contains your queue.

4. **Click OK in the Assign to a Queue or User dialog box.**

    You return to the customer's e-mail.

5. **Click Save and Close to assign the e-mail and save your changes.**

    The e-mail is assigned to that queue. However, it isn't removed from your activities list unless you reassign the owner.

Accepting e-mail

If you assign an e-mail to a queue (or user), it follows naturally that someone will have to accept it, so let's take a walk over to your service department. Susie is your company's Heavy-Duty Super-Sucker X1138 expert, and she's spotted Mr. Wayne's e-mail in the queue she works with (the queue you assigned it to). Or say you really appreciate Mr. Wayne's business and want the best expert to handle his vacuum problem; because Susie's your expert, you've asked her to look at the e-mail personally.

Here's how you would go to that e-mail and accept it into your workload:

1. **At the bottom of the main navigation pane, click the Workplace button. Then, at the top of the pane, select Queues.**

    The Queues window appears.

2. **Double-click the appropriate queue to open it.**

    Keep in mind that the Queues window shows In Progress and Assigned, plus the queues of which this technician or user is a part.

3. **Click the e-mail message you assigned to this queue to highlight it.**

    You can select multiple e-mail messages by holding the Ctrl key and clicking.

4. **In the window's toolbar, click the Accept button.**

   The Confirm Assignment dialog box appears, asking for confirmation.

5. **Click OK.**

   After the e-mails are assigned, the Confirm Assignment dialog box closes and the queue is displayed again. The accepted e-mail is now in the In Progress folder.

You can follow these steps also to accept e-mail in a user's Assigned folder under My Work.

If your assignments and acceptances of e-mail don't show up in the workspace right away, click the green arrows in the upper-right corner of the workspace. This will refresh the workspace with the updated information.

Duplicate E-Mail Addresses

Microsoft CRM does not have duplicate e-mail checking, so you can enter the same e-mail address in, say, both a contact and an account. When you send an e-mail, the e-mail will not automatically link to both the contact and account, despite the fact that they both have the same e-mail address.

For example, suppose you have Mr. Wayne as a contact and his Cobweb Catchers business as an account, with the same e-mail address assigned to both records. You can see the conundrum: When you send an e-mail, whose history does it go under? Normally, it would default to the contact record's history. However, can you imagine trying to find the e-mail if you didn't know the name of the contact to which the e-mail was sent? You'd have to search contacts *and* accounts.

Too much? Yes, we agree. You'll be happy to know that this issue can be easily solved. All you have to do is go to the Regarding field and select an account (or contact or whatever).

When the account (or contact) is in the Regarding field, you can view the sent e-mail in the History tabs of *both* the contact (Mr. Wayne) and the account (Cobweb Catchers). Now it doesn't matter whether you look under contacts or accounts; the e-mail is in both places. This also ties in nicely with the next section. (Subtle segue, isn't it?)

Relating E-Mails to Other Records

So far, you've seen how an e-mail message may be related, or associated, with an account or a contact. But did you know that you can relate that e-mail to other things, such as a contract or a quote? Here's the full list of activities and records (along with their chapter references) that you can relate to an e-mail:

- Accounts (Chapter 13)
- Campaign activities (Chapter 22)
- Cases (Chapter 23)
- Contacts (Chapter 13)
- Contracts (Chapter 27)
- Invoices (Chapter 18)
- Leads (Chapter 17)
- Opportunities (Chapter 17)
- Orders (Chapter 18)
- Quick campaigns (Chapter 22)
- Quotes (Chapter 18)

Linking an e-mail to a record is just like correcting the problem of duplicate e-mails mentioned in the preceding section. But we'll go over the steps again here:

1. **On the menu bar (at the top of the screen), choose New⇨New Activity⇨E-mail.**

   The E-mail: New window appears. You can also link a received e-mail or your own draft e-mail.

2. **Fill in all the appropriate fields (To, Subject, and the like).**

   For details, refer to the "Creating Outgoing E-Mail" section, earlier in the chapter.

3. **To the right of the Regarding field, click the magnifying glass icon.**

   The Look Up Records dialog box appears.

4. **Click the drop-down arrow to the right of the Look For field and select one of the 12 record types in the list.**

   All available records of that type appear.

5. **Double-click the appropriate record.**

   The Look Up Records dialog box closes, and your selection appears in the Regarding field of the E-mail: New window.

Direct E-Mail

Every day, when I check my e-mail, I find that roughly 30 percent is legitimate e-mails from business associates or friends, updating me on projects, current events, and so on. The other 70 percent, unfortunately, is crrrrrrap! I do not need to refinance my mortgage, find a date, aid dethroned despots in laundering their 10 million dollars, or protect my computer from e-mail spamming. (For one, that's why IT guys were invented. And two, spam against spam?!?) Heck, our office manager gets spam in foreign languages. How crazy is that?

Now, I'm going to make an educated guess and say that you're in the same boat. The promise of easy, efficient, and inexpensive mass communication has caused a feeding frenzy among a new breed of marketers. The spam's the bait, and we're the suckers! At its worst, e-mail marketing has turned into an irritating, insulting inconvenience, imposing itself right into the heart of our workday.

E-mail marketing or spam?

The world of e-mail marketing is a bit like the days of the Old West; there was a code, there was honor . . . okay, so maybe e-mail marketing isn't like the Old West. What I'm trying to say is that there is a fine line (or a wide gray area) about the rules. More than a few scoundrels are giving e-mail marketing and the people who conduct it a bad name. That said, they should not be allowed to ruin the landscape for legitimate e-mail marketers. We recommend that you consider a few things when you're ready to do direct e-mail (a.k.a. e-mail marketing).

✔ **Offer an opt-out:** Whenever you send an e-mail campaign (commonly referred to as a *blast*), the body of the message should include boilerplate text, usually at the bottom, telling the recipient how he or she came to be included in the mailing and offering the recipient the option to be removed from your mailing list.

✔ **Update a field:** Make sure that you process all opt-out requests immediately by updating the Contact Methods information. On a contact record, click the Administration tab and, under Contact Methods, check the box for E-Mail: Do Not Allow. The same process works for accounts. See Chapter 13 for more information on adding and defining new contacts and accounts.

✔ **Be ready for bounces:** Any client we've worked with is surprised at how many e-mail messages *bounce* (come back as undeliverable). So having a plan in place to clean up these addresses is a good idea. The tough part is that the plan usually requires a manual process of locating the records associated with the bounced e-mails and contacting the accounts to update their e-mail information.

With some planning and a little perseverance, you can take advantage of this efficient and highly cost-effective method of e-mail marketing.

On the other hand, we shouldn't walk away from the potential to responsibly market our products and services. If you follow a few basic rules and stick to them, you have every right to take part in the wild world that is e-marketing. Microsoft CRM has the ability to conduct mass e-mailings of messages to your recipient lists.

Creating an e-mail template

Let's touch briefly on templates. Basically, a template is an instrument of communication (in this instance) where almost everything is done for you. All that's left to do is fill in the blanks.

With Microsoft CRM, you can define templates to your specifications or you can use a predesigned template. Why would you want a template, you ask? For a number of reasons, if only to prevent retyping information over and over again. Templates are a great tool for letters and e-mail, especially if you have a product or service for which people are constantly requesting information. Make a template, pull it up to attach it to the e-mail when you're ready, fill in the blanks, and you're ready to shoot it out to whoever asks for it.

In this section, you find out how to create an e-mail template and then merge the template with a list of recipients:

1. **At the bottom of the navigation pane, click the Settings button.**

2. **Click Templates.**

3. **Click E-mail Templates.**

   The E-Mail Templates window appears, as shown in Figure 16-7.

4. **In the window's toolbar, click the New button.**

   The E-mail Template Type dialog box appears.

5. **In the drop-down box for Template Type, make a selection.**

   Keep in mind that the template you're creating here can be used only with the selection you choose in this step. Basically, if you assign the template type Leads, you would be able to send it only to customers marked as leads.

6. **Click OK.**

   The Template Type dialog box closes and the E-mail Template: New window appears, as shown in Figure 16-8. The three required fields are Type (which is filled out based on what you chose in Step 5), Title, and Subject.

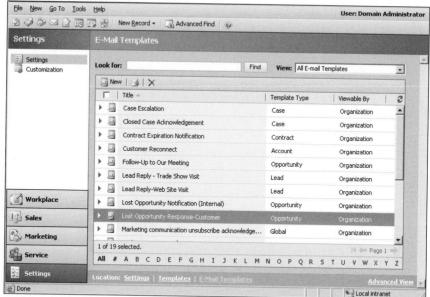

Figure 16-7:
All kinds of e-mail templates are found here.

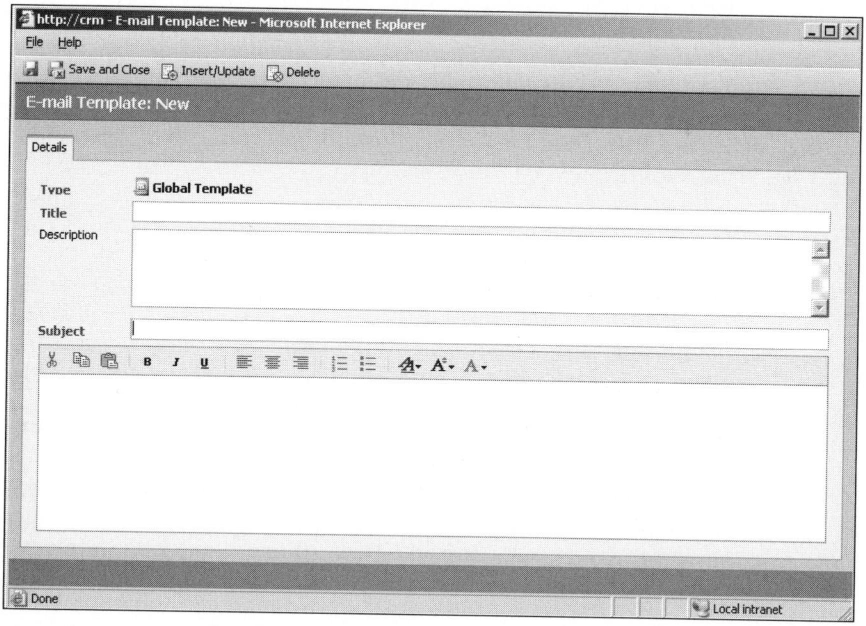

Figure 16-8:
The second step in creating an e-mail template.

7. **Enter a title.**

   The title describes or names the template (for example, Summer Deal Buster Template) and is used only for your company's internal purposes. That is, the title is visible only within Microsoft CRM and is not seen in the e-mail body or by the recipient.

8. **Enter a description for this e-mail template.**

   You might find it useful to include the purpose of the template or who made it.

9. **Enter your subject for the e-mail template.**

   The subject is for the e-mail body itself (for example, Now That Summer's Here, Do You Have Your Wake-n-Bake Breakfast-A-Go-Go Kit?). This is the line your customers will see in their Inbox.

10. **Click Save (the disk icon) in the upper-left corner of the window.**

    Use the Save icon, not the Save and Close button, to leave this e-mail template open. We're going to work on the body in the next section.

Adding data fields to a template

Body, body, body. Do you ever notice it's easier to work on the body of a document than it is on your own body? Of course, to some, creating an e-mail template might be like running a marathon. Keep this in mind: The body of your e-mail template is pretty much a blank slate, for you to customize as you want with text, italics, color, and more.

One of the cool things that Microsoft CRM lets you do with its e-mail templates is to add data fields that pull information from contacts and accounts, such as names and addresses. For example, you're sending one thousand e-mails regarding the Wake-n-Bake Set. If you define what information to pull from the contact records, each person will see an e-mail personalized with his or her name. In other words, you can create an e-mail template that has the full name of the contact as its first line. In fact, full name is a data field we use all the time.

Here's how you create those data fields and add the information:

1. **Insert your cursor into the body of the e-mail template you created in the last section, and click the Insert/Update button on the toolbar.**

   The Data Field Values dialog box appears, as shown in Figure 16-9.

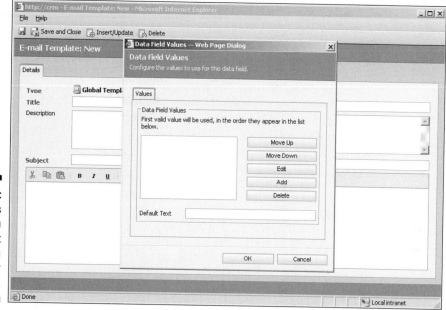

Figure 16-9:
This is
where you
start
defining
your
parameters.

2. Click the Add button.

The Add Data Value dialog box appears, as shown in Figure 16-10. This is
where you tell the template which data fields to pull from the records.

Figure 16-10:
The Add
Data Value
dialog box.

3. In the Record Type field, choose an option from the drop-down menu.

4. In the Field list, select the field from which you want the program to pull information.

5. Click OK.

Note that the data field you just chose has been added to your template,
but the Data Field Values dialog box remains open.

6. **To add additional fields, repeat Steps 2–5.**

   It's important to know that if you want multiple data fields to appear on your template, you must add each data field individually. If, for example, you want to add fields to the Template for the Microsoft CRM User's first name and last name, you must add each one separately — once to create a data field for the first name, and again to create a data field for the last name. If you add multiple fields to the Data Field Values dialog box at one time before clicking OK, Microsoft CRM automatically adds a semicolon between each data field in the Template, treating it as an *either/or.*

   So, in the example of first and last name, Microsoft CRM looks for a first name and, if it finds one, displays it. If no first name is available, Microsoft CRM looks for a last name and displays it. Microsoft CRM will not display both first name and last name. With a little bit of practice, you find out how intuitive this can be. An e-mail template can be all things to all contacts, even if the data isn't consistent from one record to the next. Thoughtful construction of the template results in the template's ability to look for data in a secondary field if the primary data field is empty.

   You can add dozens of data fields to an e-mail template. The Add Data Value dialog box offers fields associated with the following record types: user, account, contact, and opportunity.

7. **Click OK to close the Data Field Values dialog box.**

   The dialog box closes, and you can see all the data fields added to the body of your e-mail template. The data fields are highlighted in yellow, surrounded by exclamation points and semicolons, and separated by brackets.

8. **Click the Save and Close icon on your E-mail screen.**

   The E-mail Template dialog box closes, and your template is saved. All e-mail templates are visible in the Home: E-mail Templates window. The subject of the template now serves as the template's name.

Reverting to a personal e-mail template

Templates start out as organization-wide, but you can change them to personal e-mail templates. Here's how:

1. **While you're still in the E-mail templates window, open a template.**

2. **In the menu bar (at the top of the screen), choose Actions⇨Revert to Personal.**

3. **Click Save (the disk icon) if you want to do some more work on the template, or click Save and Close to return to the E-mail Templates window.**

Back in the E-mail Templates window, you'll see that the Viewable By column now says Individual for the template you converted.

4. **To change the template back to where it can be viewed by the entire organization, choose Actions⇨Make Template Available to Organization.**

5. **Click Save (the disk icon) to continue working on the e-mail, or click Save and Close.**

When you return to the E-mail Templates window, you'll see that it now says Organization under the Viewable By column.

Sending direct e-mail

Now that you know how to create templates, it's time to send out the first wave of your marketing campaign. Here's how:

1. **At the bottom of the navigation pane, click the Sales button. At the top of the pane, select Accounts.**

   You can also choose Service or Marketing in the navigation pane. You can access the direct e-mail function also through the contacts listed under each option.

2. **Click the account to which you want to send the e-mail.**

3. **Click the Send Direct E-mail icon in the toolbar at the top of the list of accounts.**

   The Send Direct E-Mail dialog box appears, as shown in Figure 16-11.

4. **Select a template from the top pane.**

   All templates are designated as Global or Account Templates. Note that when you highlight a template, its description appears on the right.

5. **Choose a direct e-mail option from the following:**

   - **Selected records on current page:** The template will be sent to all the accounts you had checked in the main display. You can select multiple accounts by holding down the Ctrl key while clicking each account.

   - **All records on current page:** The template will be sent to all accounts currently listed in the main display.

   - **All records on all pages:** The template will be sent to all accounts included in the selection in the View field in the upper-right corner of the Send Direct E-Mail dialog box. For example, if the View is My Active Accounts and there were enough such accounts to fill three pages of the main display, this option would send the template to the accounts on all three pages.

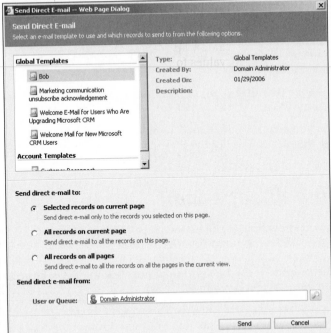

Figure 16-11:
Get to work
and send
direct
e-mail.

6. **Choose the user or queue sending the direct e-mail.**

   Use the magnifying glass to the right of the field to display the Look Up Records dialog box, and then choose the user or queue.

7. **Click the Send button.**

   The e-mail template is personalized to each selected account and sent.

Using Advanced Find to send direct e-mail

Suppose that you want to send direct e-mail to your clients in New York and New Jersey. You can use Advanced Find to filter all your records for everyone in those two states. Follow these steps to do just that:

1. **At the bottom of the navigation pane, click the Sales button. Then, at the top of the pane, select Accounts or Contacts.**

   Remember, you can also follow these steps for Service and Marketing. The Sales (or Service or Marketing) window appears with the accounts or contacts you selected.

2. **On the menu bar (at the top of the screen), choose Tools⇨Advanced Find.**

   The Advanced Find window appears, as shown in Figure 16-12. This is where you define the values for your search.

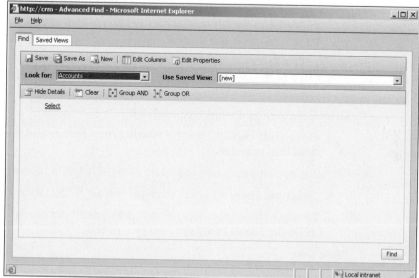

Figure 16-12:
Use
Advanced
Find to set
up your
mailing list.

3. **Click the drop-down arrow to the right of the Look For field and select Accounts.**

   The list has 49 items. Browse through them to see the available options. The options in the Use Saved View field depend on the category you select in the Look For field. Experiment by selecting various options in the Look For field and then seeing your options in the Use Saved View field.

4. **Choose your search criteria.**

   a. **Move your cursor to the word *Select* below the window's toolbar in the Advanced Find window.**

   A field appears with a drop-down menu.

   b. **Click the field to open the drop-down box.**

   c. **Because we want to send our direct e-mail to all our New York and New Jersey clients, select Address1:State/Province from the options provided.**

   This tells Microsoft CRM that the search you're about to conduct will look first in the State/Province field.

Note that after you make the State/Province selection, the word *Equals* appears next to it. To the right of *Equals* is the phrase *Enter Value*. The options in this third lookup file depend on the choices made earlier in Steps 3 and 4.

5. Choose the modifier.

a. Hover your cursor over the word *Equals* to display the field.

This should default to Equals, but always check before continuing. We want Equals in this case, but you also have Does Not Equal, Contains, Does Not Contain, and so on.

b. Click in the field to open the drop-down box, and select the option you need.

6. Enter the value you want to search for.

a. Move your cursor over the words *Enter Value*, and click in the field that appears.

Again, these options depend on choices made in the previous steps.

b. To follow along with the example, enter NY;NJ in the field.

By using the semicolon, you can define multiple possible values for this field. For our example, we've entered: NY;NJ.

7. Click Save.

A window pops up, asking for the title of your search.

8. Enter a name for your search and click OK.

This convenient feature saves your search for future use.

 Click the arrow by the Use Saved View field to see all saved searches. Searches in System Views are available to everyone. Those in My Views (including the one you just saved) are available to you.

9. In the Advanced Find window, click Find (in the lower-right corner) to activate the search.

A new window appears showing you a list of all accounts meeting your search criteria, as shown in Figure 16-13.

Now that you have your search results, here's how to send a direct e-mail to them:

1. Click the Send Direct E-mail icon at the top of the screen.

The Send Direct E-mail dialog box appears (refer to Figure 16-11). Remember, if you want to send your direct e-mail to a selection from the search results, you must hold down the Ctrl key and click each record to select them.

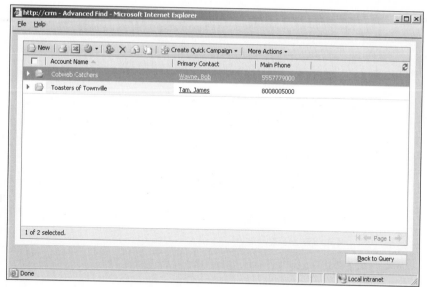

Figure 16-13:
Voila! Your
search
results!

2. **In the Account Templates list, select the template you want to send.**

3. **Choose who you want the e-mail to go to.**

   For details on these options, see Step 5 in the preceding section.

4. **Next, choose the user or queue to send the direct e-mail from.**

   Use the magnifying glass to the right of the field to display the Look Up
   Records dialog box, and then make your selection.

5. **Click the Send button.**

   The Send Direct E-Mail dialog box closes, and you're returned to the
   Advanced Find window. Woo-hoo! Your e-mails have been sent.

You can use Advanced Find to search for records based on the values in sev-
eral fields. For example, you could search for all accounts in New York or New
Jersey (as we just did) that also have an e-mail address ("E-mail Contains
Data"). We recommend that you make this last condition ("E-mail Contains
Data") a standard part of every direct e-mail campaign. After all, it's a little
hard to send e-mail to someone with no e-mail address.

On that note, having the option to search for "E-mail Contains Data" or its
counterpart "Does Not Contain Data" is worth its weight in gold. The resulting list can tell who you should be contacting for e-mail information so that
they can be included in future e-mail merge campaigns.

Managing the unsubscribe request

Suppose you manage a mailing list, and several recipients have decided they don't want to get your informative and witty newsletter. You can have them click an unsubscribe link in the campaign e-mail, which will set their record to no longer receive e-mail marketing material. Then when you create a campaign later, they will not receive e-mail — even if they are a member of the list you selected.

To set this up, follow these steps:

1. **At the bottom of the navigation pane, click Settings. At the top of the pane, click Organization Settings.**

2. **Click System Settings.**

3. **Click the Marketing tab.**

4. **Set the two auto-unsubscribe settings to Yes.**

   If you click Yes on the Subject option, you'll be able to send an e-mail to the folks who are requesting removal to verify their removal.

Note that you can edit the acknowledgment e-mail template in any way you want. Then when you create an e-mail in a campaign, include something like "Click here to no longer receive marketing material" at the bottom of the e-mail. Highlight that text and click the Unsubscribe button in the e-mail's formatting toolbar to change the text to a hyperlink. When the recipients click that link in the e-mail, it changes the Send Marketing Materials field in their records from Yes to No and also sends them the acknowledgment e-mail to let them know they have been removed from the marketing list.

Chapter 17

Handling Leads and Opportunities

In This Chapter

▶ Creating and modifying leads

▶ Changing a lead to an opportunity

▶ Creating, assigning, and sharing opportunities

*I*n CRM-speak, a *suspect* is a person or a company with whom you may do business someday. In all likelihood, your suspect has not yet heard of you. A *prospect* is the next level up. Your prospect has heard of you and may have even expressed some interest in doing business with you. Microsoft CRM refers to both suspects and prospects as *leads.*

An *opportunity* is a lead that has matured enough to deserve serious attention. But before you can begin to turn leads into opportunities, you need to enter your lead data (such as contact information, the source of the lead, and what the prospect is interested in) into CRM.

Actually, a lead can be promoted to either an account record, a contact record, or an opportunity record. The subtle benefit of promoting a lead to an opportunity is that you can forecast a sale associated with an opportunity. Each opportunity is also linked to a price list, which helps determine the pricing in a quote.

And just as you need to create a lead record before developing an opportunity, you need to create an opportunity record before you close your opportunity (whether by winning or losing the deal). You create opportunity records manually by just typing them in, by importing them from outside files (such as Excel), or by converting them from leads.

Workflow rules enable almost complete automation of your selling process, moving opportunities from one sales stage to the next. Workflow is part of the process of handling opportunities and is discussed in some detail in Chapter 8.

In Chapter 18, we discuss what happens when you close an opportunity and turn it into the real deal. In this chapter, we talk about entering leads and moving them through your sales process with the intention of turning them into full-fledged opportunities.

Processing Leads from Suspects to Opportunities

Leads may come to you from many sources. Some of the most common sources are referrals from existing customers, mailing lists you've rented or purchased, inquiries from your Web site, and responses to marketing campaigns.

Leads get into CRM in essentially two ways. You can enter them manually or you can import them, typically from an Excel file. You're probably going to enter leads manually if you have only a few sporadic leads or if you don't have them available in a convenient electronic format. In this section, we discuss getting leads into your CRM system and what to do with them after they're there.

Getting to the Leads window

Everything about leads and opportunities is accessed from the Sales module. And everything about leads starts at the Leads window, which is shown in Figure 17-1. To get to that window, click the Sales button at the bottom of the navigation pane. Then, at the top of the pane, select Leads. That's it.

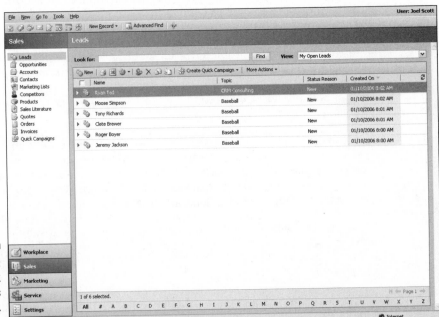

Figure 17-1:
Your work
with leads
starts here.

As you go through the standard Lead windows, you can see about 20 data fields. As with most data entry windows throughout CRM, many more fields than that are available. Those fields have been hard-coded into the database structure but remain invisible unless your system design people make them available. In the case of lead records, for example, 95 fields are available, should you need to track more information about your leads. Your administrator or dealer can add additional fields, if needed.

Creating a lead

Your marketing department's efforts are supposed to create leads. Microsoft CRM thinks of a lead as a potential customer that may or may not have expressed interest in your company's products. For example, the marketing department might purchase a list of potential users. Or various types of advertising might generate inquiries. In any case, the resulting contact information has to get into the CRM database.

Unless you have an electronic list or your CRM system is hooked to your web site, you're probably going to be entering leads the old-fashioned way — by typing. In this section, we discuss the easiest way to manually enter those hard-won leads:

1. **In the Leads window toolbar, click the New button.**

   The Lead: New window appears, as shown in Figure 17-2, with four tabs: General, Details, Administration, and Notes.

2. **Fill in at least the required fields, which are highlighted in red.**

   If the General tab isn't already selected, click it. For the Topic field, enter the product or service that the prospect is interested in.

   The Company field is a required field, so you must enter a company name even if your lead is an individual. When we encounter that situation, we simply enter X as the default company name. If you have the name of an individual or any other relevant contact information, enter that as well.

   Although E-mail and Lead source are not system-required fields (in red), they should be at least business-recommended fields (in blue). The e-mail address is on the General tab, and the Lead source is on the Details tab. Make sure you enter as much information as you can in the General, Details, and Administration tabs.

3. **When you're finished, click the Save and Close button at the top of the screen.**

   The system returns to the Leads window, where you can create another lead, access a lead, or move on to another function.

Aside from the obvious contact information, such as company name, contact person, and phone number, you should focus on collecting data that will enable you to follow up both immediately and over the long term. E-mail addresses and specific product interests are key ingredients to properly following up on a lead and are critical for campaign management and electronic marketing. These two features, both of which are new to Version 3.0, are covered in Chapters 21 and 22.

Modifying a lead

You can modify a lead by navigating to the Leads window and clicking the lead. Then make necessary changes in the various tabs of the lead's record. Remember to click Save and Close before leaving the record.

If the lead you're interested in isn't displayed in the list, check the View menu in the upper-right corner. This menu contains several options in its drop-down list that expand or contract the number of listings displayed, as shown in Figure 17-3. For example, if you're looking for a lead that has not been assigned to you, try selecting All Leads from the View drop-down list.

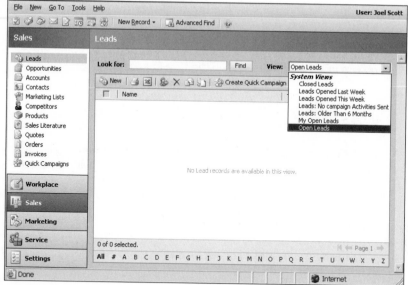

Figure 17-3:
Expanding
the list of
leads.

Your lead may have been converted to an account, a contact, or an opportunity. That's good news, but it means you have to look under those record types for your data. Accounts and contacts are discussed in Chapter 13, and opportunities are described later in this chapter. If your lead has been disqualified, refer to the upcoming "Resurrecting a lead" section.

Giving up on a lead

When you've decided that you have no hope of generating anything worthwhile from a lead, you can *disqualify* it. You do this as follows:

1. **In the Leads window (refer to Figure 17-1), double-click the specific lead you intend to give up on.**

   The General tab for that lead appears.

2. **Click the Convert Lead button.**

   The Convert Lead dialog box appears.

3. **To disqualify the lead, select the Disqualify option.**

   All the choices above the option become dimmed.

4. **Select a reason for the disqualification from the list provided, and then click OK.**

Deleting a lead is possible but not recommended. Deletions are permanent, and deleting a lead also deletes any attachments or notes associated with the lead. A far better approach is to disqualify the lead. That way, an audit trail (using that term loosely) remains if needed. And disqualifying allows you to resurrect the lead later if the situation changes.

Resurrecting a lead

Occasionally you get lucky and a lead that you thought had died comes back to life. If you disqualified the lead, you can bring it back without re-entering all the old information. If you did not heed our advice — see the preceding Warning — and instead deleted the lead, you are out of luck.

To resurrect a lead, perform the following steps:

1. **In the upper-right corner of the Leads window, change the View selection to Closed Leads.**

   The lead you previously disqualified should appear somewhere in the list.

2. **In the list, select the lead in question by double-clicking it.**

   The record for that lead appears.

3. **On the menu bar at the top of the screen, choose Actions⇨Reactivate Lead.**

   The Confirm Lead Activation dialog box appears.

4. **Click OK.**

   The original record appears. The data that had appeared dimmed while the lead was disqualified is again available for editing and general use.

5. **Click the Save and Close button and you are back in business.**

   The record is updated and the window closes.

6. **Review the list in the Leads window to make sure that your lead has been successfully brought back to life.**

   If you don't see the lead immediately, click the Refresh button near the upper-right corner of the window.

Turning a Lead into an Opportunity

Your goal is to turn all leads into opportunities. When you've reached that goal, it's time to turn your lead record into an opportunity record. Navigate to the record for that lead, and then click the Convert Lead button at the top of the screen. The screen shown in Figure 17-4 appears.

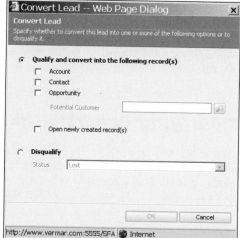

Figure 17-4:
Converting
a lead to
something
better
(or not).

The first three conversion choices in Figure 17-4 are not mutually exclusive. If you initially created a lead without establishing any related accounts or contacts, you can do all three conversions in one smooth step now. Accounts and contacts are discussed in Chapter 13.

If this potential sale is directly to a consumer (a person), select the Contact option. If you are trying to sell something to a company, choose the Account option. If you are dealing with a company, you can select the Contact in addition to selecting Account, in which case the system creates an account and a related contact record.

An *account* is a company. A *contact* is a person. A *customer* might be either one.

The third option, Opportunity, converts your lead to an opportunity. If you also elected to create an account record, that opportunity will be related to it. If you did not create an account but did create a contact, the opportunity will be related to the contact. If you had the system create both an account and a contact, the opportunity (and the contact) relates to the account.

An opportunity record can't stand on its own without an associated account or contact.

Handling Opportunities

A fine line exists between a lead and an opportunity. Generally, you've crossed the line when you're able to forecast a sale with associated revenue, a potential close date, and a probability for the sale happening. When those conditions are met, you have graduated from a lead to an opportunity, although your organization may define the transition differently. If you've already written a quotation, you're definitely over the line.

Creating and modifying opportunities

Converting a lead to an opportunity was covered in the preceding section. You can also skip the lead record entirely and go directly to an opportunity record. We like to do this when an existing client calls and asks for something — even if we're not ready to forecast a sale yet.

To create a new opportunity, follow these steps:

1. **At the bottom of the navigation pane, click the Sales button. Then, at the top of the pane, select Opportunities.**

   The Opportunities window appears, as shown in Figure 17-5.

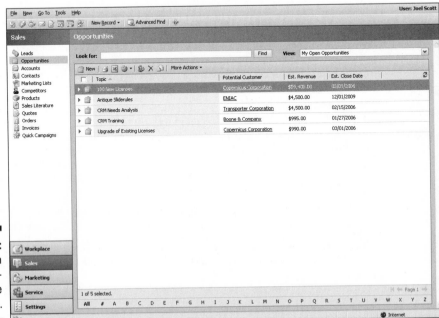

Figure 17-5: All open opportunities are displayed.

2. In the Opportunities window's toolbar, click the New button.

The Opportunity: New window appears, as shown in Figure 17-6.

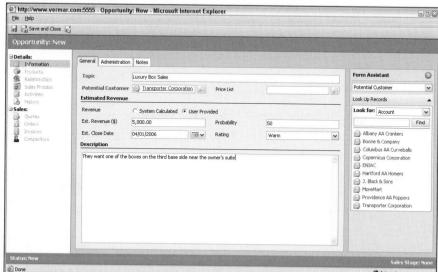

3. Enter a topic.

The topic, which is a system-required field, is just a description of what you expect to sell, for example, Consulting, Term Insurance, or Transporter System.

4. Select a Potential Customer (the second required field) to which this opportunity relates.

Remember, a customer is either an account (a company) or a contact (a person). If you click the magnifying glass to the right of the Potential Customer field, another screen appears that allows you to browse to and select either an account record or a contact record.

5. If you have a price list set up from BackOffice, select the appropriate one.

Whenever you see the term *BackOffice,* by the way, you should think *accounting system.* BackOffice integration is discussed briefly in Chapter 1.

6. For the Revenue field, if your price lists have been set up (see Chapter 10), select System Calculated; otherwise, select User Provided.

By the way, *you* are the user, so be prepared to enter a forecasted amount.

7. **Enter information in the following fields:**

a. **In the Estimated Revenue field, enter your best guess for the actual revenue you will receive when you close the deal.**

b. **In the Probability field, enter a whole number between 1 and 99.**

Although 0 and 100 are allowed, a 0 probability sale doesn't deserve to be an opportunity, and at 100 the deal must already be closed and should have been turned into an order.

c. **In the Estimated Close Date field, enter the date when you expect to close the deal.**

d. **In the Rating field, enter a rating.**

You can select Cold, Warm, or Hot to describe the rating, although the Probability field already does a good job of rating.

Although none of these are system-required fields, you won't have much of an opportunity if you don't have these estimates.

8. **Click the Save and Close button to save the opportunity record.**

From the Opportunities window, you can update an existing opportunity record by double-clicking the particular record, editing the information in any of the three tabbed areas (General, Administration, and Notes), and then saving the record.

As your opportunity progresses through the sales cycle, you'll want to update often to maintain the current status of your real pipeline.

Assigning and sharing opportunities

You can assign an opportunity to one or more other users, and you can share opportunities with other users or teams. For large or more complex opportunities, this is often a necessity.

When you *assign* an opportunity to someone else, you change the record ownership to that user. *Sharing* enables other users to see the opportunity in their My Opportunities view just as if it were their own but does not change the record's ownership.

To assign an opportunity to another user, follow these steps:

1. **On the menu bar (at the top of the screen), choose Actions⇨Assign.**

The Assign Opportunity dialog box appears, as shown in Figure 17-7. Although you can assign one or more opportunities to yourself or to another user, you cannot assign an opportunity to multiple users or to a team.

2. Select the second option, Assign to another user.

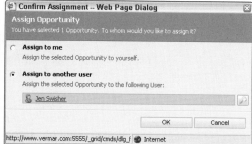

Figure 17-7:
You can
assign an
opportunity
to yourself
or to
another
user.

3. Click the magnifying glass to the right of the blank field.

A list of users appears.

4. Select the user to whom you want to assign this opportunity.

The blank field shown in Figure 17-7 is automatically filled in with that user's name.

5. Click OK.

The system returns to the General tab of that record, even though the opportunity is no longer yours.

You share opportunities as follows:

1. In the Opportunities window, click the More Actions button.

A short list of options appears.

2. Choose Sharing.

The window shown in Figure 17-8 appears.

3. Select which users or teams you want to share this opportunity with and what rights you want to give them.

Unlike assigning, sharing allows you to choose multiple users and even teams of users. For each user or team, you can decide how much authority to give. For example, you might decide to allow everyone to see the opportunity but not make changes to it. Or, if you're going away on vacation, you might share the opportunity with another user and give him or her complete rights to make changes (Write) and to share the opportunity with yet another user. Those choices and selections are shown in Figure 17-8. Chapter 5 has further details on security and rights.

4. Click OK after you've chosen the people or teams and their rights.

The system returns to the Opportunities window.

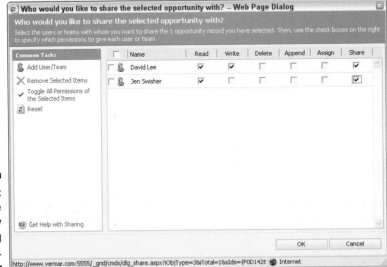

Figure 17-8:
The Opportunity sharing window.

If you decide to share an opportunity, examine the permissions you grant to other team members. For example, you may want to be judicious about allowing other members the ability to delete or close an opportunity.

Relating opportunities to activities or other records

Opportunity records are often associated with many other types of records. Opportunities can be, and should be, related to accounts, or contacts, or both. This makes sense because you are planning to sell something to either a company or a person. You may also want to relate activities, quotes, orders, invoices, notes, or attachments to an opportunity.

While working on an opportunity, chances are you're generating one or more quotes, making notes, and saving documents or data files that are associated with the opportunity. For example, in our business, CRM consulting, we often need to save sample data files so we can analyze how best to convert a legacy system's data into Microsoft CRM files. All these various files can be linked to the opportunity record.

Here are the steps to link activities or files to an opportunity:

1. **In the Opportunities window, click an opportunity record to see its details.**

2. **On the menu bar (at the top of the screen), choose Actions.**

3. **Select Add Activity, Add Related, or Add a Note.**

   If you select Add Related, this associates a quote, an order, or an invoice to the opportunity.

4. **Click the Save and Close button.**

Stages and relationships

Workflow rules automate your sales process — assuming your organization has a process and the workflow rules have been set up to emulate that process. Typically, a sales process has 3 to 12 stages ranging from initial contact, to generating a quote, negotiating, and closing the deal. Every company has a different process with different stages. In fact, a single company may have a different process for every type of product or service it sells.

Setting up your processes is usually the domain of your sales management team, an outside consultant, or a combination of the two.

From the Actions menu, you can advance an opportunity through your predefined sequence of sales steps. We highly recommend this approach, but an intelligently designed workflow is key. Workflow rules are discussed in Chapters 7 and 8.

The Relationships function enables you to link various accounts and contacts. This is often important, particularly in more complex deals. For example, you may have a pending deal with a prospect, and both an outside consultant and a leasing company are involved. Because the consultant and the leasing company are each separate records in your database, you would use the Relationship function to link them.

From the Opportunities window, you would select the appropriate opportunity, select Relationships from the navigation pane on the left, and begin adding new customers to the opportunity.

Closing, reopening, and deleting opportunities

Eventually, whether you win or lose the deal, you need to close the opportunity. This is easy enough to do. To close an opportunity properly, follow these steps:

1. **On the menu bar (at the top of the screen), choose Actions⇨Close Opportunity.**

   The Close Opportunity window appears.

2. **Under Status, click the appropriate option to indicate whether you won or lost the opportunity.**

3. **In the Status Reason field, select one of the drop-down choices.**

   Microsoft CRM provides two reasons for losing a deal: The order was canceled or you were outsold. We've never seen a salesperson select that second choice. Many other reasons exist for losing a deal, and your system administrator or dealer should help expand this list.

4. **Do one of the following:**

   - If you won, modify the Actual Revenue field to reflect the agreed-upon price and then enter the Close Date.

   - If you lost the opportunity, enter the competitor to whom you lost, if you know that information.

5. **In the Description field, enter a sentence or two with your final comments.**

   An example is shown in Figure 17-9.

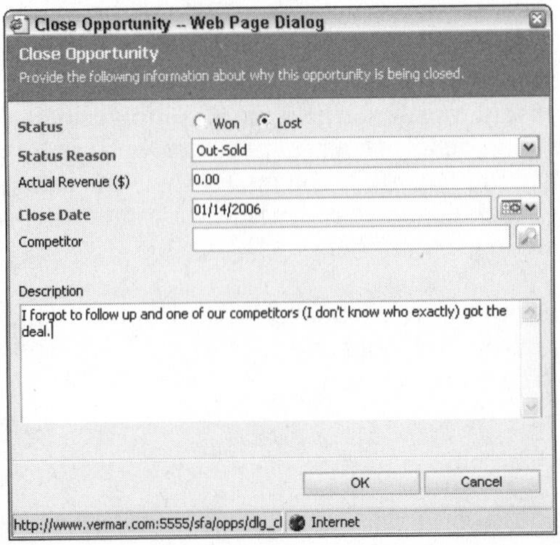

Figure 17-9:
Closing an opportunity.

6. **Click OK to close the opportunity.**

   The system returns to the General tab of the opportunity itself.

A previously closed opportunity may resurface and need to be reopened. If so, follow these steps:

1. **In the Opportunities window, make sure the View menu displays Closed Opportunities.**

2. **In the window's list, select the appropriate opportunity.**

   The opportunity's record appears.

3. **On the menu bar (at the top of the screen), choose Actions⇨Reopen Opportunity.**

   The Opportunity's status changes immediately, and you can edit it just as you would any other active or open opportunity record.

You can also delete an opportunity. This may seem like a good idea, particularly if you're upset that you lost a deal. In the long run, however, it's a bad idea because you never know when a deal may come back to life or you may need to refer to your notes on it. Don't do it. Instead, close it and attach a note if need be.

Chapter 18

Generating Quotes, Orders, and Invoices

. . . .

In This Chapter

▶ Creating and activating a quote

▶ Creating associations between opportunities and quotes

▶ Printing your quote

▶ Changing your quote to an order

▶ Changing your order to an invoice

. . . .

*M*icrosoft CRM manages the entire process of generating quotations, orders, and invoices. An essential ingredient in developing quotes is the product catalog, which is described in Chapter 10. The product catalog contains your list of products and their prices and discount structures. Microsoft CRM's quotation system draws from these products, prices, and discounts to create pricing specific to each customer.

After you generate a quote and give it to a customer, the best scenario is that the quote comes back as a signed order. The second-best scenario is that the quote comes back for revisions. Even after a quote is converted to an order, however, it can still be revised (until it has been sent to the accounting system). After an order goes to accounting, it becomes an invoice.

Although the logical flow is from quote to order to invoice, you can also create an order without creating a quote. And, in the same way, you can create an invoice without having created either a quote or an invoice. As you can see, you can start anywhere in the cycle.

In this chapter, we cover how to use Microsoft CRM to create a quotation, turn the quote into an order, and make the order into an invoice.

Creating and Activating Quotes

Several years ago we met with a very large distributor of paper products. They had been in business for more than a hundred years and had a hundred million dollars of revenue. Their entire quotation procedure was a verbal system. They never even wrote down what price they had quoted. When the customer called back to order something, the salespeople would simply ask what price they'd been given! We never got the go-ahead on installing a quotation system because they didn't think such a thing could possibly work.

If your quotation system involves something more formal than just telling your clients their price during a phone conversation, you need to generate a formal, written quotation.

Most quotes go through more than one iteration. Initially, you create a draft of your quote. You can continue editing your draft quote until it's ready to be sent. At that point, you activate the quote and send it to the customer. It is now read-only.

You can make multiple revisions of an activated quote, and each revision is stored as a separate record. The quote is then either accepted if it's won or closed if it's lost. If it's accepted, it is recorded as part of the order history.

Creating a quote

Most significant sales are preceded by a series of quotes or proposals. Many people confuse proposals with quotations. *Proposals* are quotations on steroids; they include a great deal more background, discussion, and analysis in addition to the more typical one- or two-page quotation. CRM doesn't have a built-in proposal system, but you can find third-party proposal systems that integrate with Microsoft CRM in Chapter 28.

To create a new quote, follow these steps:

1. **At the bottom of the navigation pane, click the Sales button. In the upper pane, select Quotes.**

   The Quotes window appears, displaying all your existing quotes.

2. **In the Quotes window's toolbar, click the New button.**

   The quote record appears, as shown in Figure 18-1, with General, Shipping, Addresses, Administration, and Notes tabs.

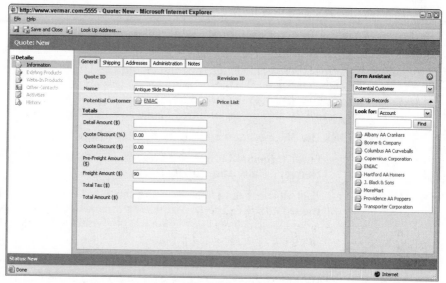

Figure 18-1:
Developing
a new
quote.

The quote ID is a unique, system-generated number that can help you identify the quote later. The revision ID is also created and maintained by the system and enables you (and the system) to track all the various versions of quotes that you have created and activated. The quote ID and revision ID fields are filled in *after* you save the quote. For that reason, clicking the Save button (the disk icon) after you enter the Name, Potential Customer, and Price List fields is essential. You do not need to click Save and Close until you have filled in all the relevant fields in each of the five tab areas.

3. **In the Name field, enter some text that describes what this quote is all about.**

   For example, you might type Microsoft CRM Training Class in Maui. After you save all the details of the quote, the text in this Name field will appear in Quotes window.

4. **In the Potential Customer field, select an account or a contact to associate with the quote.**

   To do so, click the magnifying glass to the right of the field to display the Look Up Records dialog box for Accounts and Contacts. Alternatively, you can select a customer from the Form Assistant on the right. Whichever method you choose, select the appropriate record from the list and click OK. The system returns you to the General tab.

5. **In the Price List field, use the magnifying glass or the Form Assistant to select a price list.**

6. **Now is a good time to click Save (the disk icon).**

7. **In the Totals section of the General tab, enter the Quote Discount and Freight Amount.**

   Microsoft CRM calculates the total amount and displays it in the last field in the General tab. Several fields on this screen, such as Detail Amount and Pre-Freight Amount, are system generated. You can tell because these field are outlined in black rather than blue.

8. **Click the Shipping tab and fill in the following:**

   a. **Enter information into the Effective From and To, Requested Delivery Date, and Due By fields.**

   Each of these date fields has an associated calendar display just to the right (see Figure 18-2). Clicking the calendar and then choosing a date is usually easier than manually typing a date directly into the field.

   b. **Enter the Shipping Method, Payment Terms, and Freight Terms.**

   Each of these fields has an associated drop-down menu. If your system is integrated with an accounting system, these fields can be filled in automatically.

9. **Click the Addresses tab (see Figure 18-3) and enter the Bill To and Ship To information.**

   To look up this address information, click the Look Up Address button on the toolbar.

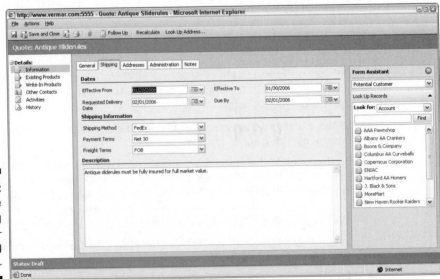

Figure 18-2:
The Shipping tab — delivering the goods.

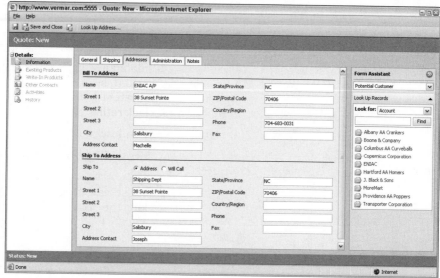

Figure 18-3:
You don't
always ship
to the same
place you
send the bill.

If the customer will be picking up the items, select Will Call for the Ship
To option (the first option in the Ship To Address section).

10. **If you want to associate your quote with an opportunity, start the
    quote from the opportunity screen or do the following:**

    a. **Click the Administration tab (see Figure 18-4).**

    b. **Use the magnifying glass in the Opportunity field to find and
       select that opportunity.**

    c. **Click OK.**

11. **Click the Save and Close button to save your quote.**

    The system returns to the Quotes window.

Activating a quote

When you first create a quotation, it is officially a draft. You can modify the
draft as many times as necessary. But before sending the quote to a customer, you must activate the quote. Follow these steps to do so:

1. **In the Quotes window, select the quote you want to activate.**

   The details of the quote appear.

2. **On the menu bar (at the top of the screen), choose Actions⇨Activate
   Quote.**

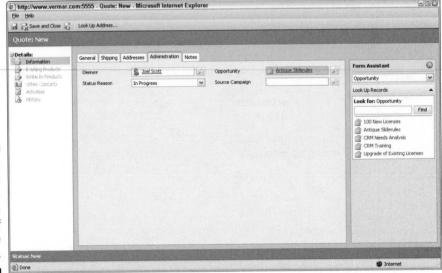

Figure 18-4:
Store
admin-
istrative
details of
the quote
here.

The quote now becomes read-only and can be turned into an order when the time comes.

3. **To save changes and continue working, click Save (the disk icon); to save changes and close the form, click the Save and Close button.**

After you have activated the quote, it's no longer a draft and the system creates an official quotation with its own quote ID number. If the customer then requests a revision to the quote, you can modify that quote. The system stores an additional record with its own revision ID for each modified quote, so you may have a long series of quotes as you continue to revise activated quotes.

The Effective To date is the date after which the quotation expires. It is meant as a deadline by which the customer needs to make a decision. So what happens when the Effective To date has come and gone but the order has not shown up? Nothing special, unless you have set some workflow rules or have some reports that list expired quotations.

Associating Opportunities and Quotes

Opportunity records house all your sales forecast information. By associating an opportunity with a quote, you allow the system to calculate the estimated revenue for the opportunity automatically. As you revise an associated quotation by changing products or discounts, those changes to the revenue stream are reflected in your overall forecast.

You can associate a quote with an opportunity or vice versa. If the opportunity doesn't exist yet, you need to create it before you can associate it with a quote.

We'll go through the steps of associating a quote with an opportunity record:

1. **In the Opportunities window, select the opportunity that needs an associated quote.**

2. **With the opportunity record displayed, click Quotes in the navigation pane (under Sales).**

   A list of all associated quotes appears in the main window.

3. **If no quotes are yet associated with the opportunity, click the New Quote button in the window's toolbar. If quotes already exist, you can edit them if necessary.**

4. **Whether you are entering a new quote or editing an existing quote, proceed with entering the information as detailed in Step 3 of the "Creating a quote" section, earlier in this chapter.**

5. **Assemble the individual items you want listed in your quote by clicking Existing Products from the navigation pane or, if you're quoting a custom product or something that isn't in the products list, select Write-In Products from the navigation pane.**

Because we started this exercise from an opportunity record, the quote we just created is automatically associated with this opportunity. No need to do any further association!

Printing a Quote

After you have finished developing a quote and have activated it, it's a good idea to do a quick Microsoft CRM print. Follow these steps:

1. **From the Quotes window, select the quote you want to print.**

   Your quote record appears on the screen.

2. **Choose File⇨Print.**

   A preview of your quote appears so you can review it for accuracy.

3. **When your previewed quote looks okay, you can send it to your printer by clicking the print button.**

   Your bare-bones quotation prints, displaying the information from each of the tab areas of your quote.

Before printing, make sure your SQL Reporting Service is started.

In most cases, this information will not be formatted in your organization's style. The good news is that you're not locked into a specific quotation format. The bad news is that you need to create a format rather than select from some canned ones.

Your system administrator or dealer can assist with the development of specially formatted printouts and reports.

Converting a Quote to an Order

A successfully presented quote becomes an order. Only a previously activated (status = active) quote can be turned into an order. The steps to change a quote into an order are easy:

1. **In the Quotes window, click the active quote.**

   The details of the quote appear.

2. **In the Quotes window's toolbar, click Create Order.**

   The Create Order dialog box appears, as shown in Figure 18-5. The Status Reason of the quote has automatically changed to Won. You can see the Status in the list of quotes as long as the View is All Quotes. The opportunity is no longer part of your forecasted sales because it's now a done deal. Today's date is automatically filled in, although you can modify this if necessary.

Figure 18-5:
Creating an order.

Create Order -- Web Page Dialog
Create Order
Use this quote to create an order.

Quote ID:	QUO-01001-FBKZ3F	**Revision ID:**	0
Status Reason	Won		
Date Won	01/11/2006		

Description

This is a pre-publication order

○ Close Opportunity

    Actual revenue is ($): ○

        ● Calculated from quotes

○ Don't update opportunity

OK   Cancel

http://www.vermar.com:5555/sfa/quotes/dlg_accept.as   Internet

3. **Select the Close Opportunity option.**

   The opportunity no longer appears in the list of Active Opportunities (that is, when the View is set to Active Opportunities).

4. **In the upper part of the navigation pane, select Orders.**

5. **In the View drop-down list (in the upper-right corner), select My Orders.**

   Your new order appears in the list. Good, so far!

Generating Invoices from Orders

When you're ready to ship your goods or services to the customer, you use the information in the order to generate an invoice to the customer. Follow these steps:

1. **In the lower part of the navigation pane, click the Sales button. In the upper part of the pane, select Orders.**

   The Orders window appears.

2. **Make sure the View menu (in the upper right) is set to All Orders.**

3. **Select the order you want to make into an invoice.**

4. **Click the Create Invoice button.**

   Microsoft CRM automatically generates and displays the invoice for you. Unless your system is integrated to a Dynamics accounting application, however, that invoice goes nowhere. Your invoice is typically printed (or delivered in some other electronic way) from your accounting system.

5. **Click Save and Close.**

One of the most compelling things about generating quotes, orders, and invoices is CRM's ability to integrate with accounting software. The extent or ease of this integration depends on the accounting software you're using. If you're using Microsoft Dynamics GP, for example, Microsoft has the integration you need. If you're using accounting software not from Microsoft, you'll probably need a third-party module to integrate the two. See Chapter 28 for information on sources for this type of integration.

Chapter 19

Setting Up Your Sales Literature

· ·

In This Chapter

▶ Adding sales literature

▶ Making changes to literature

▶ Relating literature to other records

▶ Adding and tracking competitors

· ·

*T*he Sales Literature area is really a document management system. After you set up your subjects (formerly known as the Subject Manager) to provide the structure for your company's document library, you can file individual pieces of sales literature for future reference. (See Chapter 25 for full details about how to set up the subjects.)

Subjects create an organizational structure for your literature, documents, and brochures. Think of it as the Dewey Decimal System for your own library. The Sales Literature area allows you to stock the shelves. And the shelves, by the way, are on the server — not your local computer.

Other CRM packages enable a salesperson (or any user) to be on the phone with a client and easily assemble e-mail attachments from the Sales Literature area and send the documents. If e-mail isn't the preferred communication method, faxing or printing and mailing works.

Unfortunately, Microsoft CRM missed the boat here. After you put a document into the Sales Literature area, all you can easily do is read the document. Well, that's not completely true. There is a multistep, cumbersome process whereby you can browse the area, download the document to your local computer, and manually attach it to an outgoing e-mail. But if organizing and reading your documents is what you have in mind, this chapter is for you.

You may also want to keep track of your competitors and their sales literature. This information is particularly important when competing for projects. What you find out (even in a losing battle) may help you win the next one.

Adding Literature

All new literature must be categorized by subject. This means your subjects must have already been set up with a structure to house your documents. (As mentioned, see Chapter 25 for information on subjects.)

To add a piece of literature — or any document or file — to the Sales Literature area, follow these steps:

1. **In the lower part of the navigation pane, click the Sales button. In the upper part of the pane, select Sales Literature.**

   The Sales Literature window appears, as shown in Figure 19-1.

2. **In the Sales Literature window's toolbar, click the New button.**

   The Sales Literature: New window appears, as shown in Figure 19-2. This is the main information screen for entering and cataloging your literature.

3. **In the Title field, enter a title for your article.**

4. **In the Subject field, select a subject as follows:**

   a. **Click the magnifying glass to the right of the Subject field.**

   The Look Up Records window appears.

   b. **Select a subject from the list.**

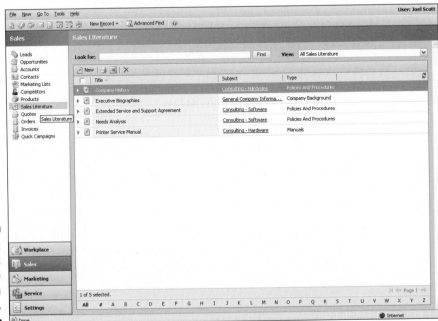

Figure 19-1: Your sales literature appears in a typical view.

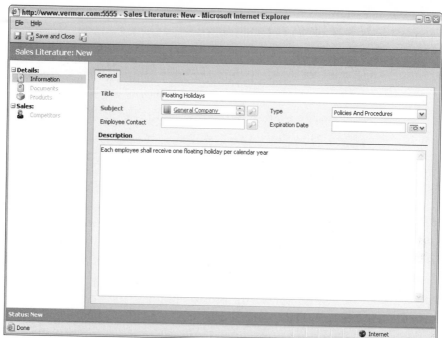

Figure 19-2:
Entering a
new article.

5. **In the Type field, click the arrow and choose an item from the list.**

   This list displays likely topic descriptions for your literature.

6. **If you want, associate a user with this literature as follows:**

   a. **Click the magnifying glass to the right of the Employee Contact field.**

   b. **Select an employee to associate with the literature.**

   This is probably the person on your staff who developed the literature or the one who is responsible for the documentation.

7. **In the Expiration Date field, click the calendar icon and select a date for your document to expire.**

   For example, you may have a sale advertisement or a company policy that expires on a particular date.

8. **If you want, enter an abstract of the document in the Description field.**

9. **Click Save (the disk icon) or the Save and Close button.**

   If you select Save, the system saves what you've entered so far but remains on this same New Literature screen awaiting further edits. If you click Save and Close, the system returns to the Sales Literature window.

So far, you've only entered general information about the document. You still need to attach the document to the listing you just created. Follow these steps:

1. **In the Sales Literature window, click the listing to which you want to add one or more documents.**

2. **In the window's pane on the left, select Documents (under Details).**

3. **In the window's toolbar, click the New Document button.**

   The Document: New window appears, as shown in Figure 19-3.

4. **Fill in the window as follows:**

   a. **Title:** Enter a descriptive title of the document, possibly including a version number or a date.

   b. **Author:** Enter either the author's name or the name of the person responsible for the document.

   c. **Keywords:** Enter one or more keywords that can be used later to locate any document with one keyword or a combination of keywords.

   d. **Abstract:** This is a short summary of the document's contents.

   e. **File Name:** This field connects Microsoft CRM to the stored file. You can use the Browse button to the right of the File Name field to locate the document.

5. **Click the Attach button in the lower-right corner of the window.**

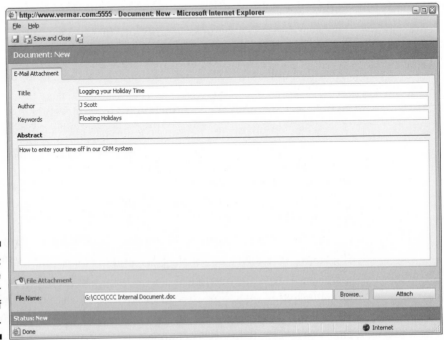

Figure 19-3:
Entering the specifics for a piece of literature.

Doing so attaches the document entered in the File Name field and uploads the document to the server.

6. **Click the Save and Close button at the top of the window.**

   The system returns to the listing of documents associated with this particular subject.

Each title can be associated with multiple documents. The structure is similar to an organization chart with each parent record capable of having multiple children. For example, you might have a document with pricing and terms and a separate document dealing with confidentiality associated with consulting agreements.

All documents are stored on the server. If you attach a document that's currently stored locally on your hard drive, Microsoft CRM makes a copy of the document on the server. This way, other users (if they have access rights) will have access to the document. When you need to retrieve the document, you have a choice of downloading it from the server or just opening it directly from the server.

Modifying Literature

Microsoft CRM copies documents to the server so all authorized team members can use them. Therefore, at least two copies of the same document exist — one on your local computer and one on the server. Users may have their own original copy of the document on their own machine. Keep in mind that you want everyone to always be working from the same version of the document.

Several document management systems allow multiple users to contribute to the same document, more or less simultaneously. Even Microsoft Word has a facility called Track Changes. Each contributor is automatically assigned a color, and it is easy to see who has done what to the document. It's also easy to gracefully remove all signs of editing before printing the final edition.

You need one central repository for the current copies of all literature. That could be the Microsoft CRM server, or it could be another readily accessible server, as long as everyone understands where the active documents are stored.

Assuming the CRM server is the central library for current documents, follow these steps to edit an existing piece of literature:

1. **In the Sales Literature window, click the row that contains the document you want to edit.**

   The General tab for that subject appears (refer to Figure 19-2). You will soon have access to the documents so you can edit one or more of them.

2. **In the pane on the left, select Documents.**

   You see a listing of all the documents related to this subject.

3. **Click the document you need to edit.**

   At the bottom of the window is a link to that document. This document, or attachment, is housed on the CRM server.

4. **Click the link to the document and save it on your local drive.**

   You can't edit the document while it's on the CRM server.

5. **Edit the document and save your changes on your local drive.**

6. **Upload the document to the CRM server so other users can access it.**

   If you simply reattach the document, it will upload automatically. Revision numbers are not automatically associated with revised documents, so you might want to include a revision number in the file name or title of the document. In addition, you can track revisions, at least a little, by checking the Modified On date that appears in the Sales Literature window.

Relating Literature to Competitors

One of the more compelling aspects of the design of Microsoft CRM is the ability to relate one kind of record to another. Suppose you want to associate a piece of sales literature with a competitor. You collect sample brochures from each of your competitors. You then catalog them in the Sales Literature area and then relate each brochure to the appropriate competitor. To do this, follow these steps:

1. **In the lower part of the navigation pane, click the Sales button. In the upper part of the pane, select Competitors.**

   A listing of all competitors appears in the window on the right.

2. **Select the appropriate competitor.**

   The General tab for that competitor's information appears.

3. **In the pane on the left, select Sales Literature (under Sales).**

   The Sales Literature window appears, showing all existing sales literature associated with the competitor you selected.

4. **Select the piece of literature that you want to associate with this competitor by clicking the appropriate row in the list.**

   You can also set up a new piece of sales literature from here, as shown in the "Adding Literature" section, earlier in this chapter.

5. **In the window's toolbar, click the Save button to save your association of sales literature with the competitor.**

Finding your competitors

You may occasionally find yourself in a competitive situation but not know exactly who your competitor is. Maybe you know the general geographic location of your competitor. The Advanced Find feature may come to your rescue. For example, if you are competing to sell computer clones against another dealer somewhere in Connecticut, you could use the specifications shown in the figure to find likely contenders. Choose Tools⇨Advanced Find in the Competitors window to access the Advanced Find feature.

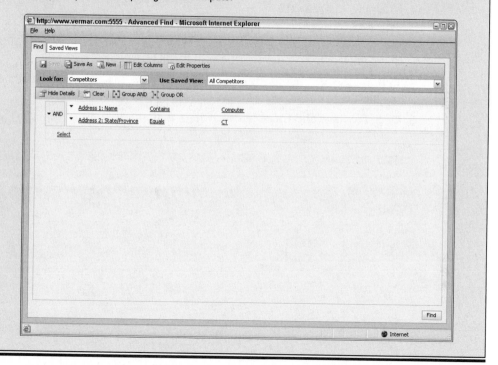

Adding and Tracking Competitors

Whenever you're in a competitive situation, knowing as much as possible about the opposition is a good idea. You want to track their strengths so you can anticipate the ammunition they will use against you. You want to know their weaknesses so you can exploit them. Yes, it's a tough world out there.

It's a good idea not only to track the products they sell but also to compile as much literature about those products as possible. Your competitor's Web site is a great place to go to compile, download, and cut and paste all the information you can find. To add a new competitor to the database, follow these steps:

1. **At the bottom of the navigation pane, click the Sales button. At the top of the pane, select Competitors.**

2. **In the Competitors window's toolbar, click the New button.**

   The data entry window shown in Figure 19-4 appears.

3. **Enter at least the one required field, Name, and as many of the other fields as you can.**

   Filling in the Key Product and Address fields may come in handy.

4. **Click the Analysis tab.**

   The Analysis tab has five general, text-based topics for you to fill in. If you've ever taken any Miller Heiman sales training, some of these topics may look familiar.

5. **In these five fields, enter everything you know or suspect about the competitor.**

6. **Click the Save and Close button.**

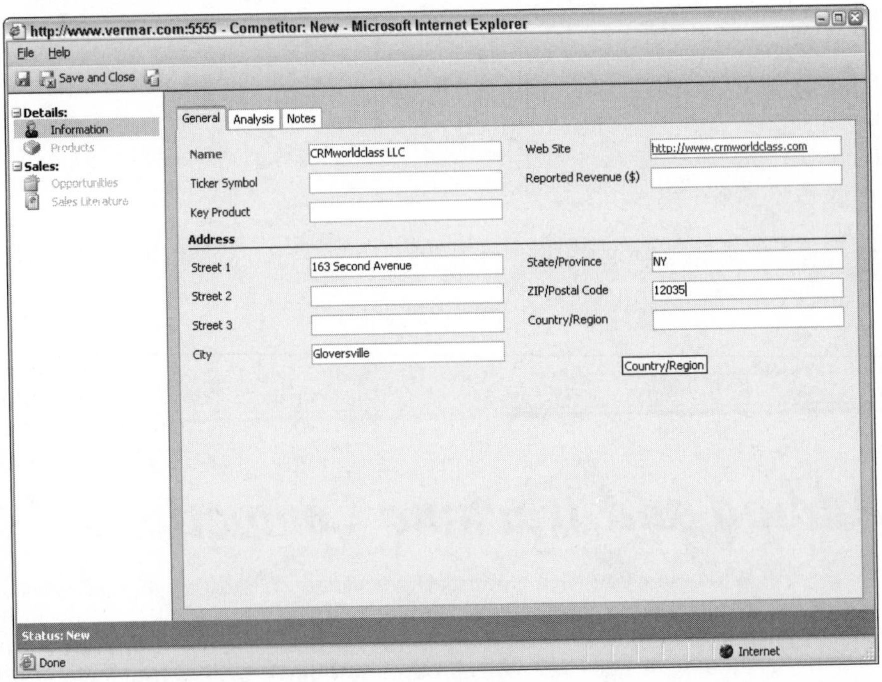

Figure 19-4:
Entering data on another annoying competitor.

Compiling a library of your organization's literature is one of the more useful things you can do for the group. Whether it's just for internal consumption or, ultimately, for distribution to prospects and customers, having current literature organized in one place and available to everyone will speed up your sales and support efforts. Do it and then make sure you keep it all up-to-date.

Chapter 20

Using Notes and Attachments

*A*lmost every type of record in the Microsoft CRM system enables you to post notes and link attachments. Think of a *note* as information that you manually type into the system. For example, if you find out that your main contact at an account is about to leave, you probably want to document that and create an action plan. Meetings and phone calls deserve this kind of follow-up documentation as well. At our company, every meeting and phone call and almost every kind of activity is documented with notes so we have an audit trail of what has been promised or accomplished.

Attachments include a variety of files that are linked to individual records. These files may be the typical Word documents or Excel spreadsheets, or they may be PowerPoint presentations, digital photos, contracts, images of faxes, and so on — almost anything.

In this chapter, you find out how to create and maintain notes and attachments, processes that have been significantly streamlined in Version 3.

Creating Notes

Notes can be associated with any kind of existing record, whether it's an account, a contact, or a case from the Customer Service area. All these types of records include a Notes tab. For example, Figure 20-1 shows the Notes tab for a typical account record.

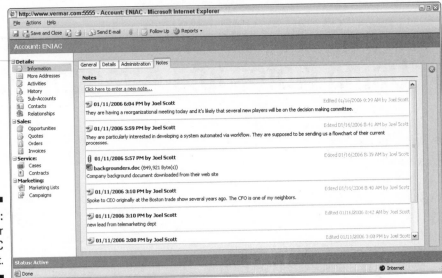

Figure 20-1:
My notes for
the ENIAC
account.

To create a new note relating to a particular account, follow these steps:

1. **At the top of the navigation pane, click Accounts.**

   The system displays the Accounts window. We are using accounts here as an example, but remember that what you do here applies equally well to contact, lead, opportunity, and case records. In fact, almost every type of record in CRM has a Notes field.

2. **Select the specific account to which you want to attach a note.**

3. **Click the Notes tab at the top of the account's screen.**

4. **Click the blue hyperlink that reads "Click here to enter a new note."**

5. **Type your text in the rectangular area, as shown in Figure 20-2.**

6. **When you've finished entering text, click another tab or a selection in the navigation pane.**

The next time you return to the Notes tab for this account, you'll see the note you entered as well as the date and time and your name. This is one of the few areas in Microsoft CRM where you don't have to manually save your work. You can see this in Figure 20-3.

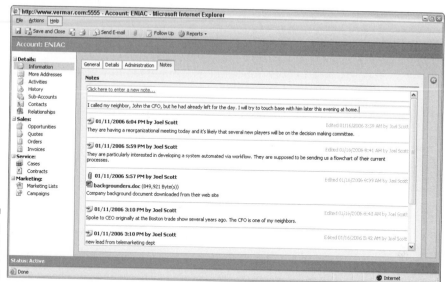

Figure 20-2:
Entering a
new note.

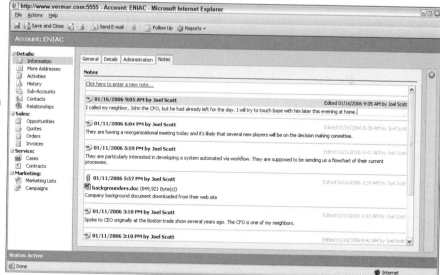

Figure 20-3:
The
evidence of
a completed
and saved
note. The
most recent
note is
always at
the top.

Notes don't have spell checking or grammar checking. If you're challenged in this department and think that others may end up reviewing your notes (and they probably will), use Word to create your notes and spell check and grammar check them there. Then either cut and paste the Word text into the notes section, or attach the Word file, as explained in the next section.

Creating Attachments

Attachments are separate files that you may associate with individual records such as accounts, contacts, opportunities, and cases. An attachment could be a Word document, but it could just as well be, say, an electronic set of blueprints, or a series of digital photos, or a spreadsheet.

You can add a note but not an associated attachment by using the Notes tab at the top of most records. You can add a single attachment, but you can't make notes, by choosing Actions➪Attach a File. A better and more general approach follows.

To add a note as an attachment, follow these steps:

1. **Navigate to the record to which you want to attach a note or a file.**

2. **On the menu bar (at the top of the screen), choose Actions➪Add a Note.**

   The Note: New window appears, as shown in Figure 20-4. The system automatically fills in the Regarding field.

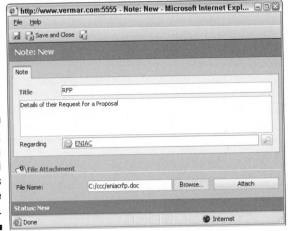

Figure 20-4:
Adding notes and attachments at the same time.

3. **Enter a title in the small entry box (next to the word *Title*).**

4. **Enter a description in the large entry box (below the word *Title*).**

   The information you type in the larger field is displayed in the listing of all associated notes — *not* what you enter in the Title field.

5. **Use the Browse button to locate and select the file you want to attach.**

6. **Click the Attach button.**

   The system uploads your file to the server for storage. This gives other users (with the proper access rights) the ability to see the file and also gives you access to it from any other computer you may be using later.

 You can attach only one file per note. All attachments are stored on the server, so when you're first attaching a file or using it in some way, the system will need to move it using your Internet connection. Virtually any kind of file is a candidate for an attachment. There are no size limitations, but if you expect to be uploading or downloading these attachments from the server frequently, try not to bog the system down with enormous files. (Video clips, fax images, and the like are often pretty big.)

Deleting a Note or an Attachment

If you need to change the file attached to a record, perhaps because the file itself has changed, you need to delete the original attachment. After an attachment is attached to the note, you can delete the attachment by clicking the Remove button.

To delete a note associated with a record, follow these steps:

1. **Navigate to the record.**

   If you were deleting a note associated with an account, for example, you'd select Accounts from the upper part of the navigation pane and then select the specific record from the Accounts window.

2. **Click the record's Notes tab.**

   All notes associated with this record appear.

3. **Double-click the note you want to delete.**

   The text of the note appears.

4. **On the menu bar (at the top of the screen), choose Actions⇨Delete Note.**

   The Confirm Deletion dialog box appears (see Figure 20-5), telling you that you are about to delete not only this particular note but also any associated attachment.

5. **Click OK to proceed.**

Figure 20-5:
Your note is
about to bite
the dust.

Deleting an attachment without deleting the associated note is now much easier than in prior versions of CRM. Follow these steps:

1. **Navigate to the record.**

2. **Click the record's Notes tab.**

   All notes associated with this record appear.

3. **Double-click the note with an attachment that you want to delete.**

   The text of the note appears.

4. **Click the Remove button in the lower-right corner.**

   A confirmation screen appears with a warning that once you remove the attachment it's really gone. However, you can always reattach the same file anytime you want to.

5. **Click OK.**

   Another confirmation screen appears.

6. **Click Save and Close to complete this action.**

With regard to relating notes and attachments to other records — you can't do it. Notes and attachments are assigned to the one record they are initially attached to — and that's it. Sorry.

Part IV
Making the Most of Marketing

The 5th Wave   By Rich Tennant

"Look—you've got Project Manager, Acct Manager, and Opportunity Manager, but Sucking Up to the Manager just isn't a field the program comes with."

In this part . . .

Marketing is a new feature in Version 3.0. Targeting your accounts, which is covered in Chapter 21, is a way to group just those accounts or records that have something in common. For example, you could target every customer or prospect in your state that might be interested in a new line of products you're about to release.

Any marketing person worth his or her salt wants to measure the cost and effectiveness of each marketing campaign, so we cover that in Chapter 22.

Chapter 21

Targeting Accounts and Contacts

*W*hether you market to companies (accounts) or individuals (contacts) or both, you need to plan the processes and the marketing campaigns you have in mind. Although your campaigns will always evolve, certain fixtures are key ingredients. Your marketing needs to differentiate between suspects, prospects, and current clients. You'll target clients based on different factors, such as how important they are, what products they have expressed interest in or have already purchased, and perhaps the type and frequency of communication they want.

Your exact marketing plan will determine what information you need to collect and store in CRM. In this chapter, we define some typical fields that are available or that you should add to your system.

After you collect the data you need for your marketing campaign, you need a way to identify all the records within the groups you want to target. The new Advanced Find feature in Version 3 allows you to save the search criteria for different groups of targeted records. As a result, you can now have many different criteria set up to identify various target groups.

In this chapter, we mostly refer to accounts, but the concepts apply equally to contacts and leads. After you've set up and populated targeted lists, you can use these lists in your marketing campaigns. You get a taste of that later in this chapter.

Important Fields for Targeting Customers

Although it may not be obvious, one of the most important pieces of data to collect for each customer or prospect is whether or not you should be marketing to them and, if so, through what medium. Microsoft CRM has a series of fields you can use to indicate "if and how." You can find these fields on the Administrative tab of each account, contact, and lead record, as shown in Figure 21-1. Interestingly, these same fields are nowhere to be found in an Opportunity record.

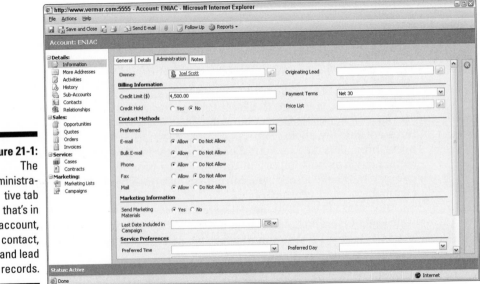

Figure 21-1:
The Administrative tab that's in account, contact, and lead records.

You may want to have your system administrator or dealer add this same series of marketing fields to the opportunity record. This makes sense because the normal evolution of a record is to go from a lead record to an opportunity record to a customer record.

Make sure to use these administrative fields conscientiously. More and more laws are being passed regulating spam, opt-in/opt-out marketing, and the divulging of contact details to third parties. If you violate these rules, your marketing will probably not be a benefit and may create all sorts of trouble.

A good marketing plan has some key elements. You need fields to track the following:

- ✔ What products the customer has purchased

- ✔ What products the customer is or may be interested in

- ✔ How important the customer is — this regulates how often you need to be in touch

- ✔ Who handles this customer

- ✔ Who is the entrenched competitor and when their contract expires

Each of these pieces of data should be incorporated into a targeted marketing plan. You should probably have many targeted groups defined — for example, one for prospects, one for current customers, and another for ex-customers whose business you'd like to win back. With the workflow embedded in Microsoft CRM, you can almost completely automate your marketing campaigns. The rest of this chapter focuses on how to do exactly that.

Developing and Saving Marketing Lists

Marketing lists are groups of records that you can use with campaigns. Campaigns can then be automated with workflow. The lists themselves can be from account, contact, or lead records. You populate each list by manually adding members (records) one at a time or by using the Advanced Find feature to compile larger and more complex groups.

Workflow refers to the overall flow of your business processes, whereas *workflow rules* are the specific steps you want CRM to take to implement a business process. However, *workflow* and *workflow rules* are often used interchangeably.

Creating marketing lists

Before you can populate a list, you must create the structure for that list. Essentially, that means you must name the list, add a few basic details, and then save the list. Follow these steps:

1. **At the bottom of the navigation pane, click the Marketing button. In the upper part of the pane, select Marketing Lists.**

    The Marketing Lists window appears, as shown in Figure 21-2.

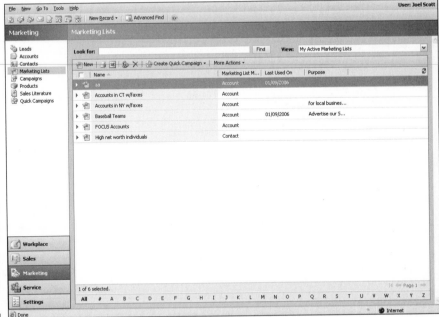

Figure 21-2:
All your
existing
marketing
lists are
displayed.

2. **In the window's toolbar, click the New button.**

   The Marketing List: New screen appears, as shown in Figure 21-3. Three fields are required: Name, Member Type, and Owner.

3. **In the Name field, enter a unique name for your new list.**

4. **Select a Member Type from the drop-down list.**

   The Member Type simply indicates whether you are building the list from your accounts, contacts, or leads. You can only use one of these per list.

5. **Enter information in the other fields, as desired.**

   If you plan to track your marketing based on this list, you should fill in the Source field (where you initially got these records) and the Cost field (how much you paid for these records). You can enter notes either in the Description field or in the Notes tab. If you use the Notes tab, each note is date- and time-stamped.

6. **Click the Save and Close button.**

   You return to the Marketing Lists window, which now displays your new marketing list.

Now you have a list, but it has no records in it yet. The next sections describe two ways to populate your list.

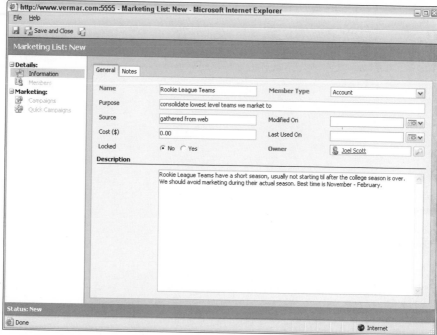

Figure 21-3:
Making
a new
targeted
group
for your
marketing.

Populating a marketing list using Look Up

The Look Up feature is the simplest way to build a list. If your intent is to build and maintain the membership in a list based only on the name of the account, the Look Up feature may be all you'll need. It probably won't be enough for every list, but it's a good place to start for the simple ones.

1. **At the bottom of the navigation pane, click the Marketing button. At the top of the pane, select Marketing Lists.**

2. **Click to select the marketing list you want to populate.**

   The same screen you were just working on (see Figure 21-3) appears, but now the Members selection in the navigation pane is available.

3. **At the top of the navigation pane, select Members.**

   The screen in Figure 21-4 appears.

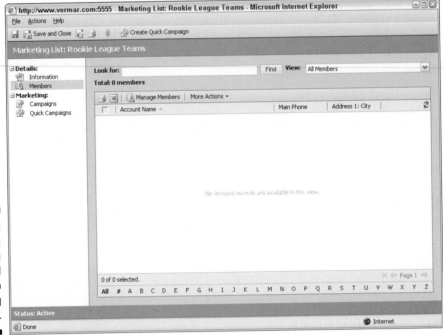

Figure 21-4:
Deciding
how you
want to add
members to
a marketing
list.

4. In the window's toolbar, click the Manage Members button.

The Manage Members dialog box appears, as shown in Figure 21-5.

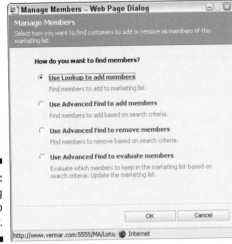

Figure 21-5:
Adding
members to
a new list.

5. Click the first option, Use Lookup to add members, and then click OK.

The Look Up Records dialog box appears.

6. In the Look For field, enter the name of the account(s) you want to add to your list.

You can enter all or part of the name. We entered *aa*. The asterisk (*) is a wildcard that matches any sequence of characters. The *aa* finds any account record whose name has two sequential *a*'s in it. The characters are not case sensitive.

7. Click the Find button.

All the accounts with *aa* in their name appear in the Available records pane, as shown in Figure 21-6. This list may include records you don't want. For example, the figure shows four AA baseball teams (the records we wanted) as well as a pawnshop we don't want to include.

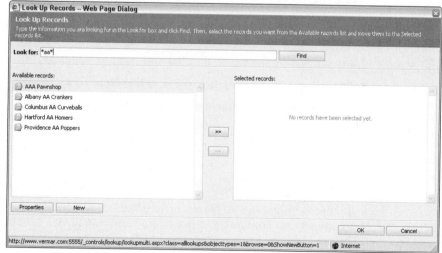

Figure 21-6:
We don't
want to
include the
pawnshop
in this list.

8. Highlight the records you want to include in your marketing list, and then click the >> button.

You can use the Shift key or the Ctrl key to include multiple records.

9. Click the OK button when you're finished.

The system flashes a message, telling you that it's adding records to your list, and then returns to the Marketing Lists window.

Populating a marketing list using Advanced Find

The next step up in sophistication is to use Advanced Find rather than the simpler Look Up feature to build a targeted list. These two methods have several key differences:

- ✓ Advanced Find can look at any field in a record, not just the Name field.

- ✓ Advanced Find can look at more than one field in a search. For example, Advanced Find can locate all the accounts in New York that also have fax numbers.

- ✓ You can save criteria you create with Advanced Find and use them again later.

To create a targeted list using Advanced Find, follow these steps:

1. **At the bottom of the navigation pane, click the Marketing button. At the top of the pane, select Marketing Lists.**

2. **Click to select the marketing list you want to populate.**

3. **At the top of the navigation pane, select Members.**

4. **In the window's toolbar, click the Manage Members button.**

   The Manage Members dialog box appears.

5. **Click the second option, Use Advanced Find to add members, and then click OK.**

6. **Select the type of record on which you are basing your search.**

   In this example, we are using account records and looking for all accounts that contain *aa* in their name and also have a fax number. See Figure 21-7.

7. **In the window's toolbar, click Save As.**

   The screen shown in Figure 21-8 appears

8. **Fill in the required Name field and add some descriptive text.**

9. **Click OK to save this new entry as one of your marketing lists.**

No matter which method you use to create a marketing list, your list is static rather than dynamic. This means the list contains only those records that you just added; it does not automatically update as you add or change records. If, for example, you add five more baseball teams to your database, they are *not* automatically included in the baseball list. You must add these five to the list if you want them to be part of your marketing plan. In Figure 21-5, the fourth option allows you to use Advanced Find to perform this update.

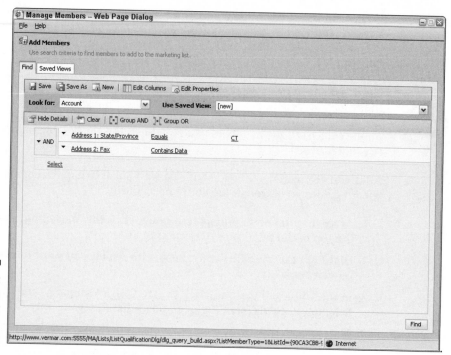

Figure 21-7:
Searching
for account
records.

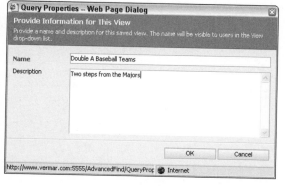

Figure 21-8:
Naming
your
marketing
list after
creating it
with
Advanced
Find.

Developing Campaigns and Quick Campaigns

Although you can send e-mails and faxes to individual customers, the real power of a marketing system is the marriage of marketing lists with marketing campaigns. After you develop a target list with either of the two methods just discussed, you can easily create a quick campaign to send out information or schedule activities. This is a powerful tool that has been greatly expanded in Version 3.

In addition to regular campaigns, which allow you to track associated finances and results, Microsoft CRM has linked a Quick Campaign Wizard to the marketing lists. After you create a target list, using the wizard is a logical next step.

If your goal is to track what you're spending on each campaign, and to track the results as well, stick with the full-fledged campaign system described in Chapter 22. If you want to send out a quick e-mail or fax blast, or schedule phone calls to all the members of a target list, the Quick Campaign Wizard is the tool for you.

After you've created a target list, it's easy to link it to a quick campaign. The wizard guides you through the entire procedure:

1. **At the bottom of the navigation pane, click the Marketing button. At the top of the pane, select Marketing Lists.**

2. **Highlight the specific list (or lists) with which you want to associate a quick campaign.**

3. **In the window's toolbar, click Create Quick Campaign and choose For Selected Records from the drop-down list (it's your only choice).**

   The Quick Campaign Wizard launches and displays the screen shown in Figure 21-9.

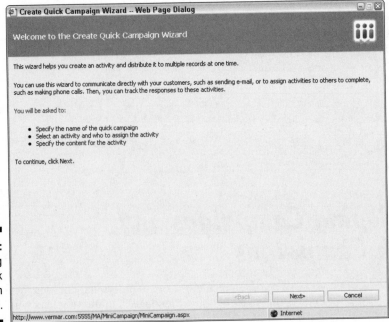

Figure 21-9:
Launching the Quick Campaign Wizard.

4. Follow the wizard's instructions as it guides you through the setup of the Quick Campaign.

Figure 21-10 is the most detailed screen during the process of setting up an e-mail blast. CRM saves you the trouble of filling out most of these fields by filling them automatically. Following is a description of the ones that you should fill in manually:

   a. Owner: This required field is automatically filled in by the system, although you can manually change it if you need to.

   b. Duration: This is an indication of how long the entire campaign should take.

   c. Priority: Your choices are Low, Normal, and High. These selections do not trigger any system-generated selections; they just give you the ability to prioritize your day.

   d. Due: This is a two-part field containing a date and a time when the campaign should begin.

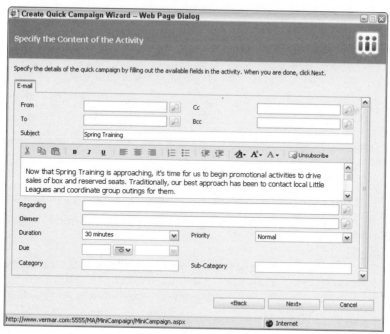

Figure 21-10:
E-mail blast
campaign
details.

      e. **Category and Sub-Category:** These two fields allow you to further define the campaign. You might enter something like "Service Contract Renewal" in the Category field and "Focus Customers" in the Sub-Category field.

5. **Click OK to exit the wizard.**

When you complete all the screens in the wizard, the system returns you to the listing of all your quick campaigns. Each line in the listing includes the current Status Reason of the campaign, as shown in Figure 21-11.

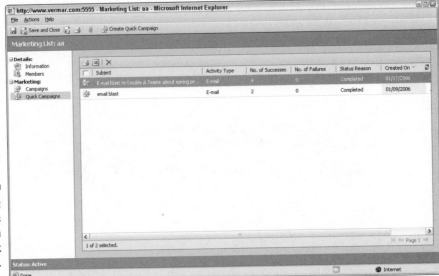

Figure 21-11:
The status report on your quick campaigns.

6. **Click the icon to the left of any subject in Figure 21-11.**

You see an area with additional reporting on the quick campaign, as shown in Figure 21-12.

The marketing module of CRM provides you with a solid tool for staying in touch with prospects and customers. Integrating targeted account lists with well-designed workflow creates a powerful automated marketing system that will help build your business and reduce your manual workload.

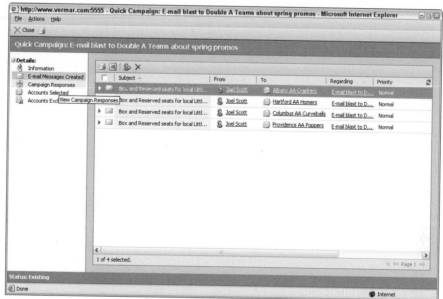

Chapter 22

Managing Campaigns

· ·

· ·

*L*et's talk campaign management — no, we're not leading 30,000 foot soldiers to take Carpathia. (Think of the logistics of that campaign!) We're talking about managing your marketing and sales campaigns using Microsoft CRM's campaign management. Use it wisely, and it will help you lead an organized campaign and (we hope) increase your profits and customer base.

The thorough and powerful Microsoft CRM campaign management feature helps you through the campaign planning process itself, tracks campaign costs and results, and allows links to other parts of the program, such as products and sales literature. Microsoft CRM also lets you adjust your campaign on the fly. Is your supplier offering a new incentive? No problem. You can easily incorporate that new discount or new product into the current campaign.

So let's go basic here: Campaign Manager allows real-time modification of your campaigns. Your marketing folks can access sales information and look at each step in the campaign. On the other side, your sales department is enjoying life because they can finally see what the customers are getting, without having to bribe Mel the marketing assistant. We know, we know. You're saying that having the sales and marketing departments talking to one another can't be done. I bet that's what someone told Orville and Wilbur Wright too, once upon a time.

Planning Your Campaign

As with most things in business, your marketing campaign will work better for you and provide more satisfying results if you plan. Now, actually planning the campaign is outside the scope of this book, so we'll touch on the basics of marketing plans and take a moment to shamelessly plug *Small Business Marketing For Dummies* and *Marketing For Dummies, 2nd Edition*. For the rest of this chapter, we'll focus on building your marketing campaign using Microsoft CRM.

Even though we're leaving the planning of your marketing campaign to the experts, we should touch on a few things, just so you have a reference point for stuff mentioned later in the chapter. Microsoft CRM lets you plan a campaign that can be as manual or as automated as you like. A manual campaign is one in which someone has to go into the system and launch the letters, e-mails, or mailing. This option offers you the most control and flexibility.

On the flip side, say you want to set up a campaign so that all you have to do is go in every week, make sure things are on track, and go back to work — that's the automatic version. You can set up the campaign steps to launch automatically. For example, suppose you want to notify customers when their help-desk agreements are about to expire. You can set up a campaign to run automatically so that these customers receive a notice 30 days before expiration, then another notice 15 days before expiration, and then a stop-the-presses e-mail the day before expiration. If you define the campaign well, you can set it up so that clients who have renewed do not get another reminder.

The following list outlines several other important aspects of your marketing campaign:

- **Track budget versus expenses:** Money, money, money. Your budget is extremely important, and you'll want to make sure you have one established before you start. Then, as the campaign progresses, the cost is automatically calculated in Microsoft CRM. You can enter and adjust information for the total budget of the campaign, the expected revenue, miscellaneous costs, or the total actual cost.

- **Assign promotion codes:** Remember these? The coupon says "Enter Code FREEBIE9 online." Plug it in and bingo, you get that free travel mug or a discount. When you assign promotion codes and people respond with them, you can use them to measure the effectiveness of your campaign (by tracking the resulting lead and sale back to the campaign). This feedback allows you to improve your marketing processes.

- **Target products:** Microsoft CRM will let you associate products and price lists with your campaigns so you can easily link to other areas of Microsoft CRM. This ramps up your Microsoft CRM to a truly integrated campaign management tool.

✔ **Define lists:** Do you want everyone in Alaska or do you want everyone in California? If you're selling parkas, Californians might not be the best group to target. You get the picture: The right list is always a critical part of a campaign. You can build detailed and drilled target lists using Advanced Find searches, based on almost any combination of data that you're tracking in your system.

✔ **Collect marketing material:** Put together the product brochures, promotional fliers, tchotchkes, or sales coupons for your campaign. Some of our favorites are a talking starfish from a hotel/resort chain (you slap it and it says "WHOA! You can do that?"). Another company sent us a pair of drumsticks to announce their new product release (and our office manager has threatened to hide them). Most people love to save money, so coupons attract attention.

As you can see, marketing and sales campaigns have fingers in almost all parts of your Microsoft CRM system, from price lists, to sales literature, to tracking leads and incoming sales.

If you're still waiting for some of your marketing materials to arrive, we recommend creating blank documents with the correct titles so you can at least have a framework for your campaign. You can always go back and put in the correct items later. And whatever you do, do not put racy or offensive messages on these blanks, even as a joke. It's been well documented that the Minions of Chaos will take this scenario and run with it, leaving you and your company in the hot seat.

You'll also want to set your revenue target and the starting and ending dates of your campaign. We suggest that you put all this together in an outline before building your campaign. That way, you can see any holes in your campaign before they become an issue.

Creating Campaigns

Now, let's say you have a plan and a budget, you successfully countered all the points your boss brought up, and you even managed to get all your materials ordered. The only thing left to do is follow these steps:

1. **At the bottom of the navigation pane, click the Marketing button. Then, at the top of the pane, click Campaigns.**

   The Campaigns window appears, as shown in Figure 22-1. (You can get here also by clicking Workplace in the navigation pane and then clicking Campaigns, under Marketing.) Click the arrow to the right of the View field to display the following categories of campaigns: All Campaigns and Campaign Templates, Campaign Templates, Launched Campaigns, and My Campaigns.

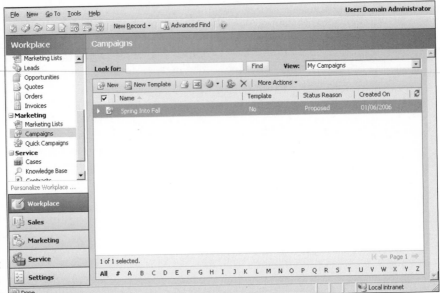

Figure 22-1:
All cam-
paigns start
here.

2. **In the window's toolbar, click the New button.**

   The Campaign: New window appears, as shown in Figure 22-2. By
   default, the window appears with the General tab selected. As with most
   fields in Microsoft CRM, the bold (red on your screen) fields are mandatory. If you take a look at the navigation pane, you'll see that you are in
   the Details section. The other options and sections become available
   when you save the campaign.

3. **Enter a name for your campaign.**

4. **Click the arrow to the right of the Status Reason field to select an
   option from the drop-down box.**

   Because we're creating a campaign here, we want Proposed. After your
   campaign is defined and everything is in place, you can change the
   status to Ready to Launch. The other options are self-explanatory.

5. **Enter your Campaign Code.**

   You can enter a code (perhaps as part of a marketing gimmick) or let the
   program assign the code (just leave it blank for now). The campaign
   code helps you link responses to the campaign for those important
   reports and demographic data.

6. **Choose your Campaign Type.**

   Use the arrow to the right of the field to open the drop-down box. Your
   options are Advertisement, Direct Marketing, Event, Co-branding, and
   Other.

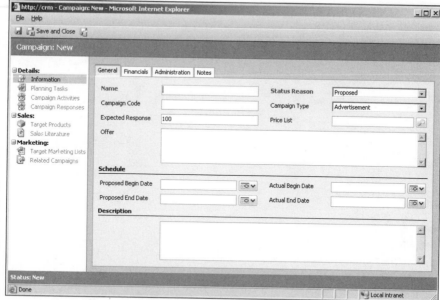

Figure 22-2:
Technically,
building
your
campaign
starts here.

7. **Next, enter your expected response.**

   This is where you would put the expected number of responses. For example, if you're sending 500 mailers and expect a 1 percent response rate, you would put 5 here. This allows you to measure the actual response rate against what you estimated.

8. **Select a price list to associate with this campaign.**

   Even if you don't fill in any of the other optional fields, we recommend that you at least choose a price list so that the campaign has something to work from.

9. **In the Offer field, describe your offer.**

10. **Click Save (the disk icon).**

    Your data is saved, and you can move on to the other tabs.

Now enter information on the Financials tab as follows:

1. **Click the Financials tab (see Figure 22-3).**

2. **Complete the Budget Allocated, Miscellaneous Cost, and Estimated Revenue fields.**

   The other two fields (Total Cost of Campaign Activities and Total Cost of Campaign) are calculated automatically as you define and run your campaign.

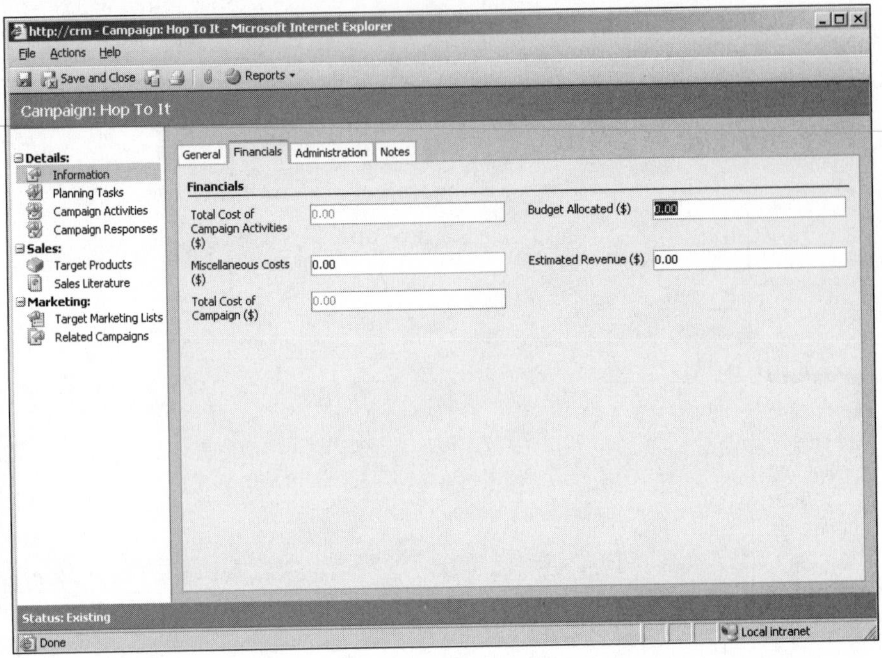

Figure 22-3:
Money
makes the
campaign
go round.

3. **Remember to click Save (the disk icon).**

   We suggest that you save your data each time you move to a new tab or option within your campaign.

After you've entered your financial information, you can either click the Save and Close button or enter notes in the Notes tab.

The Administration tab contains basic campaign administration notes (Owner, Created date, date of last modification, and who did the change), which are filled in automatically. The only field you can edit on this tab is Owner. The Owner field defaults to the logged-in username; you can change the owner by clicking the hourglass to the right of the field.

Now, let's take a look at those now active options in the navigation pane (refer to Figure 22-3). These will help you tune your campaign from the family station wagon into a hotrod.

Planning Tasks

Consider this section as your campaign check list. In the Planning Tasks area, you can enter as many tasks as you need to, whether it's ordering the tchotchkes, picking up paper, selecting graphics, and more. You can also complete or close tasks from this area and keep track of where you are in processing the campaign. All tasks you add here are also added automatically to your Outlook task list, so you can keep them in a central place. Let's take a look at entering a planning task:

1. **Get to an open campaign window (like the one we created earlier).**

2. **In the navigation pane, select Planning Tasks.**

   The Planning Tasks window appears, as shown in Figure 22-4.

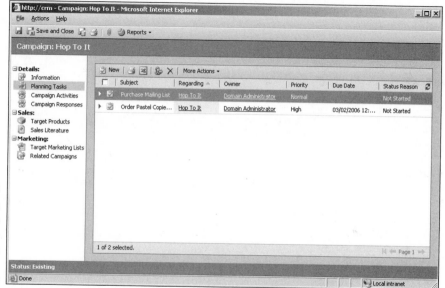

Figure 22-4: Setting up campaign tasks is easy.

3. **In the window's toolbar, click the New button to create a new task.**

   The Task: New window appears, as shown in Figure 22-5. This window is similar to the one you see when scheduling activities (see Chapter 14).

4. **Fill in the Subject and Owner fields, which are required.**

5. **Fill in the Regarding field.**

   Why would you want to do this? Easy. Say your task is to obtain a mailing list from Listzilla. By selecting Listzilla in the Regarding field, you can link this task to that contact and still have the task listed under the campaign. The cool thing here is that you don't have to link to just contacts. You can link to other Microsoft CRM records, such as cases, contacts, and leads.

6. **If desired, fill in the remaining optional fields.**

   Remember, the more information you have, the better you can complete a task.

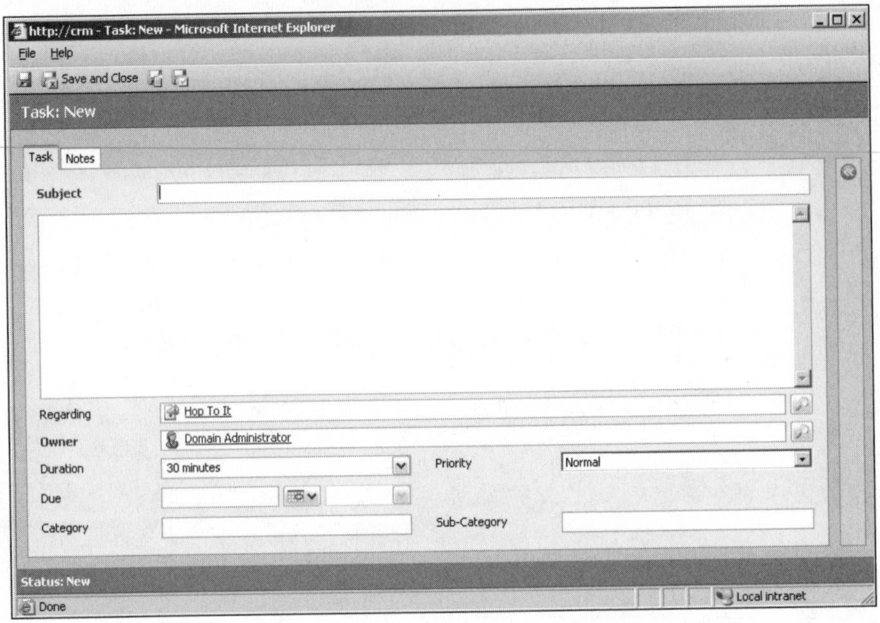

Figure 22-5:
See what
we mean?

7. **To add notes to this task, click the Notes tab and enter away.**

   As with other note fields in Microsoft CRM, you can enter information free-form.

8. **Click the Save and Close button.**

   This saves the task and returns you to the planning tasks workspace.

Campaign Activities

Campaign Activities is the next option in the navigation pane of your open campaign window (see Figure 22-6). Here, you can list the phases, or waves, of your campaign, select target literature, or distribute campaign activity.

To create a campaign activity, follow these steps:

1. **With a campaign window open, click the New button.**

   The Campaign Activity: New window appears, as shown in Figure 22-7. In this window, the Parent Campaign, Subject, and Owner fields are required. The Parent Campaign and Status Reason fields are filled in automatically.

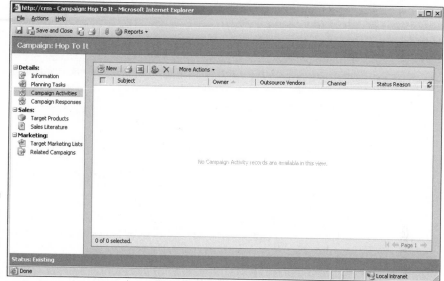

Figure 22-6:
Activities
are different
from tasks.

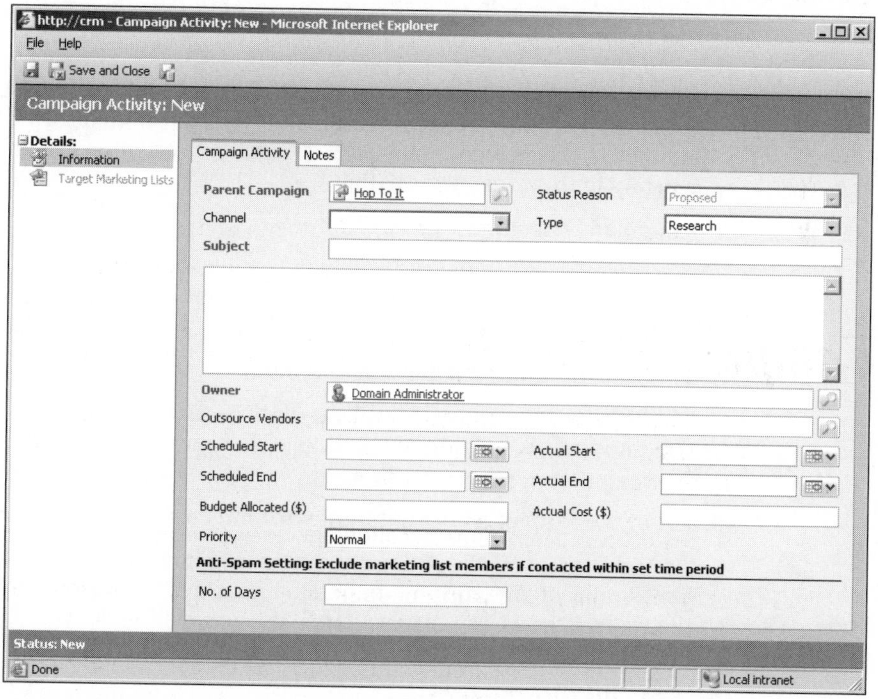

Figure 22-7:
Start by
creating the
first wave of
your
campaign.

2. **Select a Channel using the arrow on the right of the field to open the drop-down box.**

   This is where you tell the program how you want this phase carried out: phone, fax, letter, e-mail, appointment, and so on. To clarify, this is not a marketing channel, such as direct marketing or distribution. By the way, this selection must be made to distribute campaign activities, a topic covered later in this chapter.

3. **Choose a type for this campaign activity.**

   The Type is the purpose of the campaign activity, such as research or lead qualification.

4. **Enter a subject for your campaign activity.**

   Although you can call the activity anything you want, we suggest that you keep the subject logical and self-explanatory. Calling your campaign activity 'Fluffy Bunny Slippers" tells people nothing unless you're really sending out fluffy bunny slippers.

5. **Fill in the open field under the Subject field.**

   This is a free-form area for notes or a description for your campaign activity. We'll flog the developers later for not labeling the field.

6. **Choose an owner.**

   The Owner field automatically defaults to the user creating the campaign activity, but you can change it. If you want to delegate tasks in the campaign, this is where you do it. Assign the owner here, and the task appears in the owner's activities.

7. **Assign an outsource vendor.**

   Use the magnifying glass to search for and select a vendor. For example, if the local printing company, Ink, Inc., is printing the invitations to your webinar, they are your outsource vendor.

8. **Choose a scheduled start and end date.**

   This is self-explanatory. To the left of these fields, you'll see Actual Start and End Date, which are not enabled. These are filled in automatically when you start the campaign.

9. **Fill in the Budget Allocated field with the cost of your budget.**

   This way, you can check your budget at a glance instead of having to e-mail folks or rifle through papers on your desk. The companion field to the right, Actual Cost, is just that — the actual tally of everything related to this campaign.

10. **Fill in the Priority field.**

11. **Click Save (the disk icon) or the Save and Close button.**

    Remember, if you want to do some more work on the campaign activity, just click Save. Your campaign activity will be saved and the option in the navigation pane will be enabled.

Marketing always walks a fine line, especially today, with people highly sensitive to spam and their rights as a consumer. So what should you do when you want an aggressive marketing campaign but not one so aggressive that people become tired of receiving stuff from you and immediately circular-file it? At the bottom of the campaign activity window, take a look at the Anti-Spam Setting area. Basically, you enter a number of days, and the system will automatically scan and not contact (that is, generate letters or e-mail, schedule calls, and so on) those clients who have had contact in that many days. Not only does it make customers happy by not overloading their inbox, it makes your company look more on the ball. You're not sending a third request or marketing wave if the person calls after the second one and gets in the pipeline.

Let's take a look at the other option in the Campaign: New window, Target Marketing Literature. This option refers to the documents you are going to send in this activity and have already associated with this campaign. (You find out how to add literature to a campaign later in this chapter.)

Tacking literature onto the campaign at this point is pretty simple:

1. **With the campaign window open, click Add from Campaign.**

   The Look Up Records dialog box appears, so you can search for the document.

2. **When you find the document, double-click the right-pointing arrow to move it over to the selected pane.**

3. **Click OK.**

   You return to the Campaign Activity: New window.

Now let's say that your campaign includes making telephone calls. You 1,000 leads and 25 phone-call makers. Those making the calls are not necessarily salespeople; you could have qualifiers making the calls and then directing them to salespeople. How to get those phone calls scheduled to all 25 people? Yes, the logistics can choke even a skilled planner. We know you value your staff and don't want them choking, so eyes up to the main toolbar and the Distribute Campaign Activity button.

Because calls are the most common items that require scheduling en masse, you take a look at how to handle that task in the following:

1. **In the main toolbar, click the Distribute Campaign Activity button.**

   The box that appears depends on the channel you selected in Step 3 in the steps at the beginning of this section (see Figure 22-7). Because we selected Phone as the channel, the New Phone Calls dialog box appears, as shown in Figure 22-8.

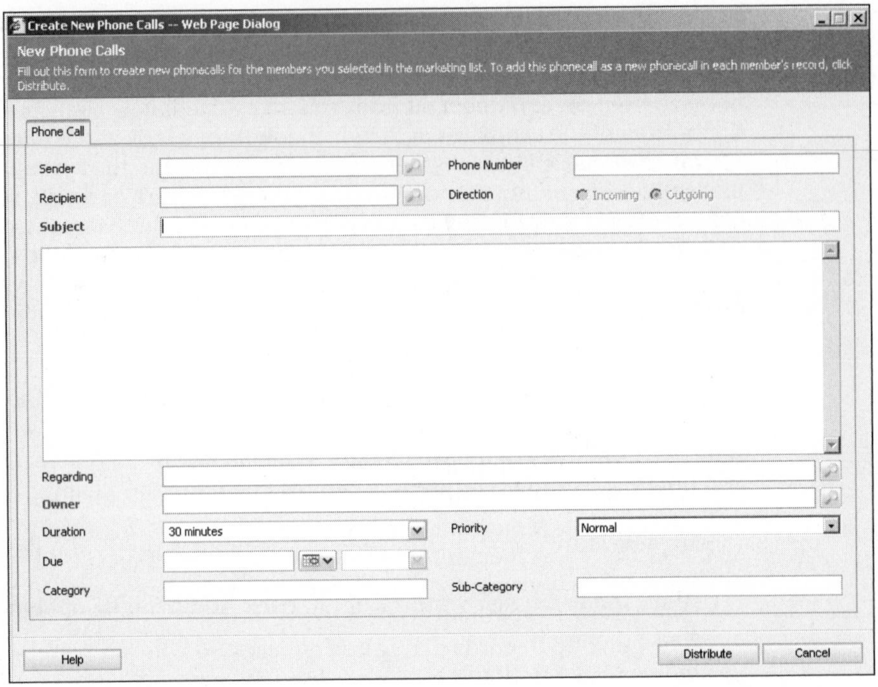

Figure 22-8:
Adding
phone calls
as activities.

2. **Enter the subject.**

   Subject is a mandatory field. You might call this Seminar Invite or Qualify Prospect. Basically, the subject is a description of the activity you're distributing.

3. **In the bottom-right corner, click Distribute.**

   Again, the dialog box that appears depends on the channel you chose to deliver this activity. Because we're using a phone call as our channel, the Distribute Phone Calls dialog box appears. You have two options here to indicate the Owner (the person the call is being assigned to) of the phone call:

   - The owners of the records in the target marketing lists
   - I will own the new phone calls

4. **Click OK.**

   You return to the campaign activity window. Take a look in the navigation pane, where you'll see added options to help you track this distribution.

5. **Click Save (the disk icon) or the Save and Close button.**

   Voila! You're done!

The phone-call option and channel will track where the phone calls went and how many failed attempts were made. As you can see, Microsoft CRM makes campaign scheduling especially easy for those in large companies and those who handle a large number of activities for marketing campaigns.

Campaign Responses

When you create a marketing campaign, you expect results or responses, whether they're negative or positive. There are even folks dedicated to determining response rates, filtering that information into percentages, and making little pie charts and bar graphs from those responses. Good news or bad, you can record it in Microsoft CRM.

Another little bonus to being able to record your responses in a central system like this is that your sales department and your marketing department can see the same information! Whoa! Who doesn't want their departments working together, in sync and harmony? (Okay, maybe not harmony as the marketing department stomped the sales department last year in the softball game, but you get the picture.)

Excited now? Good. Here's how you (or your sales staff) can record those responses:

1. **At the bottom of the navigation pane, click the Marketing button. At the top of the pane, click Campaigns.**

2. **In the Campaigns window, double-click your campaign.**

   The campaign window appears.

3. **In the navigation pane of the open campaign window, click Campaign Responses (see Figure 22-9).**

4. **In the window's toolbar, click New.**

   The Campaign Response: New window appears, as shown in Figure 22-10. Most of the fields are self-evident, but we'll touch on some of them here. You may complete them as appropriate using the magnifying glass to the right of a field or the Form Assistant (which is collapsed in Figure 22-10).

   • **Response Code:** This indicates the response of the customer. You can choose from: Interested; Not Interested; Do Not Send Marketing Materials; Error.

   • **Promotion Code:** You can link the response to a particular promotion. If the customer is calling because of the free bunny slippers, for example, you can indicate that here. Several campaigns could have the same promotion, so this is just another way of grouping data for marketing analysis.

   • **Customer:** This can be an account, a contact, or a lead.

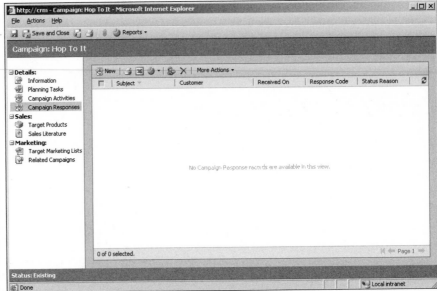

Figure 22-9:
Check and
record
responses
to all your
campaigns.

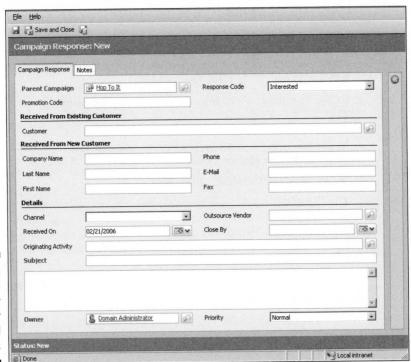

Figure 22-10:
Did the
customer
say yes or
no? Record
it here.

5. When you've completed the form, click the Save and Close button.

The Campaign Response window closes, and you return to the open campaign window.

By recording campaign responses, you can easily check the status of each campaign throughout its lifespan. This is a great feature, because you can see, for example, whether one promotion is taking off or a certain employee is having trouble making calls.

Target Products

Your target products are the products and services targeted by this campaign. If your campaign is to promote the Hop-n-Pop Toaster, the toaster is your target product. So let's add your target products to this campaign:

1. At the bottom of the navigation pane, click the Marketing button. At the top of the pane, select Campaigns.

2. In the Campaigns window, double-click your campaign.

The campaign window appears.

3. In the navigation pane of the campaign window, click Target Products.

The workspace switches to the target products view, as shown in Figure 22-11.

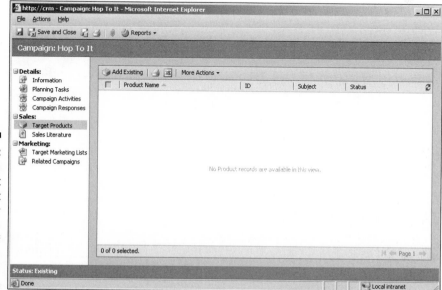

Figure 22-11: Adding a target product helps your staff keep track of what's being offered.

4. **In the window's toolbar, click Add Existing.**

   A Look Up Records dialog box appears.

5. **Find and select your intended target product, and then double-click the right-pointing arrow to move it to the right-hand pane.**

6. **Click OK.**

   Back in the target products workspace, you'll see that your new product has been added.

7. **Click the Save and Close button to close the campaign window, or go back to the navigation pane for more options.**

Adding target products is useful, especially to your call makers, who might not be that familiar with all the products in a campaign.

Sales Literature

Just like you linked a target product, you can also link sales literature for the campaign or for that product. This way, your call makers can look at the same thing the customer is looking at. Just follow these steps:

1. **In the navigation pane of the open campaign window, click Sales Literature.**

   The workspace switches to the sales literature view, as shown in Figure 22-12.

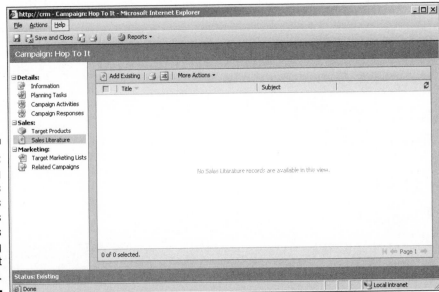

Figure 22-12:
Adding sales literature is just as helpful as adding target products.

2. **In the window's toolbar, click Add Existing.**

   A Look Up Records dialog box appears.

3. **Find and select your sales literature, and then double-click the right-pointing arrow to move it to the right-hand pane.**

4. **Click OK.**

   Back in the sales literature workspace, you'll see that your new document has been added.

5. **Click the Save and Close button to close the campaign window or go back to the navigation pane for more options.**

Target Marketing Lists

Target marketing lists are just what they sound like: the lists of people to whom you are directing this campaign. See Chapter 21 for information about building marketing lists. In this section, we show you how to link those marketing lists to your campaign. Here's how:

1. **In the navigation pane of the open campaign window, click Target Marketing Lists.**

   The workspace switches to your target marketing lists workspace, as shown in Figure 22-13.

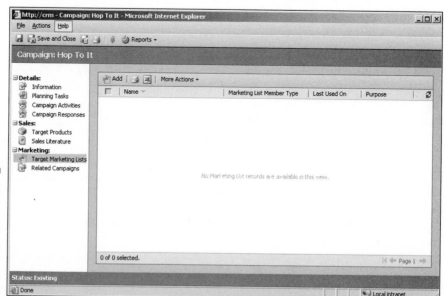

Figure 22-13: Adding the targeted marketing list can also help your staff out.

2. **In the window's toolbar, click Add.**

   As with adding target products and sales literature, the Look Up Records dialog box appears.

3. **Search for and select your records, and then click the right-pointing arrow to move them to the Selected Records pane.**

4. **Click OK.**

   Another dialog window pops up, asking whether you want to add the marketing lists to the campaign activities as well as this campaign.

5. **Make your selection in the dialog box, and then click OK.**

   You can select the box or click it again to unselect it.

6. **Click Save (the disk icon).**

   You could click the Save and Close button instead. But because we have a related item to show you in the next section, we suggest that you click Save so you can stay in the open campaign window.

Your target marketing list now appears in the workspace. Regarding the campaign activity question (Step 4), let's look at your activity lists to see exactly what changes were made:

1. **In the navigation pane of the open campaign window, click Campaign Activities.**

   The workspace view switches to your campaign activities.

2. **Double-click a campaign activity to open it.**

3. **In the navigation pane of the open campaign activity window, click Target Marketing List.**

   The list that you just linked appears here.

Related Campaigns

Now, say you're running two campaigns: one to identify interest by product category and one to reflect different marketing strategies for each product category. That's great. But what if you want to compare them? Easy! Just relate the campaigns to each other. Here's how:

1. **In the navigation pane of the open campaign window, click Related Campaigns.**

   The window switches to the related campaigns workspace, as shown in Figure 22-14.

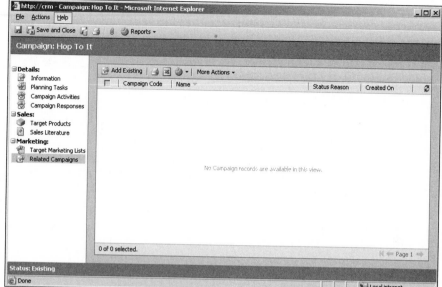

Figure 22-14:
Relating
campaigns
to each
other is also
a snap.

2. **In the window's toolbar, click Add.**

   Like the other options mentioned in this chapter, the Look Up Records dialog box appears.

3. **Search for the other campaign you want to relate to this one, select it, and click the right-pointing arrow to add it to the right-hand pane.**

4. **Click OK.**

   You return to the related campaigns workspace.

5. **Click Save (the disk icon) or the Save and Close button to save your work.**

One of the great features of Microsoft CRM is that you can do a report on just about anything, including campaign performance, which you can check by clicking the Campaign Responses or Related Campaigns selection in the navigation pane of your campaign window. Then just click the Reports icon in the window's toolbar (or select a report from the drop-down box by clicking the arrow next to the Reports icon). The report can be printed as a table or a graph. Either way, use the information to help you stay on top of what's going on in the campaign.

Part V
Taking Care of
Your Customers

The 5th Wave   By Rich Tennant

"Oh, we're doing just great. Philip and I are
selling decorative jelly jars on eBay. I run
the auctions, and Philip sort of controls
the inventory."

In this part . . .

*O*ne of the beautiful parts of Microsoft CRM is that it handles both sales and service. This integration enables your organization to coordinate activities from both sides of the fence. Salespeople, in the middle of trying to close a deal, won't be blindsided by some raging customer support issue. Customer service people will know enough to provide that little extra when a major sale is about to go down.

Customer service is one of the hot buttons in CRM and is an area in which Microsoft CRM shines. When a customer calls with an issue, it is logged as a case (Chapter 23).

Scheduling service activities is a special case of more general activity scheduling and is discussed in Chapter 24. Managing your database of subjects is handled in Chapter 25.

Cases and tasks are put into a queue for orderly disposition and management by staff members (Chapter 26).

Microsoft CRM even includes contract administration, so everyone can see what type of support a customer is entitled to and the software can properly decrement contracts and advise when renewals are in order (Chapter 27). We describe all this in Part V.

Chapter 23

Working with Cases

Microsoft CRM has taken customer service to the next generation by devoting an entire module of the program to it. The heart of the Service module is the Cases window, where you can view, resolve, and reactivate cases in an easy and comprehensible manner.

When a customer calls in with a problem, the customer service representative taking the call opens a *case* to document the problem and its eventual solution. The customer may have a faulty power supply, a new version of software that continually locks up, or a toaster that refuses to pop its contents. Some companies refer to cases as *tickets* or *issues*. Whatever they're called, active case management is the name of the game; the better you manage your cases, the better your customer service and customer satisfaction.

In this chapter, we show you how to create a case and assign it to someone on your team. You find out how to open an existing case and resolve it, scheduling activities related to gaining the solution along the way. You also find out how to reactivate a case when necessary.

Case Management Overview

The case management path looks like this: A customer service representative (CSR) takes a call. Let's say the customer is having a problem with one of your transporters. He dialed Camelot, A.D. 495 and ended up in Peoria, 1958.

The CSR creates a case and links it to the appropriate customer. The case is assigned to an engineer. The engineer sets about finding a solution, generating a few e-mails to the customer along the way. The engineer solves the problem and closes the case.

A week later, the customer calls back with the same problem. A CSR (not necessarily the same one as before) reactivates the case, and the solution process begins anew. A more thorough solution is developed and recorded, and the case is closed again. A month later, a different customer calls with the same problem. Any CSR can search the database for all cases related to the same problem. This is case management at its best.

Working in the Cases Window

Cases are listed in the main display area of the Cases window, like the one shown in Figure 23-1. You use this window to open cases, and then add notes and schedule activities, with the goal of resolving the case. The Cases window is also where you assign cases to other service representatives, share cases, or accept them yourself. The entire service team can use this window to collectively track the current status and ultimate disposition of cases.

To open the Cases window, click the Service button at the bottom of the navigation pane. Then select Cases from the list of options at the top of the pane.

Find cases   Filter cases

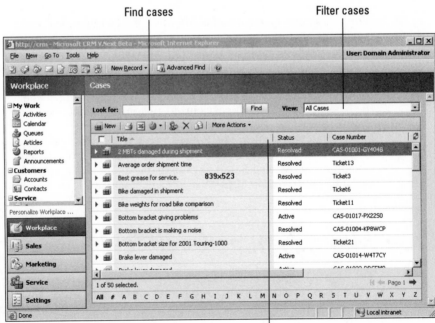

Figure 23-1:
The Cases window is where you can view and sort cases.

Sort cases by column headings

The main part of the window has a list of all your active cases. You can filter this list by choosing one of the following options from the drop-down menu next to View.

- ✔ **Active Cases:** All cases assigned to you or your fellow team members that haven't been resolved.

- ✔ **All Cases:** All cases assigned to you or your fellow team members that are open or have been resolved.

- ✔ **My Active Cases:** All cases assigned to you that haven't been resolved. During a Microsoft CRM session, when entering the Cases window for the first time or going back to it, the View option always reverts to My Active Cases (unless it has been changed by the system administrator).

- ✔ **My Resolved Cases:** All cases assigned to you that have been resolved.

- ✔ **Resolved Cases:** All cases assigned to you or your fellow team members that have been resolved.

These are the views you get "out of the box." Your implementation partner or system administrator can add, rename, and delete views.

You can sort cases also by column headings. Just click a column heading to sort as follows:

- ✔ Title displays cases alphabetically.

- ✔ Status displays the cases alphabetically by status (resolved or active).

- ✔ Case Number displays cases in numerical order.

- ✔ Priority displays cases by level of importance.

- ✔ Created On displays cases in chronological order.

Again, note that your system administrator can add columns to this list or delete columns from this list.

Click a column header a second time to display the cases in reverse order.

You have two ways to find specific cases. The Look For field at the top of the Cases window lets you search active cases by title or case number. You may type the full title or any part of it. Click the Find button, and a list of matching cases appears. Use the wildcard character * to account for text that may or may not exist. For example, searching for *porter would return Porter, Transporter, and Exporter.

You can also use the Advanced Find feature to search various fields. To do so, choose Tools⇨Advanced Find or click the Advanced Find button in the toolbar at the top of the screen. Microsoft CRM lets you define search criteria over several fields. Figure 23-2 shows just some of the case-related field that you can use to perform a search.

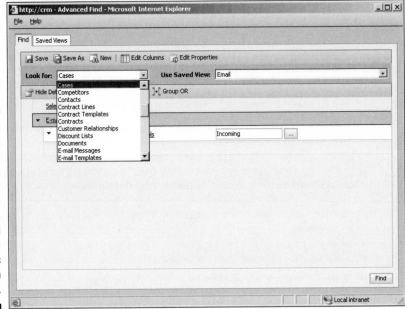

Figure 23-2: The Advanced Find feature enables you to use multiple fields and specific definitions to search for cases.

Creating Cases

Typically, a Microsoft CRM user with administrative rights creates a customer service team by assigning customer service representative (CSR) roles to users in your company. Then the CSRs can use the Microsoft CRM Service module to create, assign, and resolve cases. To create a case (assuming one of your defined roles is CSR), first you need to get to the Case: New window, as follows:

1. **At the bottom of the navigation pane, click the Service button. At the top of the pane, select Cases.**

   The Cases window appears on the right (refer to Figure 23-1).

2. **In the toolbar near the top of the screen, click New Record and then select Case from the drop-down menu.**

   The Case: New window appears, as shown in Figure 23-3.

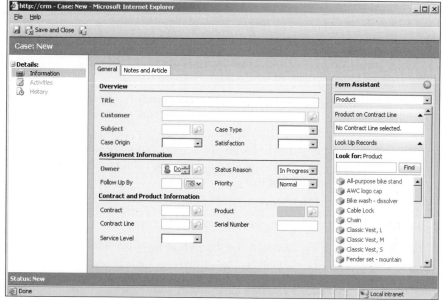

Figure 23-3:
The General
tab shows
basic
information
about the
case.

Filling in the General tab

The Case: New window has two tabs: the General tab and the Notes and Article tab. The General tab is divided into three sections: Overview, which has six fields to further define the case; Assignment Information; and Contract and Product Information.

Some fields (such as Subject) have a magnifying glass to the right of the field. This means you must use the magnifying glass or the Form Assistant to fill in the field. For more information on both options, see Chapter 2.

Remember, all fields in red are required. We'll begin with the Overview area of the General tab:

1. **In the Title box of the General tab, enter a title for the case.**

   The title should be short yet informative. For example, you could name the case after the faulty product and its part number (such as Hop-n-Pop Toaster; Part #T86258) or the problem (such as Hopless Toaster). The Title field can hold a maximum of 175 characters.

   The text in this field can be used to search for the case later, so be specific and descriptive.

2. **Use the Form Assistant to fill in the Customer field.**

   You could use the magnifying glass instead, but we'll use the Form Assistant here as an example of how it works:

   a. **Click the drop-down arrow by the Look For field and select Account or Contact.**

   b. **If you want, select an account (or contact) from the list, or use the Find field to further narrow your search.**

      Remember to use the * wildcard character to help fill in the blanks if you're not sure of the full name of the record you're looking for. If you leave the Find field blank, a list of *all* accounts or contacts will be displayed.

   c. **Click Find.**

   d. **Select the account or contact from the list.**

      The account is entered into the Customer field.

3. **Use the Form Assistant to fill in the Subject field.**

   The Subject option categorizes your cases by subject, such as Billing or Product support. You can link the case to a subject in your subject tree. (For more on the subject tree, see Chapter 25.)

4. **Back in the General tab, in the Case Origin field, click the arrow and select how you received the case.**

5. **In the Case Type box, select a value from the drop-down list.**

   The value categorizes the case as a question, problem, or request.

6. **In the Satisfaction field, select the option that best indicates the customer's level of satisfaction with your service.**

   Maybe the Rolling Stones can't get no satisfaction, but your customers can.

The Assignment Information area of the General tab has four fields. Fill them in as follows:

1. **In the Form Assistant, select the Owner option and choose who you want to assign the case to for resolution.**

   This field defaults to you, the creator of the case. You can reassign the case to another user later.

2. **In the Follow Up By box, select the date on which the owner should follow up on the case.**

   You can click the calendar or make a selection from the drop-down list.

3. **In the General tab's Status Reason field, select the option that best describes the current status of the case.**

4. **In the Priority box, set a priority for this case.**

The Contract and Product Information area offers five more fields to define your case:

1. **In the Form Assistant, select the Contract option.**

   Select a contract to link this case to.

2. **In the Form Assistant, select the Contract Line option.**

   Set the case to a contract line here.

3. **In the General tab's Service Level field, click the arrow and select the appropriate service level from the list.**

4. **In the Form Assistant, select the Product option.**

   This lets you link the case to a particular product.

5. **In the General tab's Serial Number field, enter a serial number associated with this case or with a product associated with this case.**

Now you can move on to the Notes and Article tab.

Filling in the Notes and Article tab

The other tab of the Case: New window, Notes and Article, is much simpler than the General tab, as you can see in Figure 23-4. This is where you can enter any notes and articles pertaining to the case. For example, you could note your conversation with the customer in the Notes section and attach a letter from the customer in the Article field.

Microsoft CRM calls a knowledge base item an *article*. So you could have, for example, an item, or article, on how to stop a transporter from going to Peoria.

To fill in the first area of the Notes and Article tab, follow the self-explanatory instruction to "Click here to enter a new note." A data entry area appears for you to manually enter a note. Enter as many notes as you like.

In the second area, you can link an article that ties into this particular case. If you use the Form Assistant and select the Article option, Microsoft CRM automatically displays your top ten article selections based on the links you defined in the knowledge base. (For more information on the knowledge base, see Chapter 9.) If this list doesn't show you the article you need, you can use the magnifying glass.

Click the Show Article check box to display the article you selected in the Notes and Article tab. After the article is displayed, you can e-mail it to a client from this tab by clicking Email KB Article.

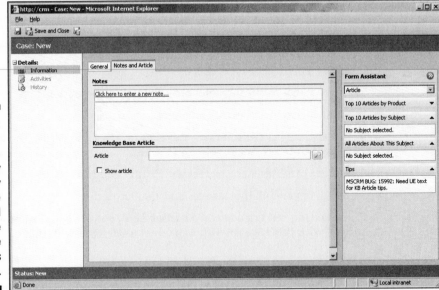

Figure 23-4:
The second
tab of the
Case: New
window
shows the
notes and
knowledge
base
articles
area.

In the last section, we showed you how to use the Form Assistant. Here, we'll describe the second technique, using the magnifying glass. To look up a knowledge base article in your library and attach it to this case, do the following:

1. **Click the magnifying glass icon at the end of the Article field.**

   The Look Up Articles dialog box appears, as shown in Figure 23-5. You have a handful of ways for searching the knowledge base.

2. **Click the arrow in the top drop-down box to choose one of the following options to search for articles:**

   - Full text search: Search the full text of articles for specific words

   - Keyword search: Search by keyword

   - Title search: Search by article title

   - Article number search: Search for an article number

   - Subject browse: Browse all the subjects to find what you want

3. **In the Search For field, enter the word or words that you want to find.**

4. **In the In Subject field, make a selection:**

   a. **Click the magnifying glass to the right of the field.**

      The Look Up a Subject dialog box appears, listing your subjects organized by headings and subheadings. You can choose a specific subject for the program to search. For example, if you select the subject Marketing, the program won't look for your text in Sales, Service, or Thank You Letters.

b. Select a subject.

c. Click OK.

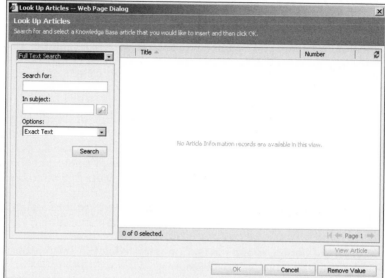

Figure 23-5:
Search the
knowledge
base for
articles
related to
the case.

5. **In the Options field, make a selection from the drop-down list.**

   You have two options: Exact Text, which means the search looks for exact matches only, and Use Like Words, which searches for the string of text you entered. For example, enter the word *pro* and you'll get everything containing that sequence of letters.

6. **Click the Search button.**

   A list of articles meeting your search criteria appears on the right.

7. **When you find the article you want, double-click it (or select it and click OK) to attach it to the case.**

   You return to the Case: New dialog box, where you can continue adding articles or exit the case altogether. Only one article can be attached at a time.

8. **To save your data, click the Save and Close button in the upper-left corner of the Case: New window.**

Congratulations, you've made your first case (and it has nothing to do with baskets). The next step in working with a case is to assign it (if you're the assigner) or accept it (if you're the assignee).

Assigning and Accepting Cases

After you create a case, you can begin to manage it. In a typical service department, managers assign cases in a number of ways. The case might be on a first-come, first-served basis or assigned by the level of complexity to the person with the experience for that level. Maybe the service staff is segmented by product lines, and cases are assigned based on the associated product. From a different perspective, cases may be *pushed* out to technicians by a manager or they may be *pulled* by the staff. In all these scenarios, cases must be managed.

After work on a case begins, your service department should have a standard operating procedure in place to determine how often a case should be reviewed. If you use workflow rules (described in Chapter 8), you can automate the case review timeline. Whether the review process is automated or manual, cases can be opened and edited as they are moved to resolution.

The first thing you want to do to start work on a case is to assign it to someone. In the following, we assign a case to a user:

1. **At the bottom of the navigation pane, click the Service button. At the top of the pane, select Cases.**

   The Cases window appears on the right.

2. **In the Cases window, select a case.**

   To select several records for an ensuing action, hold down the Ctrl key and click. Checking the little box at the top of the first column (under the New button) selects all cases.

3. **Click the Assign icon in the toolbar above the list of cases.**

   The Assign to Queue or User dialog box appears, displaying two options for managing cases. Route Case is a powerful option after you establish workflow rules. Find out more about defining workflow rules and processes in Chapter 8.

4. **Click the "Assign to another user or queue" option, and then click the magnifying glass icon to the right of the field.**

   The Look Up Records dialog box appears, as shown in Figure 23-6.

5. **In the Look For box, choose User or Queue.**

   By default, the field displays User. In this example, we're assigning the case to a fellow user, so you're all set. A brief explanation of queues appears later in this section.

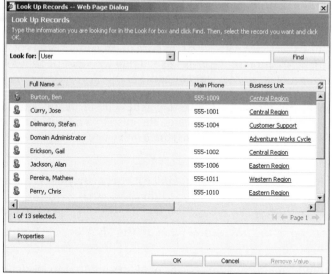

Figure 23-6:
You can
assign the
case to an
individual
CSR or
place it in a
service
queue.

6. **To narrow the search, go to the field to the left of the Find button and type the last name of the user to whom you'd like to assign the case. Then click Find.**

A list of all matching users appears. When you enter a last name, you need to enter only as many letters as it will take Microsoft CRM to select the appropriate user from the list. The search will yield all possible matches. (For example, if you type **sm** — the search is not case sensitive — you'll get Smith, Mary, and Smolinski, Gerald.)

7. **Select the name of the user to whom you want to assign the case, and click OK.**

You must highlight the appropriate user even if only one match is listed.

When you click OK, you return to the Confirm Assignment dialog box, where the username now appears.

8. **Click OK to close the Confirm Assignment dialog box.**

You return to the window of the case you were assigning, and that case has now been assigned.

9. **As with everything else in Microsoft CRM, remember to click Save or Save and Close to ensure that your changes stick.**

For you users to whom the case has been assigned, you can now view the case in your Cases window.

Microsoft CRM uses queues as a way of sorting cases for action by a specific group of customer service representatives. Think of a *queue* as an inbox for similar cases. By creating a queue based on expertise with a certain line of products or experience with a certain type of procedure, you can help streamline the solution process by associating the right people with a specific type of problem or service request.

When you're working in the Assign to Queue or User dialog box (refer to Step 3 in the preceding list), you can assign the case to a queue or route it based on workflow rules (see Chapter 8). After you've accepted a case, it appears in your My Active Cases view.

Follow these steps to check out and accept cases assigned to your queue:

1. **At the bottom of the navigation pane, click the Workplace button.**

2. **At the top of the navigation pane, in the My Work section, select Queues.**

   If a plus sign appears next to My Work, click it first to open the list. The Queues window appears on the right, with its own navigation pane and a list of queues (refer to Figure 23-7).

3. **In the Queues window, click a folder under My Work.**

   Each folder is a separate queue. All cases assigned to that queue appear in the main window.

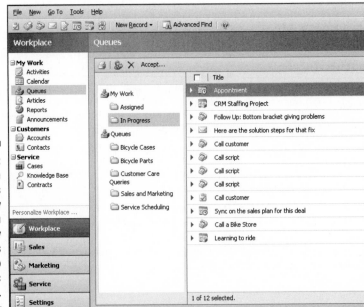

Figure 23-7:
The pane in the Queues window enables you to view all cases assigned to a specific queue.

In Microsoft CRM, you can't reject a case or an activity. (By *activity*, I mean a task, a fax, a phone call, an e-mail, a letter, or an appointment.) If you don't want to accept a case or an activity that has been assigned to you, you must reassign it to another user or queue.

   4. Click the case you want to accept.

   To select multiple cases, hold down the Ctrl key and click.

   5. At the top of the Queues window, click the Accept button.

   The Confirm Assignment dialog box appears.

   6. Click OK.

   The case is now removed from the queue and assigned to you in your In Progress queue.

Tending to Cases

As you work toward resolving a case, you typically have to perform certain activities to obtain a solution. For example, you might need to perform tests on the T-900 Transporter to see whether it will repeat the problem your customer reported. In this scenario, you would perform the following steps to log your time and associate it with the T-900 case:

   1. At the bottom of the navigation pane, click the Service button. Then, and the top of the pane, select Cases.

   The Cases window appears.

   2. In the Cases window, double-click the case you're working on.

   To follow along with the example, we double-clicked the case for which we are scheduling a test.

   3. In the navigation pane, click the Activities option.

   The window shows uncompleted activities associated with the case.

   4. In the toolbar, click the New Activity button.

   The New Activity dialog box appears. Because we're performing a test on the equipment, a task sounds like the right activity type.

   5. Highlight Task, and then click OK.

   The Task: New window appears.

   6. Enter a subject that describes the task you'll be performing.

Note that the Regarding field already displays the case title, and your name should be in the Owner field. The Duration defaults to 30 minutes, but this can be changed using the drop-down menu or on the main Task window. If appropriate, you can also complete the Due date and time; Priority; Category; and Subcategory fields.

7. Click the Save and Close icon.

The task now appears in the main display for the associated case.

To complete the task (and automatically accrue billable time against the case), follow these steps:

1. In the Cases window, double-click the appropriate case.

The Case window appears, showing the case you selected. (The title of the window includes the name of the case.)

2. In the navigation pane, click the Activities option.

You see a list of all activities associated with this case.

3. Double-click the task you want to close.

4. Click the Save as Completed icon.

In the Case window, you'll see that the task is no longer displayed under Activities in the navigation pane. But wait! Check History. If you had spent one hour performing the task, for example, the customer would now be on the hook for one hour of contract time.

Resolving a case

You can resolve cases in a number of ways. Maybe you know the solution and can resolve a case as soon as you accept it. Or you may have to research your knowledge base to see whether another service representative has solved the problem. (Chapter 9 covers the knowledge base in depth.)

You can't resolve a case until all activities associated with the case have been completed. This might require completing phone calls, tasks, and appointments, sending e-mail messages, and more. This prevents a user from accidentally closing a case before all mandated workflow and activities have been completed.

After you determine a solution to a case, follow these steps to resolve it:

1. In the Cases window, double-click the case you want to resolve.

You may find it helpful to first select My Active Cases from the View drop-down menu in the upper-right corner of the window.

2. **In the menu bar (at the top of the screen), choose Actions⇨ Resolve Case.**

   The Resolve Case dialog box appears, as shown in Figure 23-8. Note that Microsoft CRM automatically calculates and fills in the Total Time field. *Total time* is defined as the sum of time spent on all activities associated with the resolution of the case. CRM recognizes the following activities as billable (that is, automatically tracked against a case): task, fax, phone call, letter, e-mail, and appointment.

   If you need to adjust the amount of time that the customer will be billed, you may manually override the total time after the case has been resolved.

Figure 23-8:
Document the time you spent resolving a case.

Resolve Case -- Web Page Dialog	
Resolve Case	
Provide information in the following boxes to resolve this case.	

Resolution Type	Problem Solved
Resolution	Dropped Part from 3rd Story Window
Total Time	1 hour
Billable Time	1 hour

Description

OK   Cancel

3. **In the Resolution Type field, make your selection from the drop-down list.**

4. **In the Resolution field, type a short explanation of the resolution.**

5. **Choose a Billable Time increment from the drop-down menu.**

   If this activity is linked to a contract, the billable time you indicate here is applied against the total time listed in the contract.

6. **If you want, fill in the Description field.**

7. **Click OK.**

   The Resolve Case dialog box closes. Note that the case status updates to Resolved in the lower-left corner of the Case window.

Reactivating a case

If a customer calls with a recurrence of a previously resolved problem, you need to reactivate the case. Follow these steps:

1. **In the Cases window, select My Resolved Cases or All Resolved Cases from the View drop-down menu.**

   A list of all your resolved cases appears.

2. **Double-click the case you want to reactivate.**

3. **In the menu bar (at the top of the screen), choose Actions⇨Reactivate.**

   The Reactivate Confirmation dialog box appears.

4. **Click OK.**

   The case status in the lower-left corner of the Case window appears as *active*.

As you can see, Microsoft CRM offers extensive choices to help you better serve your customers, with almost everything just a few clicks away.

Chapter 24

Scheduling Services

*I*magine that it's 102 degrees and every air conditioner from here to the county line has decided to call it quits. Your customers, Mrs. Reynolds, Mr. Wayne, Mr. Cobb, and the rest are calling and starting to lose their cool. They want their units fixed ASAP, and you can't blame them.

Now, you and your guys can handle all these calls, you know you can. Besides, you have Microsoft CRM's robust service scheduling abilities (say that ten times fast) in your corner of the ring. You can schedule all your repair people with a few clicks. In this chapter, you find out how to get your resources and users into the service schedule and then how to schedule them both.

What is a resource? It can be anything you need to help your customers with their service. So if you have, say, a special wrench or an expensive air-conditioning computer to autodiagnose issues, you can assign these to your users or technicians on a job by job or daily basis. That way, you can easily prevent scheduling conflicts that might come up if you assigned the same resource to different people.

Scheduling Resources into Microsoft CRM

With Microsoft CRM, you and your staff can easily deliver timely customer service. The first thing you need to do is set up your resources — that is, your facilities and equipment — on the schedule. Later in the chapter, you define your services.

Let's see how this works:

1. **At the bottom of the navigation pane, click the Settings button.**

   The Settings window appears on the right.

2. **From the Settings window, select Business Unit Settings. Then select Local Facilities/Equipment.**

   You can now begin adding your resources. From here, you can also view your resources, local facilities and equipment, and subsidiary facilities and equipment using the View drop-down list (see Figure 24-1).

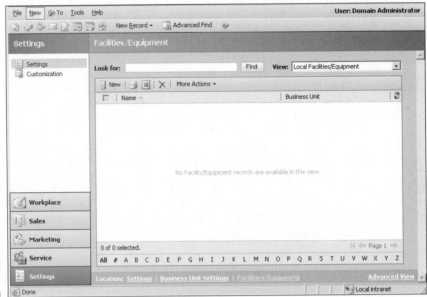

Figure 24-1: Resources are easy to add to Microsoft CRM.

3. **In the window's toolbar, click the New button.**

   The Facilities/Equipment: New window appears, as shown in Figure 24-2.

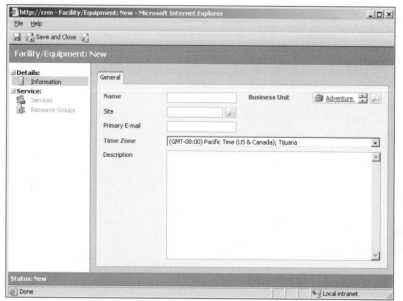

Figure 24-2:
Start with
the name
of your
resource.

4. **In the Name field, name your resource.**

We recommend you use the common name for the item, so that every-one in your company can find it. Naming the heavy-duty winch "Big Cheese" won't do any good if you're the only one that calls it that. You have up to 100 characters for the name of your resource. Remember that all fields in bold (red on your computer screen) are required.

5. **Next up, select a Business Unit.**

See Chapter 6 for more information on business units. This field auto-matically defaults to your company's business unit, but you can change it by clicking the magnifying glass.

6. **Choose a site for your resource.**

This optional field is useful if you have more than one location for your resources. For example, you might want to indicate whether you want to use the heavy-duty winch at your Newtown facility or the one at your Portville location.

7. **Enter an e-mail address.**

You can use this field to send e-mails about this resource. For instance, suppose you're taking the heavy winch out and want to notify Steve, the equipment manager. You can set up a business process so that every time you schedule this resource, an e-mail to Steve is generated. (For more on processes, see Chapter 7.)

8. **Choose a time zone.**

   The default time zone is the one for your company. However, you can change it by making a selection from the drop-down list.

9. **Last but not least, enter a description of the resource.**

   This field is optional.

10. **Click the Save and Close button.**

   You return to the Facilities/Equipment window.

Now that you've entered your resource into Microsoft CRM, you should create a schedule for it. The schedule tells everyone when the resource can be used.

For this scenario, we'll use the Big Cheese (the winch). You just purchased it on Saturday, and it's ready for deployment in the field. However, you want downtime scheduled for maintenance every Friday:

1. **In the Facilities/Equipment window, select the resource you just created by double-clicking it.**

   The window for this resource appears. Eyes up: Note that it has its own navigation pane.

2. **In the resource's navigation pane, click Work Hours.**

   A tab called Monthly View appears with a monthly calendar, as shown in Figure 24-3. To change months, click the arrow on either side of the month at the top of the calendar.

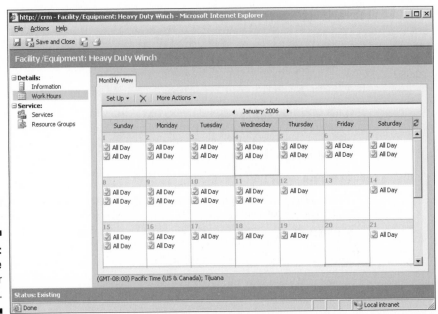

Figure 24-3: Planning the schedule for a resource.

3. **Double-click a day where you want to either restrict work or start the schedule for the resource.**

4. **Choose one of the following options and then click OK:**

   * **This day only:** Changes only the date you've selected.

   • **This date onward:** Changes the schedule from this day onward.

   • **Entire recurring weekly schedule from start to end:** Changes the schedule for all dates, including past dates.

   For our example, select the second option. The Weekly Schedule: Edit screen appears, as shown in Figure 24-4.

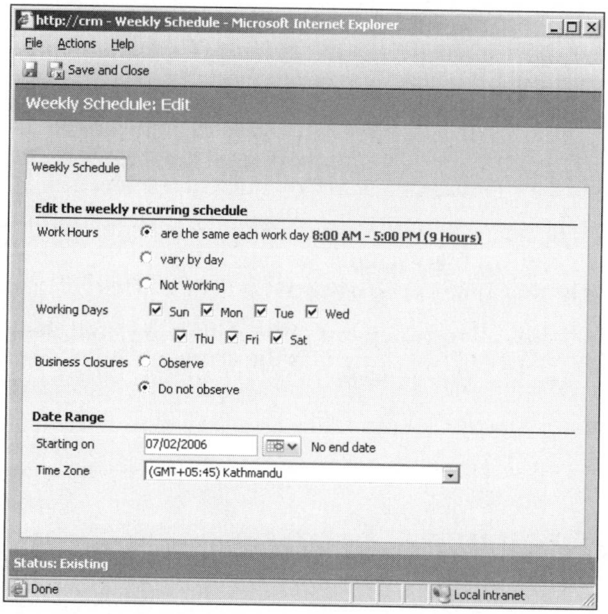

Figure 24-4: Set the days, hours, and off times on this screen

5. **Fill out this page.**

   Most of the fields in this screen are self-explanatory. You can change or select your work hours by double-clicking the bold (blue on-screen) hours listed after Work Hours. Uncheck any day that is *not* available for scheduling (the default is for everything to be checked). Business closure dates are explained later in the chapter, but here you indicate whether or not this resource is available during business closure dates.

6. **Click the Save and Close button.**

Setting Up a User's Schedule

As we mentioned earlier, you can put users as well as resources into your service schedule. Chapter 6 has more information on how to add a user to your program. This section is strictly for setting up the schedule for a previously created user so that when the person is scheduled for something, the time scheduled is compared to that user's working hours. Let's take a look:

1. **At the bottom of the navigation pane, click Settings.**
2. **Click Business Unit Settings.**
3. **Click Users.**

   The Users window appears.

4. **Double-click the user whose schedule you want to set.**
5. **In the navigation pane of this window, select Work Hours (under Details).**
6. **In the window's toolbar, click Set Up and then select Time Off.**

   You can set up a new weekly work schedule or schedule working hours for a particular day. For this example, we selected Time Off to give our person a break. Selecting Time Off displays the Schedule Time Off dialog box.

7. **Fill in the fields, all of which are self-explanatory, and then click OK.**
8. **Click the Save and Close button to return to the Users window.**

   As always, save, Save, SAVE!

Creating a Resource Group

Let's review: You have users and you have resources. A *resource group* is a group of users or resources or both that can be scheduled for a service activity. For example, suppose Brenda and Steve, who both work on commercial air conditioners, and the heavy-duty winch are inseparable as far as service calls go. So instead of scheduling three separate things, we'll group Brenda, Steve, and the Big Cheese into a resource group.

To create a resource group, follow these steps:

1. **At the bottom of the navigation pane, click Settings.**
2. **In the screen on the right, select Business Units.**
3. **Select Resource Groups.**

   The Resource Groups window appears.

4. In the window's toolbar, click the New button.

The Resource Group: New window appears, as shown in Figure 24-5.

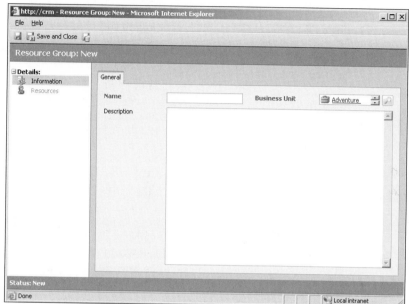

Figure 24-5:
Create
your new
resource
group here.

5. Fill in the following information:

    a. Name: This is the name of the resource group. We're calling ours Air-1.

    b. Business unit: As mentioned, the default unit is your main business unit, but this can be changed by clicking the magnifying glass and making a selection.

    c. Description: This is optional but recommended.

6. Click Save.

Because we're moving to another part of this window, we don't want to click Save and Close just yet.

7. In the Resource Group: New navigation pane, select Resources.

The Resources option is not live (active) until you click Save in Step 6. Also, eyes up and note that the title of the window has now changed to Resource Group: Air-1 (because the group we created is Air-1).

8. In the window's toolbar, click Add Resources.

The Look Up Records dialog box appears.

9. **In the Look For field, make a selection.**

   You can look for Facility/Equipment, Resource Group, Team, or User. For our example, we want look in both User and Facility/Equipment.

10. **If you want to add another resource, repeat Steps 8 and 9.**

11. **Click OK.**

   You are returned to the Resources window of your new resource group.

12. **Remember to click Save and Close.**

You can include resource groups as members of other resource groups. For example, you could have a resource group called Engineers — Virginia that consists of resource groups of technicians in each county.

Creating a Site

Sites are basically your service and sales locations, whether it's in Kathmandu or Hollywood. In Microsoft CRM, you can set up as many sites as you want, therefore creating a more efficient and effective service and scheduling system. Resources and users can be assigned to sites as well.

To create a site, follow these steps:

1. **At the bottom of the navigation pane, click the Settings button.**

2. **In the window on the right, select Sites.**

   The Sites window appears, as shown in Figure 24-6.

3. **In the window's toolbar, click the New button.**

   The Site: New window appears, with two tabs: General and Address. Remember fields in bold (red on your screen) are required.

4. **In the General tab, enter the name, which is required, and any other information you can.**

5. **On the Address tab, enter the address and select a time zone for that site.**

   The Time Zone default is the time zone of your primary location, but you can change this.

6. **Click Save (the disk icon).**

   We still have some things to do with the site before we can click the Save and Close button.

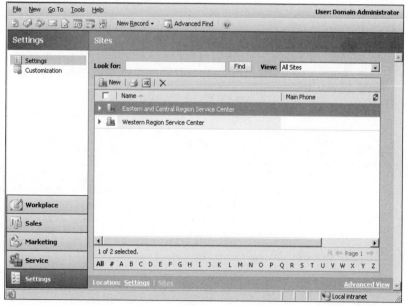

Figure 24-6:
Create and
define all
your sites
from this
page.

Now that you've created your site and saved it, you can add resources to it. Follow these steps:

1. **In the navigation pane of the Site: New window, select Resources.**

   Keep in mind that the Resources options in the navigation pane will not be live until you click Save.

2. **On the window's toolbar, click the Add Resources button.**

   The Look Up Records dialog box appears.

3. **In the Look Up Records dialog box, you can search for your selections using the Look For list and the Find field.**

   You can search for User or Facility/Equipment. Make your selection, enter the user or facility (or equipment) in the field to the left of the Find button, and then click Find. Your results will appear in the Available Records pane.

4. **Double-click the desired record to move it to the Selected Records pane.**

   You can also click the record once and then click the arrows to add or remove items from the Selected Records pane.

5. **Click OK.**

   You return to the window of the site you're working on.

6. **If you want to add more resources, go back to Step 2.**

7. **When you've finished adding resources, click Save and Close.**

   The site window closes, and your site is saved.

Creating Services

Now that you've added users, sites, and resources, it's time to add your services. Don't despair; you're almost finished with your setup. To create a service:

1. **In the navigation pane, click Settings.**

2. **In the window on the right, select Services.**

   The Services window appears.

3. **In the window's toolbar, click the New button.**

   The Service: New window appears, as shown in Figure 24-7, with two tabs: General and Required Resources. The screen opens to the General tab, which has two sections; a general area and a Scheduling area.

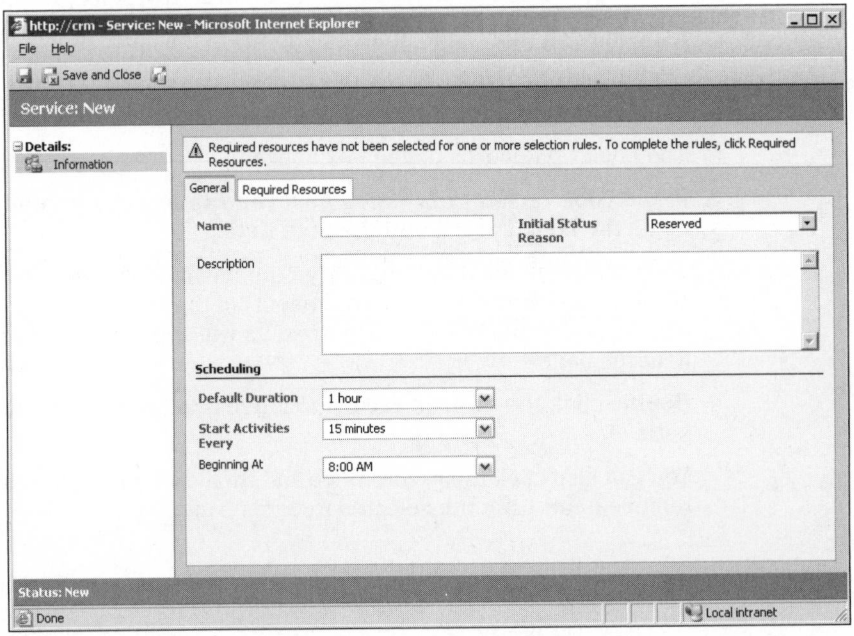

Figure 24-7:
Add your
new
services
here.

4. **In the General tab, fill in the following fields:**

   a. **Name:** Use something descriptive so that everyone will recognize the service.

   b. **Initial Status Reason:** This field lets you set the initial service activity status when an activity is created. (In case you don't speak Microsoft CRMese, this means your company can establish an approval process for services entered into your system.)

   c. **Description:** This is self-explanatory.

   d. **Default Duration:** If most of your Toaster Tune-Ups, for example, require about an hour, you would indicate that here.

   e. **Start Activities Every:** Select how far apart you want to stagger the activity. If your Toaster Tune-Up takes an hour, you can indicate that you want the service to start every 1.5 hours, giving your techs a 15-minute break.

   f. **Beginning At:** Choose a time to start the services every day.

5. **Click the Required Resources tab (see Figure 24-8).**

   You can't define a service without assigning one required resource and one selection rule. Note that the Required Resources tab has a Common Tasks pane, where you can add, edit, or remove selection items or resources. The right side of the screen shows all selection rules, resources, and resource groups assigned to this service.

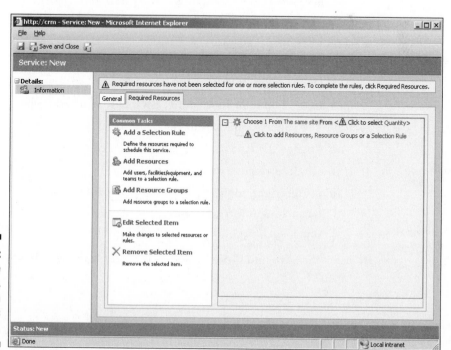

Figure 24-8: As the title indicates, filling in this tab is required.

6. **Choose a selection rule as follows:**

   a. **In the Common Tasks pane, click Add a Selection Rule.**

      The Edit a Selection Rule dialog box appears.

   b. **Select a quantity from the drop-down box (required).**

   c. **Type a description (optional).**

   d. **Choose a selection site.**

      This tells the program whether your resources can be any site or from the same site.

   e. **Click OK.**

7. **Add a resource or resource group as follows:**

   a. **In the Common Tasks pane, select Add Resources or Add Resource Groups.**

      With either choice, the Look Up Records dialog box appears.

   b. **If you chose Add Resources, select and search for a User, Facility/Equipment, Team, or Resource Group. If you chose Add Resource Groups, enter the name of the resource group you want to add in the field to the left of the Find button, and click Find.**

   c. **With either choice, double-click your choice and then click the arrow to move the highlighted option to the Selected Records pane.**

   d. **Click OK.**

8. **If you want to change an item:**

   a. **On the right, highlight the item you want to change.**

   b. **In the Common Tasks pane, click Edit Selected Items.**

      The Edit a Selection Rule dialog box appears.

   c. **Change the rule as desired, and then click OK.**

9. **If you want to remove an item:**

   a. **On the right, highlight the item you want to remove.**

   b. **In the Common Tasks pane, click Remove Selected Items.**

   c. **When the prompt appears, click OK.**

10. **Click the Save and Close button to close the window and save your changes.**

Scheduling Service Activities

Okay, pat yourself on the back and give your IT folks a bonus. You've added all the pieces — users, sites, resources, and services — and can now start scheduling. Because this is organized during system design and installation, your users (that is, your sales staff) will not have to face doing this setup every day. So, when Mrs. Reynolds calls to get her air conditioner fixed, your staff can schedule her into their workload with just a few clicks.

As mentioned in Chapter 3, some aspects of Microsoft CRM are available only in the Internet Explorer Client of Microsoft CRM. On the flip side, a few features are only in the Outlook Client of Microsoft CRM. With that in mind, remember that the Service Calendar is not found in the Outlook Client.

Let's have a look at how you actually schedule a service in Microsoft CRM:

1. **At the bottom of the navigation pane, click the Service button. At the top of the pane, select Service Calendar.**

   Your Service Calendar appears.

2. **In the Type field (next to the Look For field), select Service Activity from the drop-down list.**

   You see all service activities scheduled for today.

3. **Choose a day for the service.**

   You can navigate to different dates using the calendar and navigation tools in the window's right pane. (The calendar pane is collapsible, so you may need to open it to view the calendar.) You can choose the date also by using the calendar selections at the bottom of the schedule pane.

4. **In the window's toolbar, Click the New button and make your selection.**

   To follow along with the example, choose Service Activity. The Service Activity: New window appears, as shown in Figure 24-9.

5. **In the Subject field, enter a name for this service activity.**

6. **In the Service field, select the service you want to schedule.**

   To select the service, you can use the magnifying glass or the Form Assistant.

7. **The following fields are optional:**

   a. **Site:** If certain resources are available at only one site, you can indicate that site here. That way, the service activity is assigned to the appropriate site. Also, only resources linked to that site will be available for this service.

    b. **Customers:** The customer (account or contact) for whom you're scheduling the service activity.

    c. **Resources:** Choose your resources here. For example, if you need the Big Cheese winch for this activity, you'd indicate that here. (Or you can leave this field empty and let the person in charge of scheduling enter the resources.)

    d. **Location:** Where the service activity is taking place. Using our air conditioner service example, if the unit is located out behind the chicken shed or on the rooftop, you would put that here.

    e. **Show Time As:** Indicate whether the activity is Open or Scheduled. You have the options Requested and Tentative under Open and Pending, Reserved, In Progress, and Arrived under Schedule. If you choose Scheduled or one its options, the time is marked on the calendar and you can't schedule other activities for that time.

8. **Choose your start and end times as well as the duration.**

   Or if you want to mark the entire day on the calendar, you can select the All Day Event check box.

9. **Add any notes.**

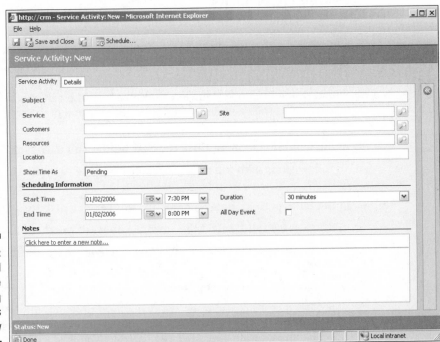

Figure 24-9:
Start all
your service
scheduling
from this
window

10. **Click the Details tab and fill it in as required.**

   Here, you can assign ownership and a priority to the activity as well as link this activity to another account or contact (or more). You can also assign a category and even a subcategory to the activity under this tab.

11. **Click the Save and Close button to schedule the activity.**

   You return to the Service Calendar window, where your newly scheduled activity appears.

You can also schedule appointments in this calendar.

For those of you who want to check your resources and users from the main working area of Microsoft CRM, you can go to the Service Calendar. Just follow these steps:

1. **At the bottom of the navigation pane, click the Service button.**

2. **At the top of the pane, select Service Calendar.**

3. **Click any resource, and you will see the schedule for that resource in the calendar area.**

The screen is split into a resources area and a calendar area, as shown in Figure 24-10. It looks a little busy but we wanted to show you just how many options are available.

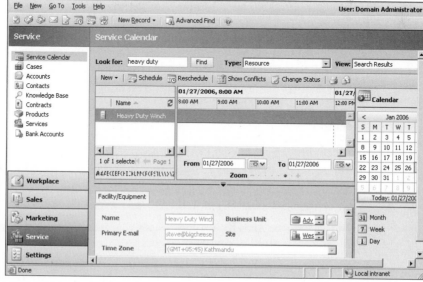

Figure 24-10: The first step to excellent customer service.

You can customize the screen by shrinking the resources pane or the calendar pane (just click the line separating the two and drag it). You can also collapse the bottom part, showing the resource information, by clicking the black triangle under the word *Zoom.* The graphical calendar on the right can be collapsed by clicking the arrow in the little calendar to the left of the word *Calendar.* The Zoom feature allows you to choose the increments the calendar is shown in, from 1-day to 15-minute increments.

The Service Activity Volume Report

Want to know what kinds of cases your staff handled, how long the work took, and what was accomplished? Then the Service Activity Volume report is for you.

You can reorganize the report seven ways from Sunday and filter it to pare down the data. The default grouping is by number of service activities by month, sorted by month, week, or date in ascending order. You can analyze your service activities from a number of viewpoints so that you can better manage your service department and maintain peak efficiency and responsiveness. You can see either the duration or number of service activities, grouped by services, resources, time periods, or other groupings.

Now that you know how to schedule — and your business has been running smoothly as people are processed in and out of the customer database — let's look at putting all that information together into a readable format. Here's how:

1. **At the bottom of the navigation pane click the Workplace button. At the top of the pane, select Reports (under My Work).**

   The Reports window appears, as shown in Figure 24-11.

2. **In the Look For field, type** Service Activity **and then click the Find button.**

   The Service Activity Volume report appears.

3. **Double-click the report to open it.**

   Another, less direct way to find this report is to select Service Reports in the Category list and then select it from the options presented.

4. **In the Service Activity Volume window, enter how many days' worth of service activities you want to see.**

   On your screen, the number is underlined. But as soon as you move your cursor over it, you'll get a free-form entry field. For our example, we're going to use 30 days, as shown in Figure 24-12.

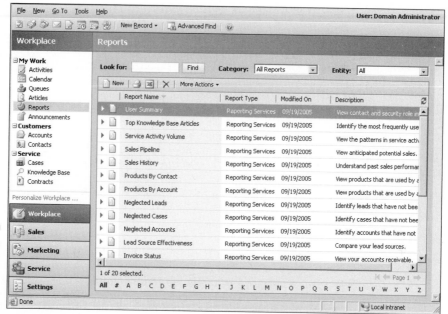

Figure 24-11:
Set up and
find reports
here.

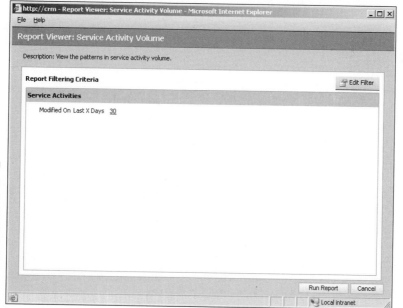

Figure 24-12:
Here's
where you
find out
who's
making it
and who's
breaking it.

5. **If you need to change the selection criteria for the report, click Edit Filter in the top-right corner and make the necessary changes.**

   You return to the screen shown in Figure 24-12 so you can make your changes. The filter is initially set to select the number of days. You can change the criteria or add additional criteria. You can also clear the selection criteria from this page.

6. **Click Run Report in the lower-right corner.**

   After a few seconds, you get a comprehensive report that you can organize in many ways. You can choose a display method (Activity Count or Activity Duration). You can also group your information using the options in the drop-down box under Group By and choose at what size you want to view the report. Figure 24-13 shows the report. You can also export or print from this page. If you change the criteria using the options on this page, just click View Report to view your refreshed information.

Now that you've found out how to set up your services and how to schedule and run reports, you are well on your way to not only more efficient servicing processes but also happier customers (and a happier bank account).

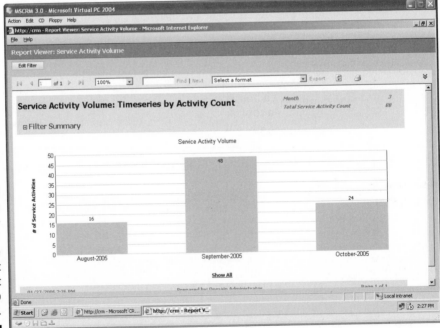

Figure 24-13:
Très magnifique! A sample of what Microsoft CRM can do in reports.

Chapter 25

Managing Your Subjects

- -

In This Chapter

▶ Adding subjects

▶ Editing subjects

▶ Removing subjects

▶ Relating subjects to other activities

- -

*W*hen managing your subjects (no, not the evil-overlord-type subjects), you can organize all your cases, sales materials, knowledge base articles, and products — creating a hierarchical tree of information that we call a *subject tree*. At the trunk of the subject tree are your main topics. The tree has branches, which also have branches, which can also have branches. With Microsoft CRM, the subject groups get narrower until you're down to that last, specific article — or, using our tree example, you're down to that last spindly twig.

Suppose you have a hospital supply company. The trunk of the subject tree contains your main topics, such as the hospital supplies you manufacture and sell. You might add subjects (big branches) representing your products and services, such as surgical supplies, dressings, drugs, prosthetics, cleaning supplies, and beds. For the subject Surgical Supplies, you might add the different types of surgical supplies that you sell, such as gloves, pumps, and sutures (more branches off that main one).

Want another level of detail? Under the subject Gloves, add the different types of gloves you sell. Under Sutures, add the different brands or different thicknesses.

Also remember that Microsoft CRM subjects can be not only products but also services. For this chapter, we'll use Bikes, Clothing and Accessories, and Company Information as our subjects.

Structuring your subjects and their relationship to one another is important. We'll show you how to create your subjects and add items or more subjects to them in this chapter.

Tips for Defining Your Subjects

Microsoft CRM uses a collapsible tree system much like the one that Windows and Microsoft Outlook use. Creating a subject tree offers the following benefits:

- ✔ A consistent hierarchy for associating contacts with products, sales literature, and knowledge base information
- ✔ Easy access to information related to specific subjects
- ✔ Centralized management of subjects (including creating, editing, and removing subjects) and their relationship to one another in the subject tree

Building a subject tree is easy, but figuring out what to put on which branch can be difficult. We recommend scheduling a brainstorming session with different departments in your company. Define your products and services into categories and topics. If those categories and topics can be further divided (such as surgical supplies to gloves to different sizes of gloves), create your subtopics.

Brainstorming can become perplexing and lead to lengthy discussions. Don't worry — spending time on the subject tree at the beginning is far better than building the subject tree on the fly. And moving things around in the subject tree later isn't as easy as placing them at their appropriate level in the first place. Additionally, ad hoc subject design may not account for the needs of your entire organization. You can save yourself time and aggravation by having a blueprint in place first.

No hard-and-fast rules exist when defining the structure of a subject tree. Each company has its own priorities. But you might want to consider the following items when defining your subject tree structure:

- ✔ Price lists
- ✔ Sales literature
- ✔ Product specs
- ✔ Warranty information
- ✔ Service contracts
- ✔ Knowledge base articles

Only users with the appropriate access rights can create subjects and add items to a subject tree. (See Chapter 6 for more information.)

You can also relate items such as product catalogs and sales literature to subjects.

Accessing the Subjects Window

After you have created the outline or blueprint for your company's subject tree, be sure to save it where it can be easily accessed when you're ready to build it. A good idea is to have the administrative assistant (who as we all know, truly runs the company) create the outline in a Word document.

In the Subjects window, you can add subjects, edit them, and remove them. We perform all those tasks in this chapter. First, however, you need to get to that window. Just follow these steps:

1. **At the bottom part of the navigation pane, click the Settings button.**

   The Settings window appears on the right.

2. **In the Settings window, click Subjects.**

   The Subjects window appears, as shown in Figure 25-1.

Figure 25-1: Begin managing your subjects here.

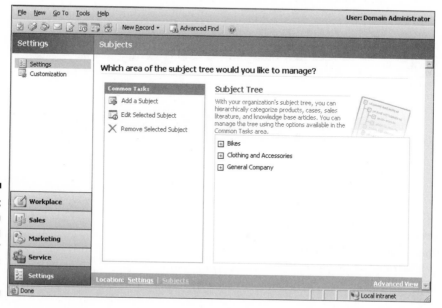

Three options appear in the Common Tasks pane, which is to the left of the main display: Add a Subject, Edit Selected Subject, and Remove Selected Subject. We cover each of these in the following sections.

Adding a Subject

Now that you've followed the bread crumbs to the Tree of Microsoft CRM, you can start adding your subjects. We suggest adding the subjects you've designated as the trunk of your subject tree, in other words, the main categories or topics. Modifying and updating the subject tree is part of the evolutionary process of any business.

To add subjects, follow these steps:

1. **In the Common Tasks area of the Subjects window, click Add a Subject.**

   The Add Subject dialog box appears.

2. **Enter a title for the subject and (if desired) a description.**

3. **To place the new subject under a previously created subject, click the magnifying glass icon next to the Parent Subject field.**

   The Subject Lookup dialog box appears, as shown in Figure 25-2.

   If you navigate to the selected parent and child before you click Add a Subject, the Parent Subject field is automatically populated with your highlighted selection.

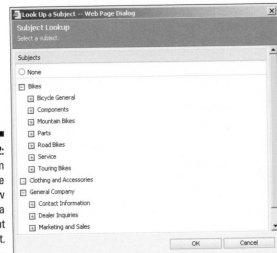

Figure 25-2:
You can associate the new subject to a parent subject.

4. **Click the appropriate plus sign (+) to the left of a subject to open the subject tree, highlight the subject you want as the parent, and click OK.**

   The new subject is added to the subject tree. This design flexibility enables you to create a sophisticated hierarchy to match the blueprint you came up with at the brainstorming session.

   The desired parent could be the child of another subject.

5. **If you selected a parent subject and you want to display the subject you just added, you must click the plus sign to the left of the parent.**

   If the new subject was added as the child of a child, continue clicking plus signs until you've drilled down to the appropriate level.

Clicking the plus sign to the left of a subject displays its children (if any exist) and is the easiest way to drill down into a subject. If the plus sign turns into a dot, you know that you're at the end of the line for that subject.

Note: Whenever you make an addition or revision to the subject tree, Microsoft CRM has an annoying habit of refreshing the entire window. If you had drilled down several levels to add a new subject and clicked OK, the screen refresh will take you all the way back to the top-level view of the subject tree (arrgh!). It does this so you will always have an up-to-date view of your subject tree, but be prepared to spend a few extra mouse clicks when adding lots of subjects.

Editing a Subject

The Edit Selected Subject option is the second option in the Common Tasks pane (refer to Figure 25-1). This option enables you to rename a subject or move it to another location in the subject tree.

To edit a subject, follow these steps:

1. **In the Subject Tree area of the Subjects window, highlight the subject.**

2. **In the Common Tasks pane, click Edit Selected Subject.**

   The Edit Subject dialog box appears.

3. **Edit the subject's title, change the subject's parent/child relationship in the subject tree, or revise the description notes, all by entering text into the respective fields.**

   To change the parent subject, you must use the magnifying glass at the end of the field. The title and description can be modified by entering text.

Moving a subject to a new parent subject will move *all* the selected subject's associated children. This action could lead to an unpleasant surprise for your co-workers the next time they look for a subject.

4. **Click OK.**

The Edit Subject dialog box closes, and your edits are saved.

Removing a Subject

The Remove Selected Subject option, the last option in the Common Tasks pane, enables you to delete a subject from the subject tree. You might choose this option if a product line has been discontinued or a service can no longer be offered.

To remove a subject, follow these steps:

1. **In the Subject Tree area of the Subjects window, highlight the subject you want to remove.**

2. **In the Common Tasks pane, click Remove Selected Subject.**

3. **When a window appears asking whether you're sure you want to delete the subject, click OK.**

   The window closes and the subject tree refreshes, minus the subject you removed.

Removing a subject could have serious consequences to product catalogs or knowledge base entries. If you remove a subject such as Video Card listed under the parent Hardware, and the card had several knowledge base articles linked to it, the links will be broken and the related knowledge will be useless if a future issue regarding the video card occurs.

One nice safety feature here is that you get an error message if the subject you're attempting to delete is associated with a case, a product, or a knowledge base article or has any other object associated with it. Thanks, Microsoft!

Relating Subjects to Other Activities

Another great option that Microsoft CRM offers is the ability to link, or relate, your subjects to activities (tasks, cases, and so on). In this way, you can find subjects with fewer clicks.

For example, let's assume that Sally in the service department opens a new case pertaining to a software problem that Mr. Wayne is having with the Series 211 Transporter. Something about this case strikes her as familiar. Because other cases were associated to the subject "Series 211 Transporter," Sally can search for those cases and get a list of them almost instantly. Barry, her cube neighbor, gets a request for sales literature on the Series 411 Transporter. He conducts a search for all sales literature linked to the subject "Series 411 Transporter" and gets a list of all related documents. Last but not least, there's Jim, in the cube across the way. At a potential customer's request, he is researching the electrical requirements of all backup power supplies that your company sells. He performs a knowledge base search of all articles related to the subject called "Power Supplies" and prints those articles.

By associating and organizing subject trees with logical, explanatory details, you can easily retrieve your company's data and information.

Relating subjects to cases

Let's go back to Sally and the case she just opened with Mr. Wayne. She wants to make sure this case is linked to the "Series 211 Transporter" subject. Others might come across the same problem and she knows that this is important information for any of the CSRs in her company.

You can link new or existing cases to subjects by following these steps:

1. **At the bottom of the navigation pane, click the Workplace button. At the top of the pane, click Cases (under Service).**

2. **To start a new case, click the New button. Or to open an active case, double-click it.**

   Both options display the Case window.

3. **In the Case window, click the magnifying glass icon to the right of the Subject field.**

   The Subject Lookup window displays the subject tree. Although you may have only one subject tree for your company, you can design the subject tree with as much complexity as you need.

4. **Locate the subject to which you want to link the case.**

   You may need to click a plus sign or two to drill down to the appropriate subject.

5. **After you've located the subject you want, double-click it.**

   The subject you selected is displayed in the subject field of the Case window.

6. **Click the Save and Close icon in the upper-left corner of the window.**

   Your case is now related to the subject you selected.

We recommend that cases be related to subjects when you first create the case. However, if you're not sure of the best subject to link to, you can assign or change the subject later. Keep in mind that changing a subject related to a case may cause problems if the case has been worked on and information has been related to the previous subject.

Putting the case link to work

Suppose a customer calls with a problem with one of your company's products — the Hop-n-Pop toaster just won't hop when it pops the bread out. Your customer service representatives can check to see whether any other cases are linked to the same product using the Advanced Find feature. This offers you the ability to conduct detailed searches in almost any searchable field in Microsoft CRM.

To view all cases linked to a specific subject, follow these steps:

1. **In the menu bar (at the top of the screen), choose Tools⇨ Advanced Find.**

   The Advanced Find dialog box appears, as shown in Figure 25-3. The Look For field tells the program where to look for the parameters you're going to add later. The Use Saved View lists searches you've saved previously. The area below these fields is where you'll enter the data you want to search for.

2. **In the Look For field, click the arrow to the right and choose Cases.**

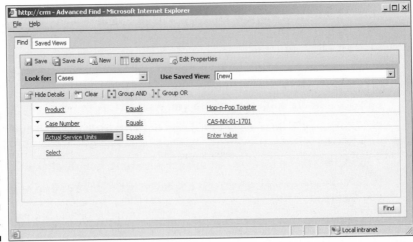

Figure 25-3:
You can search for records based on values you define.

3. **Place your cursor over the blue Select option to activate the drop-down menu, and then click the arrow to open the menu.**

   These options depend on what you chose in the Look For field in Step 2. For example, if you chose to search for Documents, your search options are File Size, Author Name, File Name, and so on. If you chose Facilities/Equipment, you can search for Name, Primary E-mail, Business Unit, and so on.

4. **Place your cursor over the word *Equals* and set the Condition for the search from the drop-down menu.**

   Again, placing your cursor over the word *Equals* activates the drop-down menu. Click it to open the menu and make your selection.

5. **Under Enter Value, select or enter the appropriate value.**

   This field is dependent on the decision made in the first column and will not appear until you've made a selection from Step 3. For example, if you chose Product in Step 3, the Value field will have a magnifying glass so you can pull up the Look Up Records dialog box to select a product. If you chose Case Number, you get a blank field in which you can simply enter the case number.

6. **Click the Find button (in the lower left).**

   A new window appears with your search results, created from the choices you made in the main Advanced Find window.

7. **To open an entry in the search results list, double-click it.**

For more on Advanced Find, see Chapter 2.

Relating a subject to a knowledge base article

The process of linking a subject to a knowledge base article is the same as that for linking subjects to cases. (We discuss the knowledge base in detail in Chapter 9.) A knowledge base article is a record (stored in the knowledge base) that contains information. It may document a process, contain the history of the company, provide details on the company's health or retirement plan, or list employee addresses and phone numbers.

You can create a link between a knowledge base article and a subject when you create the article. You can also link existing articles to existing subjects. Linking knowledge base articles to specific subjects provides your customer service representatives with a quick and easy way to search for similar problems and solutions in a specific subject.

To link a new article to a subject, follow these steps:

1. **On the menu bar (at the top of the screen), choose New⇨Article.**

   The Select a Template dialog box appears, as shown in Figure 25-4.

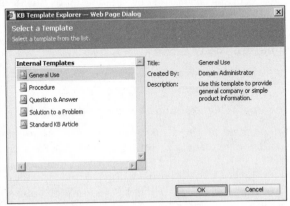

2. **Select the appropriate template.**

   Templates help format your articles so that they're uniform in appearance, making them easier to read (this is handy when you have a client on the phone). Microsoft CRM has several predefined templates, and you can also create your own. (For more on templates, see Chapter 12.) After you select a template, check the right side of the Select a Template window. You'll find basic information about the template you selected.

3. **Click OK.**

   The Article: New window appears, as shown in Figure 25-5. (You find out about creating and submitting articles in Chapter 9.)

4. **Enter a Title for your new article.**

5. **Select the subject to which you want to link your article.**

   To do so, click the magnifying glass icon to the right of the Subject field. In the Subject Lookup window that appears, select the subject from the subject tree. You may need to click a plus sign or two to drill down to the appropriate subject.

6. **Place your cursor over the text that appears under Question and click it.**

   The predefined text is removed, and a free-form field appears so you can enter your Article question.

   Text can be edited and pasted into these positions just like in a Microsoft Word document.

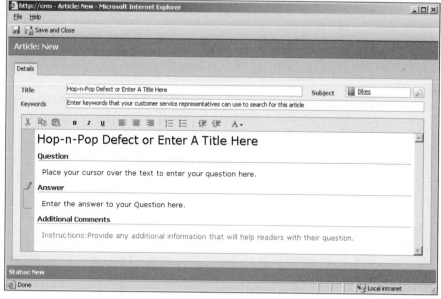

Figure 25-5:
From here,
you can
start
building
your article.

7. **Place your cursor over the text that appears under Answer and click.**

   Just like in Step 5, the predefined text is removed, and a free-form field appears so you can enter your answer.

8. **In the Additional Comments area, enter any text, if desired.**

9. **Click the Save and Close icon.**

   Your article is now related to the subject you selected.

To link a previously created knowledge base article to a subject, follow these steps:

1. **At the bottom of the navigation pane, click the Service button. At the top of the pane, select Knowledge Base.**

   The Knowledge Base window appears.

2. **Under Article Queues, select Draft, Unapproved, or Published.**

   All draft or unapproved articles are displayed in the main window. Draft articles have been composed but haven't been submitted for approval by a user with editors' rights; consider them works in progress. Unapproved articles have been submitted to a user who has been assigned the task of reviewing and approving articles. Published articles have been approved for the general population. After an article is published, the Subject link can't be altered. However, if you find you need to change a published article, you can unpublish the article to make the necessary changes.

3. **Click the desired article.**

   The Article window appears.

4. **Select the subject to which you want to link your article.**

   To do so, click the magnifying glass icon to the right of the Subject field. In the Subject Lookup window that appears, select the subject from the subject tree. You may need to click a plus sign or two to drill down to the appropriate subject.

5. **Click the Save and Close icon.**

   The article is now linked to the subject you selected.

Putting the article link to work

Let's say that another customer calls about the Hop-n-Pop toaster. She heard that an attachment is available that allows the user to toast hamburger buns. You can search the knowledge base for the article that talks specifically about the bun toaster option.

To view knowledge base articles linked to a specific subject, choose Go To⇨Workplace⇨Knowledge Base. The Workplace: Knowledge Base window appears. See Chapter 28 for more detailed searching techniques that you can use to locate articles.

Relating a subject to the product catalog

As with cases and articles, products listed in the product catalog can also be linked to a subject. This is an efficient way to set up metrics for tracking sales by department, product type, subproduct type, and so on. The Subject field related to a product catalog item may be edited at any time, as long as the product remains active (see Chapter 18).

To link a product to a subject, follow these steps:

1. **In the lower part of the navigation pane, click the Settings button.**

2. **In the upper part of the navigation pane, select Settings.**

   The Settings window appears on the right.

3. **In the Settings window, select Product Catalog.**

   The Product Catalog window appears. Detailed information on using the Product Catalog is in Chapter 18.

4. **Select Products.**

   The Products window appears, as shown in Figure 25-6.

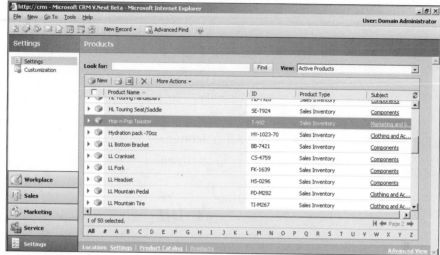

Figure 25-6:
This
window lists
all your
company's
products.

5. **In the window's toolbar, click the New button.**

   The Product: New window appears. Chapter 18 contains detailed information about this window. For now, direct your attention to the Subject field.

6. **Select the subject you want to link your product to.**

   To do so, click the magnifying glass icon to the right of the Subject field. In the Subject Lookup window that appears, select the subject from the subject tree.

7. **Click the Save and Close icon.**

   Your product is now related to the subject you selected.

Searching for products linked to a subject requires using the Advanced Find feature, which was described earlier in this chapter in "Putting the case link to work."

Relating a subject to sales literature

You follow the same steps to link a piece of sales literature to a subject as you do to link cases and articles to a subject. What's the advantage? Here's an example: Suppose you have a training manual that you sell. Your marketing department has created a two-page advertisement for the manual in PDF format. It would be handy to be able to link the ad with the product using a subject relation.

When customers call to request training information related to a specific product, you can easily search for all the training materials associated with the product, including the spiffy ad slick. You can then e-mail those documents to your customers, and within minutes they can be perusing the information and deciding about training.

To link sales literature to a subject, follow these steps:

1. **At the bottom of the navigation pane, click the Sales button. At the top of the pane, select Sales Literature.**

   The Sales Literature window appears.

2. **In the Sales Literature window's toolbar, click the New button or double-click an existing sales literature item.**

   If you click New, the Sales Literature: New window appears. Otherwise, you see the window for the existing literature item. Chapter 20 contains detailed information about this window.

3. **Select the subject you want to link your sales literature to.**

   To do so, click the magnifying glass to the right of the Subject field. In the Subject Lookup window that appears, select the subject from the subject tree.

4. **Click the Save and Close icon.**

   Your sales literature is now related to the subject you selected.

Note that subjects related to sales literature can be edited at any time. Searching for sales literature linked to a subject requires using the Advanced Find feature, which is described earlier in "Putting the case link to work."

Chapter 26

Managing Queues

*T*hink of a *queue* as a shared inbox in which related activities and similar cases can be held for processing. Call it the list du jour. *Activities* are your tasks, appointments, calls, and e-mails (see Chapter 14 for more about creating and managing activities). *Cases* are your service support tickets (see Chapter 23 for more about working with cases). *Processing* means assigning and accepting activities and cases (read on). A queue is handy not only because it gives you a centralized list of outstanding activities and cases, but also because you can sort your tasks by their subject matter or assignment.

Queues give access to issues and cases for all departments and areas of your company without having to create a new ticket or incident for each department. Say you have an issue with the Hop-n-Pop Toaster that initially comes into your Customer Service queue, but when your customer service representative (CSR) gets ahold of it, they find that it's more a service issue. After Service gets it, they figure the CSR must have been asleep because it's a billing issue. Instead of having three separate incidents running around your system (remember the Minions of Chaos), you can easily take that activity and switch it between queues.

Likewise, storage in a single queue makes it easy for customer service representatives to locate an issue they're qualified to address. Queues also enable service managers to direct activities and cases to experts for a solution or to other team members if a particular CSR is too busy.

The concepts of *pull* (in the case of your CSR) and *push* (in the case of your service manager) can be automated by using workflow rules (see Chapter 8 for more about workflow rules) to make queues a powerful service management assignment tool. In this chapter, we discuss the various queues defined by Microsoft CRM and how to use them. You also discover how to create, modify, and manage your own queues.

Queue Overview

Your company probably has a person who acts as a human router, directing service calls and e-mails to the appropriate CSRs or taking care of an escalated situation when the CSR cannot handle it. This person is usually the harried-looking individual with the perma-cup of coffee in one hand. You may call these people customer service managers, quality attention retainers, or what have you, but for this book, we call them service managers. They are the optimal choice for creating and defining your queues because they manage the front lines of your customer service department. Your service managers also know the strengths and weaknesses of your CSRs and can assign them the proper queues; in this way, your best washing machine guy isn't dealing with refrigerator issues.

When you assign your CSRs to queues and then assign activities and cases to those queues, you're giving your people (and your company) an effective and efficient means of solving problems and making customers happy.

A good, basic setup for queues is to create queues for each product or service your company offers. For example, if you sell four brands of toasters, you should create a queue for each brand of toaster. Maybe you run a cleaning service that cleans both personal homes and businesses. You could create a domestic and a corporate queue. Another way to set up queues if you sell or support only a single line is for the other area in your business to interact with support. You could also create a queue for engineering, billing, and shipping departments. Then if you need them involved in a case, you could schedule an activity or the entire case to them.

Personal and Public Queues

Microsoft CRM comes with two predefined queue areas: the My Work queue, listing folders for the activities and cases assigned to you, and the public queue. The public queue area displays all the queues that your user ID belongs to. Users who have been assigned the appropriate rights can create queues.

When you look into a public queue, you see all activities and cases associated with that queue, whether they are assigned to you or not. Everyone who is a member of that queue can see these activities and cases.

The My Work queue, shown in Figure 26-1, has two folders:

- **Assigned:** You'll find all the cases that have been assigned to you. These are cases that you have not accepted yet.
- **In Progress:** These are all the cases you have accepted and are currently working on.

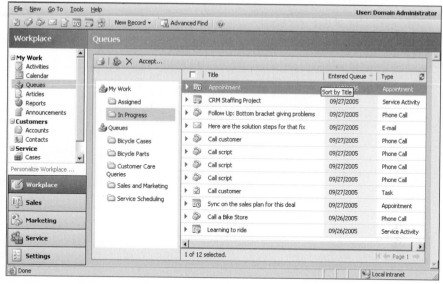

Figure 26-1:
Your folders
in the
My Work
queue.

Creating a Queue

Microsoft CRM can have as many queues as your company needs. We recommend meeting with your service manager and your customer service team to make a master plan of all your services and products and how you want to handle customer service scenarios before building your queues.

For example, let's say Mrs. Reynolds calls in about her Hop-n-Pop Toaster. The toaster won't hop when it pops. This call could be routed to the regular Toasters queue for the next available CSR. However, if she calls to report that the toaster caught fire, this is a serious issue, one that your company feels should go straight to management. So you route Mrs. Reynolds to the Toasters — Emergency queue for a manager to handle.

Another example is a collection agency that has one queue for missed payments at 30 days and another for more critical debts. Many companies offer tiered service programs and memberships. With queues, you can make a battle plan to promptly route those Gold and high-priority memberships to the faster response-time queues.

Follow these steps to add your new queues:

1. **At the bottom of the navigation pane, click the Settings button.**

   The Settings window appears on the right.

2. **Click Business Unit Settings.**

3. **Select Queues.**

    The Queues window appears, as shown in Figure 26-2. All queues are listed here.

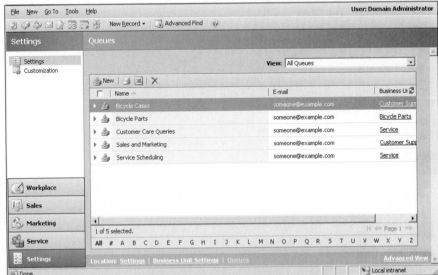

Figure 26-2:
All current queues are displayed here.

4. **In the window's toolbar, click the New button.**

    The Queue: New window appears, as shown in Figure 26-3. Three fields are required: Queue Name, Business Unit, and Owner.

5. **In the Queue Name field, enter a name for this queue.**

    Remember to keep it simple and descriptive. Naming the queue on defective merchandise after your mother-in-law, for example, won't help anyone else find it.

6. **In the Business Unit field, click the magnifying glass to display the Look Up Records window.**

    Business units are similar to departments or regions. For example, if you're in the Customer Care department or a regional center, and you want to create a queue for your staff, you would select Customer Care or the name of your regional center here. See Chapter 6 more on creating business units.

7. **In the Owner field, choose an owner for the group.**

    Click the magnifying glass will open a Look Up Records window with all your users. Choose one and click OK. You are returned to the Queue: New window. The owner essentially monitors the queue; assigning cases, shifting workloads and so on.

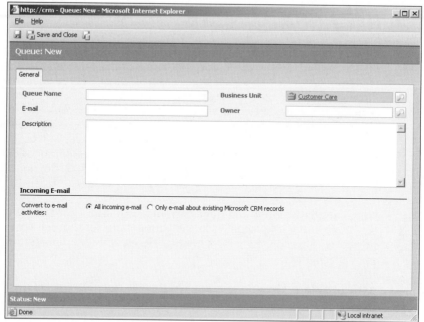

Figure 26-3:
Create your
queues in
this window.

8. **If your company handles trouble "calls" through e-mail from customers, enter the e-mail address that the trouble e-mails should go to, and they will be dropped into this queue.**

   Suppose that Mrs. Reynolds is on your web page and has a question about the Hop-n-Pop Toaster's warranty. She fills in the online form, and an e-mail is generated with the information and sent to toasters@acme. com. Enter that e-mail address in the e-mail field on this queue, and her e-mail will be dropped automatically into, say, the Toasters — General queue. In the bottom half of the window, you can choose to route all incoming e-mails or filter down to those from recognized contacts in your system. (See Chapter 13 for more on contacts.)

9. **If you want, enter a description for the queue as well as any important notes.**

10. **Click the Save and Close button.**

    The Queue: New window closes, and you return to the main Queues display, where your newly created queue is listed along with the other queues. The e-mail address and business unit for each queue is also displayed.

Activities and Queues

When a new activity (a task, a phone call, an e-mail, an appointment, and so on.) is created, the program does not automatically assign it to a queue. Here's where your service manager ensures his or her job security. They look at the activity and assess the situation: Does Mrs. Reynolds's question go to general customer service or should it be assigned to Bob, who knows the toaster warranties verbatim? Of course, your service manager assigns the activity to Bob. This efficient utilization of your company's resources (that is, the service manager, Bob's training, fancy computer equipment) saves time, prevents redundancy, and most importantly, makes Mrs. Reynolds a happy customer by getting her an answer in a timely manner.

Now, back to activities and queues. You can view all your queues and activities from your workplace. In the navigation pane, look under My Work. From here, you can also view your activities, cases, articles, reports, and announcements.

Activities should be created first and then assigned to a queue. You can't create an activity from within a queue. (See Chapter 14 for details about creating an activity.)

Assigning an activity to a queue

Let's revisit Mrs. Reynolds's problems with her Hop-n-Pop toaster and assume that you're the service manager on duty. She's getting burnt toast and can't find the switch to set the level of toastiness. Instead of sending her call to the General Toasters queue, assign her to the Hop-n-Pop Toasters queue so that she gets Barb, a specialist in Hop-n-Pop toasters. You can optimize your service staff's efficiency while promoting customer satisfaction — what a concept!

As we mentioned earlier in the chapter, activities can be assigned to a queue or to a user. The difference? Queues can have a number of users assigned to them, and a user is just that: a single individual.

Keeping that in mind, as the service manager, when should you assign activities to an individual CSR or manager and when should it be dropped into a queue for the next available CSR to pick it up?

A good service manager will be able to effectively evaluate all these situations and assign activities accordingly. Also, initiating workflow rules can easily help automate the functions of assignments and escalation (see Chapter 8 for details on rules and workflow).

TIP

Because activities (such as tasks, phone calls, appointments, and e-mails) and cases are handled the same way within your queues, we occasionally use *activities* as a generic term for them all. So within this section, we're going to call everything an activity, whether it's a customer service call or a service request.

Now you're set to start assigning activities to queues. Let's take Mrs. Reynold's issue with her toaster. Follow these steps to assign her activity to a queue or a user:

1. On the menu bar (at the top of the screen), choose Go To⇨My Work⇨Activities.

A list of all your activities is displayed.

2. Locate your activity.

You can sort the activities by clicking the column headers or filter the activities according date, type, or status (under the View drop-down list). See Chapter 11 for more on filtering.

3. Double-click the activity to open it.

4. On the menu bar, choose Actions⇨Assign.

The Confirm Assignment dialog box appears.

5. Select the queue to which you want to assign this activity:

a. Click the magnifying glass icon.

A Look Up Records dialog box appears, as shown in Figure 26-4.

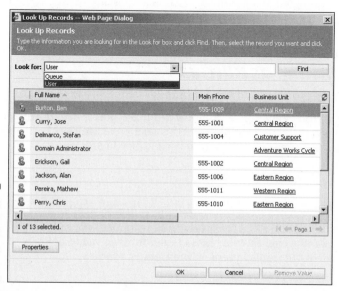

Figure 26-4:
Search for a queue and assign the activity to it.

       b. In the Look For field, click the arrow and select Queue from the list.

A list of all current queues is displayed in the lower part of the screen. You can also assign activities to users from this window.

The assigned user must still accept the activity. (We show you how to do that in the next section, "Accepting activities.")

       c. Double-click the queue, or highlight the queue and click OK.

You return to the Confirm Assignment dialog box.

You can also search for queues using the Find box or alphabetize the queues by clicking the Name column header.

6. In the Confirm Assignment dialog box, click OK.

You're back in the Activity window.

7. Click the Save and Close icon.

Note that the task is still displayed in the Workplace: Activities window display. It's still a legitimate activity. However, you can see the task also in the Queues display because you've assigned the task to a queue.

8. Under My Work in the navigation pane, select Queues and find the queue to which you assigned the activity. Double-click that queue to open it.

The Queues window appears (refer to Figure 26-1). You now see the activity assigned to that queue.

Remember to save, Save, SAVE! Always click the Save and Close button, even if you're reassigning a previously created activity. This way, you guarantee that all changes will be saved.

Accepting activities

For this section, let's become the CSR. We have our caffeine, pictures of the family, and the latest conceptual macaroni and glitter art adorning our desks. Service managers, you should read this section as well because good service managers understand the job from their subordinates' view.

You will find two types of activities:

- Activities assigned directly to you (in the Assigned folder under My Work: Queues)

- Activities assigned to a queue that your user name belongs to, which are found in the public queue in the Queues window

In either case, you have to accept the activity before you can begin work on it. If no workflow rules are in place, it's up to you to monitor your queues for outstanding activities.

To get to your queues and activities, follow these steps to first accept your activities:

1. **In the lower part of the navigation pane, click the Workplace button. In the upper part of the pane, select Queues (under My Work).**

2. **In the pane on the right, click the Assigned folder under My Work or click a folder under Queues to display any pending activities.**

3. **Click the activity to highlight it.**

4. **Click the Accept button in the toolbar.**

   The Confirm Assignment dialog box appears, asking you to verify that you want to move the selected activity to your In Progress folder.

5. **Click OK.**

   You've now accepted the activity.

After the activity moves to your In Progress folder, you can open it, create other associated activities, and ultimately complete it. You may also reassign the activity. For example, suppose Jen gets an activity about the FryjaBox refrigerator, but she's the Clean-o-matic Washing Machine whiz. Not to worry, Jen can turn that activity over to Stan, the FryjaBox guru. Or say you get a call about a problem that you know Amanda took care of just last week. You could reassign that call to her.

After the activity is completed, it will no longer be in your In Progress folder. But you can still find it in the navigation pane. Look under Activities (under My Work). Or, if it's a case, look under Cases (under Service).

Queues are a valuable tool for your company. They can be examined for up-to-the-minute information on how many customers have a specific issue or how many CSRs are engaged with issues relating to a specific product. This information can go a long way toward optimizing the efficiency of the service department and helping identify issues in other departments as well.

Chapter 27

Building Contracts

*W*hether you work as a one-man computer shop or for a multimillion dollar corporation, you will at some point come across a contract. Contracts seal the deal, make the world move . . . tell someone you have a contract and you're in.

Think about what contracts do. Basically, they outline specific services or entitlements with a certain number of hours, days, or service calls. They can also spell out things such as response time and whether the client gets a dedicated resource to call.

With Microsoft CRM, you can bill against contracts, keep track of billables (and do it consistently), set up and organize your contracts, and more. Microsoft CRM builds contracts on contract templates, as we show you in this chapter. We also explain how to create a contract and how to link the contract to a customer and set the contract's status, terms and conditions. You'll also find out how to associate cases with your new contract so you can accurately and efficiently track your services.

Creating a Contract Template

Templates are one of the best inventions of humankind, right up there with chocolate and a few actors we can't name here. Why? Because with a template, especially a contract template, you can establish or predefine the variables (required or not) so that every contract offers the same consistent appearance and information. Regardless of whether the contract is for software support or copier repair or cleaning services, you can build a contract template specifically for the services you offer.

For this chapter, we're going to visit Mr. Wayne and his Cobweb Catchers Cleaning Service. First, follow these steps to create a contract template:

1. **At the bottom of the navigation pane, click the Settings button.**

2. **In the Settings window, click Templates.**

3. **Click the Contract Templates option.**

   The Contract Templates window appears, listing all current contract templates.

4. **In the Contract Templates window's toolbar, click the New button.**

   The Contract Template: New window appears, as shown in Figure 27-1.

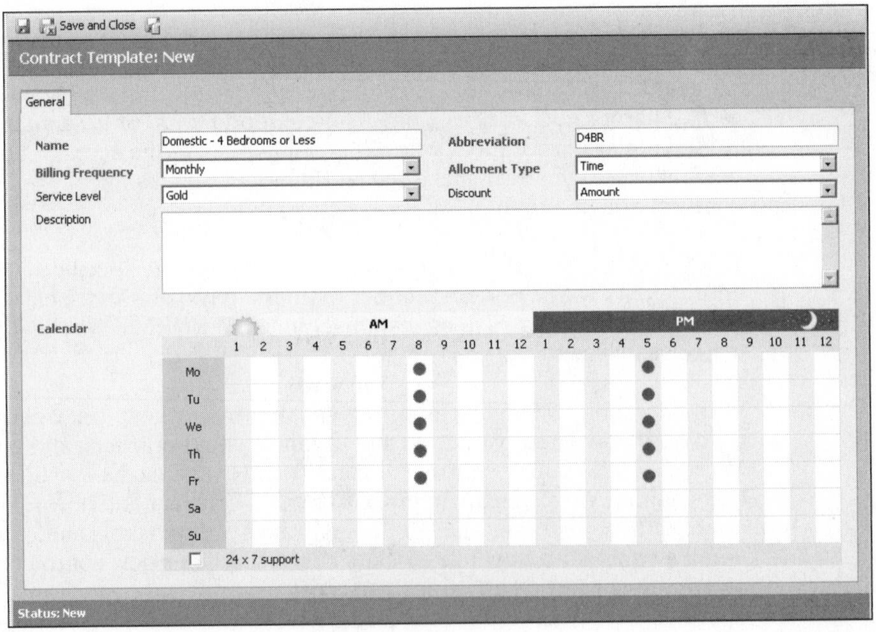

Figure 27-1: Build your contract templates using the Contract Template: New feature.

5. **Fill in the Name and Abbreviation fields.**

   The name can be anything you want. For the abbreviation, use something that you think logically abbreviates your contract name.

6. **Choose a billing frequency.**

   Choose your billing cycle, whether it's monthly, bimonthly, quarterly, semiannually, or annually.

7. **Select an Allotment Type.**

The three options for providing support are Number of Cases, Time, and Coverage Dates.

- **Number of Cases:** Offer your services by the case or call. For example, you might offer a five-call service package in which Cobweb Catchers goes to your house five times, regardless of the length of each visit.

- **Time:** You can provide your services for an amount of time, whether it's hours, days, and so on. For example, Mr. Wayne might offers his Spring Cleaning Contract as six hours of time.

- **Coverage Dates:** Set a time frame for your services. For example, Mr. Wayne's A Year Dear package covers 12 months of service.

8. **If you want, select a service level and discount, and fill in the Description field.**

Use the Service Level field to designate the contract's status.

9. **Fill in the Calendar grid.**

Set the days and hours of support this contract offers by clicking in the appropriate box. A green dot will appear in the box. In our example, Mr. Wayne provides his services from 8 A.M. to 5 P.M., Monday through Friday.

Here's a quick trick to save clicks: Let's say your hours are like Mr. Wayne's: 8–5, Monday–Friday. Place your cursor over the number 8 (AM) on the grid and click. The 8 AM hour for the entire week is filled, including Saturday and Sunday. Then go to the 5 and do the same thing. To clear times for Saturday and Sunday, just click the appropriate box.

10. **Click the Save and Close icon in the upper-left corner.**

The Contract Template: New window closes, and your new contract appears in the Contract Templates window.

Understanding Contract Status

Before we get into showing you how to create your contracts, let's go over the different levels of contract status: draft, invoiced, active, on hold, cancelled, and expired. Because everyone can see contracts, the status allows your sales and service staff to be consistent with their answers and support.

Each contract starts out as a draft and automatically moves to active status once the beginning date has been reached, regardless of whether it's still a draft or has been invoiced. Contracts expire on the end date specified in the contract. Your sales and service staff can place contracts on hold or cancel them.

Here's the list of contract status types:

- ✔ **Draft:** After a contract is created, it automatically has draft status. This is the default option and allows your staff full access to it for modifications or updates.

- ✔ **Invoiced:** After the contract is ready for use, it can be invoiced (from the Actions menu). We'll show you how to do this later in the chapter. The dates, contract names, and contract ID can't be edited after the contract has been invoiced.

- ✔ **Active:** A contract still in draft status moves to active status automatically after the beginning date set in the contract has been reached. For example, if your beginning date is July 3, 2006, the contract will go to active status on that date. As with invoiced contracts, the dates, contract names, and contract ID can't be edited after the contract becomes active.

- ✔ **Expired:** A contract expires automatically on the end date set in the contract. After this happens, no new cases can be opened against it (although existing cases can be closed). Expired contracts can only be renewed and can't be edited in any fashion.

- ✔ **Cancelled:** A contract that is active or invoiced can be canceled (from the Actions menu). Canceled contracts can't be edited.

- ✔ **On Hold:** A contract may be placed on hold (from the Actions menu). While a contract is on hold, cases may not be logged against it. To take it off hold, choose Release Hold from the Actions menu.

Creating a Contract

Now that you and Mr. Wayne have created your contract template and have been briefed on contract status, you're ready for business. That's a good thing because Mrs. Reynolds is on the phone and wants her home cleaned. After you've met with her and discussed her needs, you can create a contract for her using your spiffy new contract template.

Here's how to create a contract:

1. **In the lower part of the navigation pane, click the Service button. In the upper part of the pane, select Contracts.**

2. **In the Contracts window's toolbar, click the New button.**

   The Template Explorer dialog box appears.

3. **Double-click the contract template we created earlier.**

   The Contract: New window appears, as shown in Figure 27-2. For our example, we'll choose the D4BR Template to create the contract for Mrs. Reynolds.

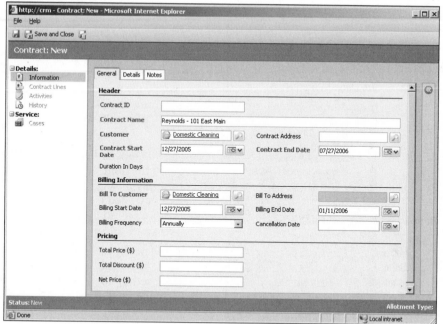

We'd like to point out two things about this Contract: New window. First, as with most of Microsoft CRM, the fields in red (on your screen) are required. Second, you can't modify the Contract ID field. The contract ID is generated automatically when you click the Save and Close button to create the contract. However, your system administrator can specify some of the characteristics of the contract ID.

4. In the Contract Name field, enter a name for the contract.

For our example, we've used Mrs. Reynolds's last name and her street address

5. Fill in the Customer field.

To do so, click the magnifying glass and select the customer from the Look Up Records window. You can also open the Form Assistant on the right of the screen, and select Customer from the drop-down list. When you do, a list of customers appears, as shown in Figure 27-3. You also have the option to search by contact or account.

6. Enter the contract start and end dates.

You can use the calendars or enter the dates manually.

7. Use the magnifying glass to select the Bill To Customer.

The Form Assistant pane is updated with the appropriate addresses. Select the one you want by double-clicking.

Figure 27-3:
Add a
customer
using the
Form
Assistant.

8. **Although the Contract Address and Bill To Address fields are not required, save yourself some time and add them now.**

   To do so, click the arrow in the top field of the Form Assistant pane, and select the Contract Address and Bill To Address options in turn. Although the addresses are not displayed in the appropriate address fields in the Contract: New window, an index card icon confirms that the addresses have been associated with the contract.

   It's worth taking the time to add these addresses now because you need them later when you change the contract's status.

9. **Click Save (the disk icon) to record these addresses.**

10. **Click the Details tab in the Contract: New window and fill it in as necessary.**

    The only required fields (Contract Template and Owner) are already filled in. You can choose the type of discount you want the customer to have (percentage or amount) and enter a description for the contract.

11. **To add a note, do so on the Notes tab.**

12. **Click Save (the disk icon).**

    Your contract is now a draft. Keep this in mind for the rest of the chapter. We'll be moving it out of draft status later.

Now that you've saved the contract, the following options are live. These options allow you to enter or view information relative to the contract during its life:

- ✔ **Information:** You entered the initial information for the contract here.

- ✔ **Contract Lines:** This option outlines what the contract covers. Several Contract Lines (for example, hardware, software, parts, and maintenance) can be associated with a single contract.

- ✔ **Activities:** This is where you find every activity scheduled as part of the support in the contract, such as phone calls, e-mails, tasks, and appointments.

- ✔ **History:** All completed or closed activities go here.

- ✔ **Cases:** All cases or trouble tickets go here.

Shortcut alert! For the most part, your contracts will contain a lot of the same information (such as billing frequency or pricing). Instead of creating a contract from the template, you can open a contract similar to the one you want to create and copy it.

Follow these steps to copy a contract:

1. **In the lower part of the navigation pane, click the Service button. In the upper part of the pane, select Contracts.**

2. **Double-click the contract you want to copy.**

We recommend that you write down the current contract ID number. When you get to Step 3, the contract is copied with all the same information except the contract ID. The program generates a new contract ID for the new contract you're creating. The only way you can tell your new contract from the old one is by the contract ID.

3. **On the main menu (at the top of the screen), choose Actions⇨ Copy Contract.**

   The Create From Existing Contract dialog box appears. You can choose to copy over cancelled contract lines as well, just by selecting the box in this window. (For more on contract lines, see the next section.)

4. **Click OK.**

   You return to the open contract window. The new contract usually takes a minute to pop up, so be sure to keep an eye on that contract ID.

5. **Check the contract ID to make sure you're using the new contract.**

6. **Go ahead and change the new contract information.**

   For our example, we made a new contract for Mrs. Reynolds's neighbor, Mr. Cobb, by copying her contract and giving it a new name, as shown in Figure 27-4.

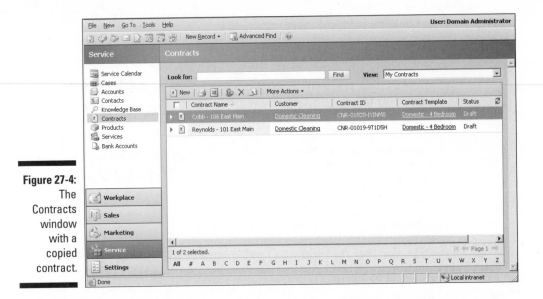

Figure 27-4:
The
Contracts
window
with a
copied
contract.

Adding Contract Lines to a New Contract

Now that you have your new contracts for Mrs. Reynolds and Mr. Cobb set up, it's time to outline the services you're offering. Keep in mind that while we're using services in our examples, you could set up contracts for selling products as well.

A description of what you're offering your client is called a *contract line*. For example, you might offer the friendly neighbors a weekly cleaning (to include dusting, vacuuming, swabbing, and polishing the furniture) every Tuesday at 10:00 AM and specialty cleaning once a month or once every two months. Let's say you're also giving them a free inspection of their carpet every six months. We'll put a variation in there and say that Mrs. Reynolds has a 100-year-old armoire she wants polished only once a month and Mr. Cobb has asked that his collection of antique telephones be excluded from the cleaning. He'll dust those himself.

The Contract Line: New window has three tabs: General, Administration, and Notes. The General tab has areas for the following:

- ✔ General information, such as the name of the contract line and the product

- ✔ Allotment details, which show the total minutes or cases, how many have been used and how many remain, and pricing

- ✔ Total price, which shows the price for the product for this contract

To add a contract line, follow these steps:

1. **In the lower part of the navigation pane, click the Service button. In the upper part of the pane, select Contracts.**

2. **Double-click the contract that you want to add a line to.**

3. **In the navigation pane, click Contract Lines.**

   The Contract Lines window for that contract appears.

4. **In the window's toolbar, click the New Contract Line button.**

   In our example, shown in Figure 27-5, we're using Mr. Cobb's antique phone collection. Note that the Form Assistant window is collapsed.

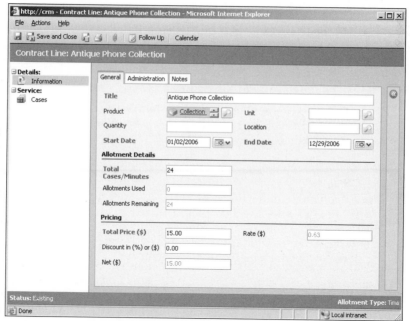

Figure 27-5: Establish Service terms that your service staff members can track as they support the customer.

5. **In the first section, type a title for this contract line and choose the start and end dates.**

   These three fields are required, but the others in the top section are not. You can enter the dates manually or select them from the drop-down boxes.

6. **In the Allotment Details section, enter the number of minutes or cases you want to specify for this contract.**

   The other two fields are optional and show how much has been used and how much is left.

7. **In the Pricing section, enter the total price for this product for this contract.**

   Of the remaining fields under Pricing, Discount is the only one you can fill in. Keep in mind that the amount or percentage of the discount is determined by what was entered for this product on the product list. The other two fields are filled in automatically based on the discount you enter. Net is the total after the discount is applied.

8. **Click Save (the disk icon).**

9. **Click the Administration tab, and check your customer. Enter a serial number if necessary.**

   The customer field is required and should already be filled in. The serial number field is optional and is a good place to track product serial numbers against the contract (say for inventory or quality assurance).

10. **On the Notes tab, enter information important to this contract.**

    The Notes tab, like the other Notes areas in Microsoft CRM, offers a free-form place to enter data.

11. **Click the Save and Close icon.**

    The new contract line appears in the Contract window's main display. You see the contract line's title, product, allotments remaining, and net (a dollar amount).

Clicking any column heading sorts the list of contract lines by that criterion.

Now that you've added the meat to the contract, you can see how Microsoft CRM can track things such as time, available cases, or remaining minutes. In just a few clicks and a glance, you can easily see the status and details of a contract. We know what that translates to: getting information to the customer quickly, which means happy customers.

As we mentioned, you can move a contract from draft to invoiced status, if the start date has not yet been reached.

Follow these steps to move a contract from draft to invoiced status:

1. **In the lower part of the navigation pane, click the Service button. In the upper part of the pane, select Contracts.**

   The Contracts window appears.

2. **Double-click the contract you created earlier.**

3. **On the menu bar (at the top of the screen), choose Actions⇨Invoice Contract.**

   The status of the contract, displayed in the lower-left corner of the window, is updated to *Invoiced* (if the start date has not yet been reached) or *Active* (if the start date has been reached).

Expired contracts are automatically updated to expired status on their end date. The other status levels — cancelled, on hold, and renew — can be updated.

Renewing a Contract

As we mentioned, you can renew cancelled or expired contracts in a few short steps:

1. **In the lower part of the navigation pane, click the Service button. In the upper part of the pane, select Contracts.**

   The Contracts window appears.

2. **Double-click the contract you want to renew.**

3. **In the menu bar (at the top of the screen), choose Actions⇨ Renew Contract.**

   The Renew Contract dialog box appears, asking for verification and whether you want to copy the cancelled contract lines as well.

4. **Click OK.**

   Keep an eye on the status in the lower-left corner. When you renew a contract, its status is changed automatically to draft.

Creating a Case and Linking It to a Contract

Now that we've set Mr. Cobb and Mrs. Reynolds up with their cleaning contracts, Mr. Wayne and his service staff can take calls. That's a good thing because Mr. Cobb is on the phone, wanting to take advantage of the Mothers Know All cleaning advice package, which is good for the life of his contract. He gets ten free phone incidents for cleaning advice. In Mr. Cobb's case, it's a doozie. Seems his pet raccoon got into the trash and grape jelly paw prints are all over his 40-year-old Persian rug.

Your customer service representative takes the call and starts a case for Mr. Cobb to track the resolution process. You find out how to create a case in Chapter 25. Here, we show you how to associate that case to the contract.

See the instructions in Chapter 25 on opening a new case. Then follow these steps to link the new case to Mr. Cobb's contract.

1. **In the newly created case, go to the Form Assistant and select Contract from the first drop-down menu.**

   Available contracts associated with the customer are listed in the Form Assistant under the lookup field. Only active and invoiced contracts appear.

2. **Find and select the contract.**

   The Contract field under Contract and Product Information in the main window should now be filled in (see Figure 27-6). Now that you've assigned the contract, you have to assign the contract line associated with this call.

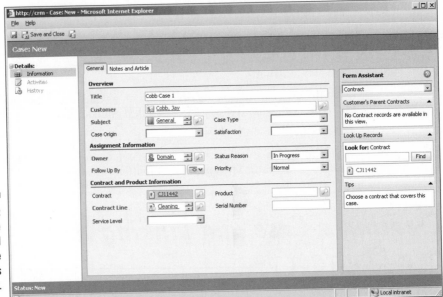

Figure 27-6: Your case assigned to the customer's contract.

3. **Click the magnifying glass icon to the right of the Contract Lines field.**

   The Look Up Records dialog box appears, listing all the contract lines associated with this contract.

4. **Find the contract line, highlight it, and click OK.**

   The case is now properly linked to the contract, and any work performed while resolving the case will be tracked against the active contract.

5. **Click the Save and Close button.**

   Remember the cardinal rule of computers: save, Save, SAVE!

Part VI
The Part of Tens

The 5th Wave   By Rich Tennant

"Your database is beyond repair, but before I tell you our backup recommendation, let me ask you a question. How many index cards do you think will fit on the walls of your computer room?"

In this part . . .

Υou can find many official and unofficial independent software vendors (ISVs), all madly developing add-on products for Microsoft CRM. We have reviewed the best products and present the top ten in Chapter 28.

Everyone needs a little help once in a while. In Chapter 29, we describe the best places for getting an essential tip, training, or consulting.

Chapter 28

Ten Add-Ons

*A*dd-on products are developed by vendors outside Microsoft who have identified some niche or integration that Microsoft has not yet filled. Because CRM has been around before Microsoft CRM, some third-party applications are also available for other CRM products.

As of this writing, there are hundreds of registered developers for Microsoft CRM products and a considerable list of products. We also maintain our own web site, with a current list of the third-party products available. We include brochures, product descriptions, and downloads from the different developers as well as the official list of registered products. You'll also find many unregistered products. You can view the list at

```
www.microsoftCRMProducts.com
```

In addition, Microsoft keeps a list of registered products at

```
http://www.microsoft.com/businesssolutions/
            industrysolutions.aspx
```

To cull the list in this chapter to just ten, we established several criteria:

- ✔ **General applicability:** CRM is about managing prospect and client data. And it's about making it easier for a team of users to work together. If an add-on module didn't address one or both of these issues, it didn't make the cut.

- ✔ **Integration with Microsoft CRM:** Many vendors advertise their products as Microsoft CRM add-ons even when little, if any, integration exists. If there is little integration or no apparent reason for the integration, the product didn't make the cut.

- ✔ **History of and support from vendor:** The CRM dealer industry is still a cottage industry, with dealers coming and going. Often a vendor writes a custom application for one client and then decides to offer it as a general product to an unsuspecting public. We've tried to check out the vendors and their motivation as well. Evaluating motivation, of course, is much more subjective than the first two criteria.

- ✔ **Updated for Version 3:** Some of the less popular add-ons for Version 1 have not been overhauled for Version 3. Any add-on we mention works with Version 3.

Just because a product doesn't appear in this chapter doesn't mean that you shouldn't be interested in it. The product may not have been available for review at the time of this writing, or it may be of special interest to your company but not of more general interest. And, conversely, just because a product appears in this chapter doesn't mean that you should buy it without further evaluation.

Many developers put out advertising materials on products that they are thinking about developing. That is *vaporware*. Before plunking down your hard-earned money, make sure that the product exists and has documentation and support — maybe even a reference site or two.

Converting and Integrating with Scribe Insight

www.scribesoft.com, 603-622-5109

According to Microsoft, most Microsoft CRM installations that use an ISV product include Scribe Insight. This is remarkable and earns Scribe our first-place vote.

Many companies using Microsoft CRM are coming from some other CRM package such as ACT! or GoldMine. It's not easy getting all your data out of one of these packages and into something else. Scribe Insight contains templates for converting the data from either of these packages into Microsoft CRM Version 3. Without such a utility, you'd be hard-pressed to get much more than just simple contact information from these packages. With Scribe, all the activities, such as appointments, phone calls, and related notes, are migrated to Microsoft CRM.

After your data is in Microsoft CRM and you're using the system, you may want to integrate CRM with some other application, such as your accounting system, your ERP system, or your data-mining application. Again, Scribe is your prime source for those migrations.

Although you could use the Microsoft Data Migration Framework, it usually involves some knowledge of programming and SQL Server. Scribe simplifies this task and makes data conversion easier.

Increasing Your Productivity

Third-party developers (like us and others out there) are here to help out Microsoft. After all, they can't think of everything (even though Microsoft CRM comes darn close). As ISV Partners with Microsoft, we can easily add to Microsoft CRM's functionality with our products, therefore increasing your return on investment. As developers, we think that two of the best are c360 and Axonom.

Productivity packs from c360

www.c360.com, 678-781-3189

According to Microsoft, c360's productivity packs are included in about half of Microsoft CRM implementations. That's more than good enough for Microsoft to have awarded c360 the 2005 Microsoft Partner Choice ISV of the year.

c360 packages groups of utilities into three productivity packs: a Core Productivity Pack, one for sales, and another for service.

The Core Productivity Pack includes the following:

- ✔ A utility for combining multiple screen views into one screen to reduce the number of clicks to get from one screen to another.
- ✔ Duplicate record detection across multiple record types. For example, if you enter a new lead record for ABC Corp., it can check to make sure that ABC Corp. does not already exist as an account record.
- ✔ Alerts that trigger pop-up windows based on any type of record.
- ✔ Roll-up summaries for all record types.
- ✔ Relationship charting to see how various records in the database relate to each other.
- ✔ E-mail linking that simplifies connecting an e-mail to a CRM record.

The Sales Pack includes:

- ✔ An enhancement to CRM's forecasting.
- ✔ A connection to your web site to automate creating and updating records. This is particularly useful if you combine this automation with workflow to automatically respond to inquiries.

The Service Pack includes:

- ✔ The ability to link e-mails to cases
- ✔ A workplace configuration that enhances the use of queues

c360 also has industry-specific vertical tools but nothing for the marketing module yet. c360's web site provides a nice tour of all features.

Axonom's Powertrak

www.axonom.com, 952-653-0351

Several Microsoft competitors have positioned themselves against Microsoft CRM by claiming Microsoft's product is not *vertically oriented,* meaning it has no solutions for particular industries. And in most cases, they're right — as long as you don't look at all the rapidly developing third-party products.

Powertrak, from Axonom, provides industry-specific templates extending the range of Microsoft CRM. They have modules for advanced marketing, technical case management, call center, multichannel portals, Ecommerce, and time and billing. The real news here may be the templates for retail, financial, nonprofit associations, and high-tech manufacturing. In particular, the wealth management system (which features *house-holding,* a method of rolling related peoples' accounts into one view) is of interest.

eBridge BizTalk Server Adapter

www.ebridgesoft.com, 800-755-6921 ext. 315

Microsoft provides links from CRM to its accounting packages. But if you're not using a Microsoft accounting system, you need third-party middleware.

The eBridge adapter provides bidirectional integration between Microsoft CRM and a long list of accounting applications to ensure that critical business information is synchronized across the enterprise. Application adapters include Microsoft Business Solutions, Microsoft Business Solutions, Solomon, Sage products, QuickBooks, and Peachtree. To see the entire list, go to

```
http://www.ebridgesoft.com/ebridgesuite/ms_crm.html
```

A thought on hosting

Hosting of various software applications and particularly CRM has become popular. The success of Salesforce.com is testament to that. While hosting CRM is not technically an add-on product, a little discussion here is appropriate.

If you don't have the infrastructure or the technical personnel for the proper care and feeding of CRM, you can have it hosted for you. CRM is a web-based application anyway, so it's a good candidate for third-party hosting. You trade much less investment in equipment and staff for a likely long-term rental commitment. Our financial analyses indicate that if your intention is to use the software for less than 36 months, it's often more cost effective to use an outside hosting facility.

A wide variety of companies provide hosting for Microsoft CRM. They range from companies who just host it to those who fully manage your customizations and much more. For a list of partners who can host Microsoft CRM for you, visit

```
http://www.microsoft.com/crm.
```

Quotes and Proposals

Quotations are usually simple, one- or two-page listings of items, prices, terms, and conditions. Proposals are usually much longer, with detailed discussions, literature, plans, references, and pricing.

Getting more from your quotes

www.quotewerks.com, 407-248-1481

Microsoft CRM includes a pretty good quotation system, but if you need something more configurable, you may want to look at QuoteWerks from Aspire. We've been using their quoting products for many years (long before Microsoft CRM Version 1 appeared).

QuoteWerks is a solid, cost-effective product that allows you to develop configurable quotes and then print and e-mail them. Forecasts and follow-ups are automatically logged in CRM. For an excellent description of the program's capabilities, go to

www.quotewerks.com/mscrm.asp

Proposals and RFPs

www.pragmatech.com, 603-672-8941

www.santcorp.com, 800-272-0047

RFPs and *proposals* are slightly different animals. RFP software is designed to recognize questions from prospective clients and organize your answers. Proposals are usually done according to your company's order and methodology. In any event, automating your proposals should allow even those not gifted with writing skills to put together professional-looking work.

Whether you're responding to a series of questions or creating your own proposals, Pragmatech's software should greatly reduce the time and effort required and should result in a higher win ratio as the quality and consistency of your responses improve. Sant Software also offers proposal and RFP generation linked to CRM.

Here's the rub. Whether you use software from Pragmatech or Sant or someone else, setting it up requires a significant amount of effort. Someone at your company who can write well and has experience with your products and sales must be involved in the initial design of the system. And for a system like this to be cost-effective, your company must send at least one or two proposals a week.

Proposal-generating systems can run as stand-alone systems without integrating with a CRM product, so we almost eliminated this entire category. But this genre of software has enough merit to be included here.

Alerts and Alarms

www.vineyardsoft.com, 802-899-1265

Workflow functionality is built into Microsoft CRM. With workflow, you can automate a variety of business rules and processes. However, workflow works only with the files that are part of Microsoft CRM. Workflow can't trigger activity based on data that might be in an accounting system or in an HR system. KnowledgeSync from VineyardSoft fills that gap.

KnowledgeSync 2000 is a business-activity monitoring application that detects and responds to critical, time-sensitive data in Microsoft CRM, in incoming e-mail, and in many other applications. KnowledgeSync 2000 updates Microsoft CRM, other databases, and users (through e-mail, faxes, pagers, and the web) with critical information. KnowledgeSync comes with many *canned* alerts (called EventPaks). To develop a customized alert, you may want to find a specialist — probably a VineyardSoft partners.

KnowledgeSync can easily alert you to a variety of conditions within your database. Here are a few examples:

- ✔ A forecasted sale is suddenly overdue.
- ✔ A lead distributed to an outside salesperson has not been pursued.
- ✔ Money has come in (or has not come in) from a client.
- ✔ A deal was closed.

Business Intelligence

www.rapidinsightinc.com, 603-447-1980

Your Microsoft CRM system contains some of the most valuable information your company owns. Just as important is the history your company has with each prospect and customer. That history is like an audit trail of everything that has been done, whether it was done well or not. And there is much to be learned by analyzing that history.

Business intelligence systems provide statistical analysis and graphical tools to help analyze what has already happened and help predict what might happen. For example, it's useful to ask such questions as the following:

- ✔ How does our rate of closing deals relate to the number of times we call on a prospect or to whom we assign the prospect or to which product we are trying to sell?

- ✔ Which marketing activities are actually paying off?

- ✔ What percentage of cases has each support person successfully closed, and what percentage are still open and unresolved?

- ✔ What is our historic customer retention rate and how does our retention rate correlate with the number of contacts we make with each customer, who is assigned to handle the account, and the products we are selling?

One of the most flexible, powerful, and effective business intelligence systems comes from a new company called Rapid Insight, Inc. If you want to understand what business processes are working and which ones need adjustment, you will use a tool such as Rapid Insight Analytics. You will analyze what you have been doing, predict what is likely to happen if you continue with the same processes, and try to predict results of new processes.

Business intelligence systems is a highly specialized area that requires expertise in process design, statistics, and modeling. You can find additional information and resources on Rapid Insight Analytics and on client retention systems at www.ccc24k.com/business-intelligence.htm.

Enhancing Field Service Organization

www.fieldpoint.net, 866-336-5282

Fieldpoint has created an advanced Field Service Application for Microsoft CRM. If you're looking to extend CRM 3 to support professional service organizations such as IT and managed service providers, software companies, consultants, and repair professionals, this add-on might be just the ticket.

Chapter 29

Ten Ways to Get Help

*Y*ou can get help with Microsoft CRM in so many ways that it's hard to whittle it down to just ten. Free help is available through CRM's online help system and from the newsgroups. Then there's paid help from dealers, developers, and Microsoft itself. If you're anything like us, you'll try the free stuff first.

The newsgroups are becoming more popular as Microsoft CRM's popularity spreads. Subscribing to a newsgroup now and getting comfortable with the posting process is a good idea. As time goes by, more and more users will be sharing information, best practices, and the inevitable workarounds.

Microsoft Partners can be found all over the world, and they serve as your best and often local support. Beyond that group is a cadre of Independent Software Vendors (ISVs), ready to sell you their custom CRM add-on products (see Chapter 28). Don't overlook ISVs as resources, too. They have a lot of experience dealing with the substance of CRM's programming code and can offer insights into problems you may encounter. These developers can also help you design custom enhancements to the program. After all, that's their business.

Note: The links in this chapter were accurate when they were initially researched but may, due to the dynamic nature of the web, change or disappear over time. If a link no longer works, please accept our apologies. In addition, new sites are appearing all the time. The best way to locate information about Microsoft CRM is to open your search engine of choice and type **Microsoft CRM** in the Search field.

Using CRM's Built-in Help

No doubt about it, the quickest way to get a simple question answered is to go to the built-in help that comes with the software. The price is right and the system is easy to use and will probably answer 80 percent of the basic questions you're likely to have.

You can get to the built-in help feature by selecting Help from the main menu on most screens or by clicking the blue question mark icon on the toolbar.

The screen shown in Figure 29-1 appears, providing you with a choice of topics that relate to the area of the software you're working with.

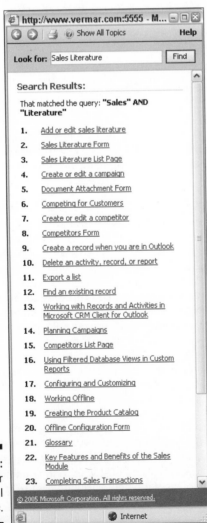

Figure 29-1:
Asking for
a special
topic.

You can drill down on any of these topics by clicking the topic of interest. Or, if this isn't exactly what you had in mind, you can search for another topic as follows:

1. **In the Look For field at the top of the pane, enter a keyword.**

2. **Click the Find button.**

   Additional topics appear below the Look For field. Each additional topics has a radio button.

3. **To find help on an additional topic, click the appropriate radio button.**

   The help text appears at the bottom of the pane.

4. **When you've finished exploring everything the built-in help has to offer, click the X in the upper-right corner to close the window and return to CRM.**

Getting the Straight Story from Newsgroups

Far and away, newsgroups are the most interesting place to find out what is really going on. They're free and Microsoft CRM makes it easy to access them. Let the buyer beware, however. You get what you pay for.

Within the newsgroup threads (a *thread* is a chain of related responses), you will find input from users, dealers, developers, and an occasional response from someone at Microsoft. Mostly the tone is polite and professional. Usually the information is correct — but not always.

If you have a question or a problem, you should first see whether an existing thread relates to your issue. If so, you read through that thread. You may be pleasantly surprised to find that your question has been addressed. If you don't find a thread that looks like your problem, you should start a new thread.

To access the newsgroups:

1. **Click Help from the main menu (on almost any screen).**

   A list of menu choices appears.

2. **Click the second option, Microsoft CRM Online.**

3. **Enter one or two keywords relating to your topic.**

   For example, we entered Sales Literature, as shown in Figure 29-2.

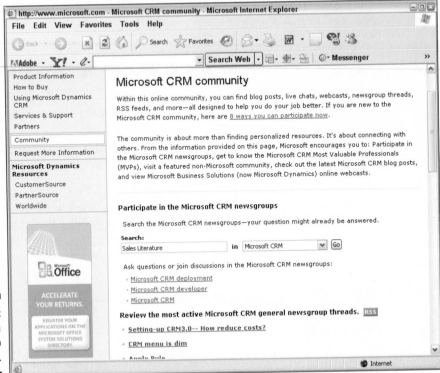

Figure 29-2:
Getting to a
newsgroup
thread.

4. **Click the Go button.**

All existing threads related to your keywords appear. Figure 29-3 shows six threads that relate to Sales Literature.

5. **Click whichever thread seems most relevant and interesting.**

6. **You can then browse through the "conversations" everyone has been having.**

If you don't find an answer to your question, you can start your own thread:

1. **From the newsgroup area, click the New button (refer to Figure 29-3).**

2. **When asked whether you want to submit a question, a suggestion, or a comment, make a selection.**

You see a screen where you can begin your new thread.

3. **Enter as much as you can about your issue, and then click Post (at the bottom of the window).**

This submits your issue to the world.

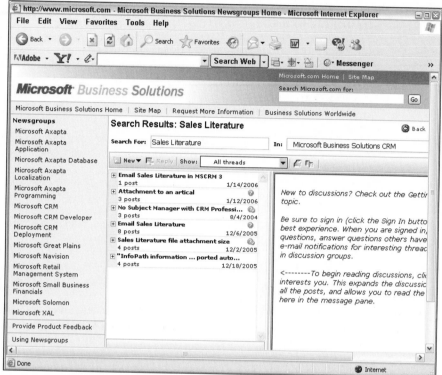

Figure 29-3:
Newsgroup
threads
regarding
the Sales
Literature
area.

4. **Go about the rest of your business for a while.**

   Please note that "a while" might be minutes, hours, or days.

5. **Return to the newsgroup area occasionally to see whether anyone has responded.**

   Chances are that within a day various people will have replied with helpful advice.

Finding an Expert

First, you should know there are a lot of dealers, many of whom are bona fide experts. Actually, Microsoft calls them partners, although one would have to use that term loosely. Finding dealers and developers is one thing; choosing the right one can be a challenge.

There are also developers. These are primarily technical shops specializing in creating custom software and various add-on products. You can almost consider them a subset of the dealer channel, except developers usually don't sell or install CRM. That said, some dealers also develop custom software, and some developers sell CRM.

The dealer and developer community is a prime place to go for serious help. If you need assistance with installation, customization, training, integration with other software, importing data, or just routine support, there is no better place to go. Expect to pay for this service. In the United States, rates range from $140 to $200 per hour.

Microsoft does not publish a comprehensive list of all their CRM dealers. One way to get a few names is to go to the following web address:

```
http://www.microsoft.com/dynamics/crm/purchase/default.
          mspx#EDAA
```

This link brings you directly to Microsoft's Inside Sales Department, which will match you up with several qualified experts.

Microsoft has a special category of consultants with serious expertise and commitment. Microsoft calls them MVPs. You can easily find them by following these steps:

1. **From the main menu of most screens, click Help.**

   A list of menu choices appears.

2. **Click the second option, Microsoft CRM Online.**

   The window we saw back in Figure 29-3 appears. Scroll down a bit until you see a hyperlink to Most Valuable Professionals (MVPs).

3. **Click the MVP hyperlink.**

4. **In the left pane, select MVP Awardees. In the center of the window, select Microsoft Dynamics CRM.**

5. **Scroll through the series of names, biographies, and contact information.**

Another way to find experts is to surf the web. We like Google, and it's certainly useful for finding almost every person or company serious about Microsoft CRM. Other search engines will also work, of course. Some key search words follow: Microsoft CRM, Microsoft CRM dealer, Microsoft CRM partner, Microsoft CRM developer, Microsoft CRM add-ons, and Microsoft CRM training.

 Don't be fooled into thinking that a shaded listing at the top or in the right pane of the Google window guarantees expertise. It guarantees only that the company is paying the most to gain your attention. Surf with caution and a little suspicion. Lowest prices and the best service usually don't go well together.

Another interesting and independent site is

```
http://www.mscrmexperts.com
```

Investing in Training

A key ingredient to a successful implementation of Microsoft CRM is training — end-user training and administrative training. Overlook these and your implementation will not be a success. New training materials and companies are appearing so rapidly that a list printed here will quickly become outdated. Again, surfing the web (using the keywords "microsoft crm training") or asking your dealer is probably the best approach to finding the right training.

Training is a tradeoff in time, budget, and commitment. In the following list, we itemize the best training at the top, with a gradual descent toward barely useful:

- Send all your users to a training facility away from your office and daily distractions. Maui is good.

- Bring an experienced Microsoft CRM trainer to the facility and make sure it really is a training facility.

- Have your own in-house trainer get trained and come back to train all your users. This is almost never as good as having an experienced CRM trainer do the job, but it is less expensive.

- Find some live web-based training that each of your users can access.

- Find a web-based or CD-based tutorial for your users.

- Attend free webinars.

- Just tell each user to use the new software. Some of them will probably get it.

Microsoft offers many types of training, not only for their CRM product but also for many of their other business software products. A good starting point to find out about all these options is

```
http://www.microsoft.com/learning/training/default.asp
```

And, of course, buy each user a copy of this *For Dummies* book. Give each one a raise after they've read it.

Microsoft Packaged Service and Support

Microsoft offers several levels of decision-making, design, and support services. They each cost real money, but it may be money well spent. Design and planning always pay off in the end. You can access the details of Microsoft's programs by going to

```
http://www.microsoft.com/BusinessSolutions/packaged_
            consulting_offerings.mspx
```

The QuickStart and QuickPlan programs are meant to help you before installation. Express Consulting and the Software Assurance programs are designed to help you once you already have the software.

QuickStart

Microsoft's QuickStart program is intended to help you in the decision-making process — before you purchase any software. There is a fee for this program. Dealers have offered similar programs for a long time, usually under the heading of needs analysis.

The advantage of going with Microsoft's QuickStart program is that you have access to Microsoft's experts in their Professional Services Organization. That's a good thing. They have a structured and tested methodology for examining your current situation and future needs. Their intent is to match your needs with their offerings. There are pros and cons to this.

The benefit to QuickStart is that you get an in-depth view of the product, an assessment of whether and how it will work for you, and the beginnings of an implementation plan.

QuickStart will most likely lead you down the path toward a Microsoft CRM implementation. Microsoft's Professional Services Group is very good, but their focus is on Microsoft's product line. They will certainly try to make Microsoft CRM fit your organization's needs. If you have not yet determined what specific CRM product is best for your situation, you may want to conduct your own independent research before signing up for QuickStart.

QuickPlan

Microsoft's QuickPlan program is the next step after QuickStart or after you've decided that Microsoft CRM is the right product for you. Although QuickPlan was designed by Microsoft, it is run through their Dealer Channel with some backup from Microsoft. That is, you'll be working with a specially trained dealer, not with Microsoft directly.

The purpose of QuickPlan is to spend two weeks designing your implementation and preparing your organization for that implementation. This is money well spent and is particularly critical if your application involves more than a handful of users or requires customization or integration with other software.

Express Consulting

Microsoft's Express Consulting is used instead of or in addition to hiring a consultant, dealer, or developer to assist you. Note, however, that relying too heavily on Microsoft's Express Consulting, or on any outside consulting, may undermine the growth of your company's own internal expertise. Any CRM implementation is a living, growing, and evolving system. Weaning your organization away from outside consultants is a good long-range goal. Official technical support and software upgrades are also available directly from Microsoft.

Software Assurance

Microsoft offers five levels and plans for CRM support. The details of Microsoft service plans can be found on their web site at this address:

```
http://www.microsoft.com/dynamics/crm/support/
            serviceplans.mspx
```

The five levels are Open or Open Value Program, Select or the Enterprise Agreement Program, Full Packaged Product Maintenance, Deluxe Support, and Flex Support. The plans you qualify for and the plan you select should reflect your need for help and for updates. Do not assume that because you purchased Microsoft Dynamics CRM 3.0 that you will never need an update. You'll definitely want to stay current with future releases of the software, and you shouldn't seriously consider a plan that doesn't include those updates.

Next, you should think about how often you're likely to call for help and your tolerance for waiting for a response. If you're a Type A personality or the application is truly mission critical for your company, the Open Value Program, offering a three-hour response, might not be ideal.

CustomerSource is a web portal that allows you access to a considerable amount of information about each of your Microsoft products. If you have any of the five plans just described, you should have access to CustomerSource. (If you have one of those plans and have paid for maintenance in the last 12 months but don't have access to CustomerSource, contact your dealer for instructions regarding access.)

CustomerSource will also provide you with detailed information about various types of training that are available. In addition, you can search the official Microsoft knowledge base, submit support incidents, and much more.

Getting in Touch with Us

We use Microsoft CRM. We write about Microsoft CRM. We even sell it occasionally. We have a team of experts who do nothing but CRM consulting. We can even help you find additional resources, if that's what's needed. You can get in touch with either of us at the following address:

```
dummies@crmworldclass.com
```

Accessing General CRM Resources Online

Not to be confusing, but the CRM in this section is not related specifically to Microsoft CRM. These CRM resources are dedicated to client relationship management in general. Much of the information on the web sites we list here doesn't deal with software. Instead, it's about the philosophy and concepts behind more actively managing your customer base.

A solid understanding of CRM concepts can enhance your Microsoft CRM investment. Here are a few resources to get you started:

- ✔ **www.crmguru.com:** Membership is free. Newsletters arrive directly in your e-mail. This site has a <u>Community Forum</u> link and a <u>Guru Panel</u> link. The site also features a searchable GuruBase.

- ✔ **www.crmdaily.com:** The site's self-proclaimed description is Real-Time CRM Industry News from Around the World, but we think it's best described as an online newspaper. Articles are fresh, and the layout is great. Each article has a brief overview on the front page with a link to the details. This site also has a searchable archive.

- ✔ **www.crm2day.com:** Excellent articles and a concise design make this page easy to read. It features an Experts Corner and a searchable library, which puts a lot of great CRM information only a few clicks away. And the free company listing is great for networking!

We hope this chapter provides you with a good start. Everyone needs a little help when they're first starting or even later when digging a little deeper into a new feature.

Index

• N •